Understanding Teaching-Learning Practice

Series Editors
Robert A. Ellis, Griffith University, Brisbane, QLD, Australia
Peter Goodyear, University of Sydney, Sydney, NSW, Australia

This series publishes research on contemporary teaching-learning practices, and in particular, studies that provide evidence of the intertwined relationship between how practice informs research and how the outcomes of research can effectively inform practice. The series publishes studies that make use of diverse methodologies and conceptual framings that foreground real-world practice and trace the connections between teaching, learning activities and experiences, and learning outcomes. Focusing on research that goes beyond disciplinary, sectoral and national borders, the series reflects the following views on understanding teaching-learning practice:

- Student learning is central: one cannot understand effective teaching without understanding successful learning.
- Evidence of the quality and character of teaching-learning practice is best understood in context; the broader landscape in which it occurs must figure prominently in its analysis.
- A real-world application of research outcomes to improve teaching-learning is best informed by a real world analysis of its practice; the challenge lies in completing the circle.
- Innovations in learning and teaching practice, including those which involve new technologies, create quality, coherence and sustainability issues, which need to be addressed.

The series acknowledges the growing complexity of learning and teaching activities in context and studies the roles of digital and material tools and new spaces in teaching and learning. In doing so, it recognises the increasingly diverse nature of educational work and aims to publish studies combining multiple data sources to create richer, robust, more interpretable, more action-oriented evidence.

The ongoing goal of the series is to improve the scholarliness of practice - helping it to be better informed by research - and synergistically, to improve the practical applicability of research designs and outcomes.

More information about this series at http://www.springer.com/series/14356

Klára Šeďová · Zuzana Šalamounová ·
Roman Švaříček · Martin Sedláček

Getting Dialogic Teaching into Classrooms

Making Change Possible

 Springer

Klára Šeďová
Masaryk University
Brno, Czech Republic

Roman Švaříček
Masaryk University
Brno, Czech Republic

Zuzana Šalamounová
Masaryk University
Brno, Czech Republic

Martin Sedláček
Masaryk University
Brno, Czech Republic

ISSN 2522-0845   ISSN 2522-0853 (electronic)
Understanding Teaching-Learning Practice
ISBN 978-981-15-9242-3   ISBN 978-981-15-9243-0 (eBook)
https://doi.org/10.1007/978-981-15-9243-0

© Masaryk University 2020
This work is subject to copyright. All rights are reserved by the Publisher, whether the whole or part of the material is concerned, specifically the rights of translation, reprinting, reuse of illustrations, recitation, broadcasting, reproduction on microfilms or in any other physical way, and transmission or information storage and retrieval, electronic adaptation, computer software, or by similar or dissimilar methodology now known or hereafter developed.
The use of general descriptive names, registered names, trademarks, service marks, etc. in this publication does not imply, even in the absence of a specific statement, that such names are exempt from the relevant protective laws and regulations and therefore free for general use.
The publisher, the authors and the editors are safe to assume that the advice and information in this book are believed to be true and accurate at the date of publication. Neither the publisher nor the authors or the editors give a warranty, expressed or implied, with respect to the material contained herein or for any errors or omissions that may have been made. The publisher remains neutral with regard to jurisdictional claims in published maps and institutional affiliations.

This Springer imprint is published by the registered company Springer Nature Singapore Pte Ltd.
The registered company address is: 152 Beach Road, #21-01/04 Gateway East, Singapore 189721, Singapore

Contents

1	**Thinking About Classroom Dialogue: Introduction and Theoretical Background**............................		1
	1.1 What is in the Book..		1
	1.2 Turning to Talk as a Springboard for Dialogic Teaching........		3
	1.3 Theoretical Background		5
		1.3.1 Sociocultural Theory and the Relation Between Thinking and Speech............................	5
		1.3.2 Zone of Proximal Development and Scaffolding	6
		1.3.3 Dialogic Theory: Voices and Communicative Approaches...................................	8
		1.3.4 Power Patterns—the Classroom as a Community of Learners....................................	10
	1.4 Summary..		12
	References...		13
2	**Elements of Dialogic Teaching and How to Get Them into Classrooms**..		17
	2.1 Elements of Dialogic Teaching		17
		2.1.1 Repertoires of Teaching Talk	17
		2.1.2 Indicators of Dialogic Teaching	18
		2.1.3 Principles of Dialogic Teaching	22
	2.2 Teacher Professional Development Programs as a Tool for Delivering Dialogic Teaching to Classrooms...............		24
	2.3 Troubles with Dialogic Teaching............................		28
		2.3.1 Organizational Constraints	28
		2.3.2 Teacher Mindset	30
		2.3.3 Unbearable Complexity of Change	31
	2.4 Summary..		32
	References...		32

3 How to Change Classroom Talk: TPD Program Design and Research Methods ... 37
- 3.1 The "Effective Classroom Dialogue" TPD Program ... 37
  - 3.1.1 The TPD Program Design ... 38
  - 3.1.2 The TPD Curriculum ... 39
  - 3.1.3 Teachers Participating in the Teacher Development Program ... 43
- 3.2 Research Aims and Data Collection Methods ... 44
  - 3.2.1 Data Collection Methods ... 44
- 3.3 Analytical Procedures ... 46
  - 3.3.1 Quantitative Analysis ... 46
  - 3.3.2 Qualitative Analysis ... 49
- 3.4 Ethical Aspects of the Research ... 51
- 3.5 Limits of the Research ... 52
- 3.6 Summary ... 53
- References ... 54

4 Did Transformation Happen? The Effects of the TPD Program on Classroom Talk ... 57
- 4.1 Research Questions and Procedure ... 57
- 4.2 Changes in Dialogic Teaching Indicators ... 58
  - 4.2.1 Open Questions of High Cognitive Demand ... 58
  - 4.2.2 Uptake ... 60
  - 4.2.3 Open Discussion ... 60
  - 4.2.4 Student Thoughts with Reasoning ... 61
- 4.3 Changes in Dialogic Teaching Principles ... 61
  - 4.3.1 Collectivity ... 61
  - 4.3.2 Purposefulness ... 62
- 4.4 Student Thoughts with Reasoning in Relation to Other Indicators and Principles ... 63
  - 4.4.1 Student Thoughts with Reasoning in Relation to Other Indicators ... 63
  - 4.4.2 Complex Model of Relationships Among Dialogic Teaching Indicators and Principles ... 65
- 4.5 Summary ... 67
- References ... 67

5 The Case of Daniela: The Nonlinear Development of Change ... 69
- 5.1 About Daniela ... 70
- 5.2 The Series of Lessons that Daniela Taught During the TPD Program ... 70
- 5.3 How to Understand the Nonlinear Development of Change ... 94
  - 5.3.1 Critical Reflection as the Motor for Change ... 95
  - 5.3.2 The Phenomenon of Unintended Consequences ... 95

		5.3.3	The Role of Gestalt in the Process of Change	96
		5.3.4	Reflection as a Way to Overcome Gestalt	98
		5.3.5	Teaching Methods as Instruments for Implementing Change	99
	5.4	Summary		100
	References			101

6 The Case of Marek: Tension and Conflict in a Dialogic Teaching System ... 103
    6.1 About Marek ... 103
    6.2 Series of Lessons Marek Taught During TPD Program ... 104
    6.3 How to Understand Inner Tensions and Conflicts in a Dialogic Teaching System ... 131
        6.3.1 When Dialogue is Not Purposeful ... 133
        6.3.2 Purposeless Riddles ... 134
        6.3.3 Quasi-Evocations ... 134
        6.3.4 Quasi-Reflections ... 135
        6.3.5 Neighborly Chatter ... 136
        6.3.6 Why Does Purposefulness Occur in Teaching? ... 136
        6.3.7 When Dialogue is Not Collective ... 137
        6.3.8 Overcoming of Inner Tension in the Dialogic Teaching ... 140
    6.4 Summary ... 141
    References ... 142

7 Teachers' Self-understanding and Emotions as the Catalysts of Change ... 145
    7.1 Concepts and Data Analysis in This Chapter ... 145
    7.2 Self-understanding of Teachers Participating in the TPD Program ... 147
        7.2.1 Perfect Teachers ... 147
        7.2.2 Eager-to-Learn Teachers ... 148
        7.2.3 Positive Teachers ... 149
        7.2.4 Insecure Teachers ... 150
    7.3 Connection Between Self-understanding, Emotions, and Change in Teaching Practices ... 151
    7.4 Why Do Emotions and Self-understanding Make a Difference? ... 153
    7.5 Summary ... 155
    References ... 155

8 Generic Processes Behind Dialogic Teaching Implementation: Discussion and Conclusion ... 157
    8.1 What Have We Found? ... 157
    8.2 What Made Change Happen? ... 159

	8.2.1	Troubles with Dialogic Teaching Overcome	160
	8.2.2	Implementation of Dialogic Teaching as Process of Appropriation	166
	8.2.3	There is No Profound Change Without Reflection	169
8.3	Concluding Remarks		173
	8.3.1	What Did We Learn About Dialogic Teaching?	173
	8.3.2	What Did We Learn About the Professional Development of Teachers?	174
	8.3.3	An Unexpected Epilog	175
	8.3.4	Where to Next?	177
8.4	Summary		178
References			179
Appendix			183

Chapter 1
Thinking About Classroom Dialogue: Introduction and Theoretical Background

Abstract This chapter is an introduction to this book. First, we reveal our motivation for writing it—to contribute to understanding how teachers can improve classroom dialogue and thereby boost student learning. Second, we present the organization of the book and the content of individual chapters. Third, we define dialogic teaching. Fourth, we outline the essential concepts and theoretical inspirations that were the basis for this study.

1.1 What is in the Book

This book is based on the assumptions that students learn through talk and that engaging students in classroom talk positively affects their learning outcomes. Not all forms of classroom talk are comparably effective. Students learn more in some kinds of classroom talk than in others (Resnick et al. 2015). One approach to classroom discourse that is seen as powerful is dialogic teaching (Alexander 2020). This is a style of teaching that harnesses talk to engage student interest, stimulate their thinking, advance their understanding, and at the same time empower them. This book is focused on dialogic teaching and the question of how to get it into the classroom.

Existing research has consistently revealed that real classroom discourse in various countries is far from the ideal of dialogic teaching. Therefore, a number of intervention projects have taken place over recent decades aimed at making classroom discourse more dialogic. We are part of this research stream, and this book expands on the results of intervention research conducted in the Czech Republic. The book describes the efforts that the participating teachers, with the help of the researchers, invested in attempting to teach differently than they were used to and to instigate a rich and authentic dialogue with their students. Our results show that if teachers change their talk patterns, this is then followed by a desirable change in their students. But the results demonstrate that it is not easy for teachers to change their teaching and talking practices.

The aim of this book is not only to report on a successful intervention, but most importantly to investigate in depth the teacher experiences and ways of learning during the intervention project. Teachers find it very difficult to change their own talk and interaction patterns. Therefore, we think it is necessary to examine thoroughly the process of teacher learning that is essential for such a transformation. Although there is an impressive body of scholarly literature in the field, we see this as an important research gap.

The book is divided into eight chapters. In this chapter, we define dialogic teaching and introduce key underlying theories and concepts. We focus on sociocultural theory, which explains the relationship between talking, thinking, and learning. We utilize the thoughts about different voices in dialogue that have been developed by dialogic theory. In Chap. 2, we offer a kind of "anatomy" of dialogic teaching, listing various features attributed to dialogic teaching such as repertoires of teaching talk and indicators and principles of dialogic teaching. Further, we survey some remarkable intervention studies striving to get dialogic teaching into classrooms. We conclude from the divergent outcomes that to make classroom discourse dialogic is not an easy task and that success in such an endeavor is never to be taken for granted. Therefore, we further analyze potential sources of trouble causing schools to resist dialogic teaching initiatives. In Chap. 3, we present our own intervention project and its methodology.

We provide information about participating teachers and their classrooms, about the nature of the development program for the teachers, and about our analytical approaches to data acquired during the project.

The next four chapters present our original research findings. Chapter 4 verifies the impact of our own teacher professional development project. Using statistical data, we prove that due to the project, the nature of classroom talk changed substantially in the participating classrooms. In other words, together with participating teachers, we succeeded in the implementation of dialogic teaching. The following chapters of the book are devoted to seeking an explanation for this success. We strive to present a rich and contextually grounded picture of teacher learning and development during the project.

Chapters 5 and 6 offer two case studies showing in detail how two teachers experienced their participation in the development program and what their development trajectories were. We show step by step how they gradually changed their teaching practices as well as their beliefs. We also focus on the challenges they faced in the process of transformation. In these two case studies, we document a number of phenomena that we observed across the whole sample of participating teachers and that we thus consider to be significant effects accompanying the process of change.

In Chap. 7, we go back to the whole sample of participating teachers. Even though they all displayed changes in their teaching practices, the extent of these changes was not the same for all of them. In this chapter, we strive to understand why. We highlight the importance of teachers' self-understanding and emotions in the process of their professional learning and demonstrate the potential of emotions to be a catalyst of change.

We conclude with a discussion of all our findings in Chap. 8. We discuss those features of our intervention program that facilitated a successful change. We interpret the implementation of dialogic teaching as a result of process appropriation in which participating teachers experimented with new teaching tools and modified them to serve their own needs and preferences. We reveal experience and reflection as the instruments for overcoming the challenges and partial failures naturally accompanying the transformation.

With this book, we hope to attract the attention of four main groups of readers: in-service teachers, pre-service teachers, teacher educators, and researchers. Teachers can find inspiration in this book for ways to deal with talk in the classroom. They can take a close look into the classrooms of their colleagues and in this light reflect upon their own practices. The stories of the teachers in this book may encourage readers from the teaching ranks to embark on the adventure that a deep transformation of teaching styles necessarily entails. Teacher educators might be interested in the description of a successful professional development program and in the analysis of what made this program effective. This book may also serve as a heartening read for them. In our analysis, we document that partial failures are an unavoidable component of the long-term developmental process, and a teacher educator must not be afraid of these challenges. On the contrary, as we show in this book, failures and frustrations can be utilized to deepen the transformation. Finally, we hope for the interest of the researchers in the field. We feel ourselves to be a link in the long chain of thorough investigations of classroom dialogue. We were inspired by many great studies when designing our research and thinking about data. We are pleased to add to the existing knowledge and hopeful that we will inspire other scholars.[1]

1.2 Turning to Talk as a Springboard for Dialogic Teaching

In the past few decades, the focus of education sciences has been turning increasingly to language, communication, and dialogue. Current research emphasizes that talk plays a central role in classroom learning and knowledge creation (Jones and Hammond 2016). A number of authors have studied how talk works in the classroom setting and what its effects are.

It is understood that students learn through talk, and their academic performance can be largely attributed to the quality of classroom discourse (e.g., Mercer and Littleton 2007; Resnick et al. 2018; Wells and Arauz 2006). Considerable empirical evidence indicates that engaging students in classroom talk positively affects learning. Recent studies have demonstrated this link at the classroom level—classrooms with more dialogic instruction had better learning results than classrooms in which the teacher did most of the talking (e.g., Applebee et al. 2003; O'Connor et al. 2015; Alexander 2018; Muhonen et al. 2018; Howe et al. 2019). Other studies have indicated a positive relationship between participation in classroom talk and learning for individual students. This association implies that the more an individual student verbally participates in classroom discussion and the higher the quality of that student's contribution, the better learning outcomes are achieved by that student (Ing et al. 2015; Webb et al. 2014; Sedova et al. 2019; Larraín et al. 2019).

---

[1] Czech names are spelled with diacritical marks. We trust that the reader will be able to recognize Sedova (Šeďová), Salamounova (Šalamounová), Svaricek (Švaříček) and Sedlacek (Sedláček).

As a direct result of this turn to talk, many authors have claimed that to improve student academic achievement, it is necessary to study the roles that language and talk have in teaching (see Mercer and Howe 2012). This perspective drives academic theory and research as well as practical applications. A number of approaches have been developed that can be grouped under the umbrella term *dialogue-intensive pedagogies* (Wilkinson et al. 2015). These approaches stem from the premise that good education motivates students to actively talk about subject matter (Lefstein and Snell 2014). Examples of these pedagogies include *dialogic teaching* (Alexander 2020), *dialogic inquiry* (Wells 1999; Wells and Arauz 2006), *dialogic education* (Phillipson and Wegerif 2016), *dialogically organized instruction* (Juzwik et al. 2012), *collaborative reasoning* (Chinn et al. 2001), *exploratory talk* (Barnes and Todd 1977; Mercer and Hodgkinson 2008), *accountable talk* (Michaels et al. 2008), and *productive talk* (Van der Veen et al. 2017). Our book subscribes to the concept of dialogic teaching (Alexander 2020). Nonetheless, we are aware of overlaps and connections with related dialogue-intensive pedagogies. Therefore, we refer to works by authors who promote other dialogic concepts.

According to Wilkinson et al. (2015), all dialogue-intensive pedagogies have several traits in common. A series of open questions that fuel discussion is central to dialogue-intensive pedagogies. The questions are cognitively demanding, which forces students to analyze, generalize, and speculate rather than simply look for facts or revise already learned knowledge. They respond with elaborate utterances, explain their perspectives, and provide evidence for their points. Teachers react to this with more questions that take into account what has already been said. Thus, the course of the discussion is to an extent influenced by the students.

Although many approaches strive to make teaching dialogic, the classroom reality often strongly diverges from them. The findings of Czech and international studies reflect the same results. Across decades, the most recurring pattern of interaction in schools is IRE (Mehan 1979): teacher *initiation* for student to talk, student *response*, and teacher *evaluation* of the response. Teachers ask many questions that tend to be closed questions of low cognitive demand and prompt students to manifest what they remember of previously taught subject matter. Student responses are in accordance with the nature of teacher questions: they are short and not elaborated, often amounting to just one word. Most commonly, such responses are memorized factual information. The reactions from teachers are brief: they merely state whether such responses are correct. They do not give students uptake to elaborate on their answers or new stimuli for further thinking. Students only rarely have the opportunity to express elaborate talk with reasoning that they have reached after performing thinking processes of high cognitive levels. These findings have been presented in a number of international studies (Gutierrez 1994; Nystrand et al. 1997; Alexander 2001; Burns and Myhill 2004; Parker and Hurry 2007; Kumpulainen and Lipponen 2010; Sedova et al. 2014).

The incongruity between the lively development in the sphere of academic interest in dialogue-intensive pedagogies and the quite rigid state of affairs at schools is disquieting and has provoked scholars to consider what they can do to change this. This book is meant as a contribution to this movement.

1.3 Theoretical Background

The concept of dialogic teaching has a rich theoretical background. Recently, Kim and Wilkinson (2019) did outstanding work in summarizing various theoretical traditions upon which dialogic teaching rests. In this chapter, we outline the major theoretical sources that formed our approach to dialogic teaching.

1.3.1 Sociocultural Theory and the Relation Between Thinking and Speech

The concept of dialogic teaching stems from the sociocultural theory related to the work of Vygotsky (1978), who postulated that there is a clear connection between speech and thought. According to Vygotsky, each higher mental function occurs twice in the development of a child: first on the social level as an inter-psychological function and second as a way of thinking on the individual level as an intrapsychological function (Vygotsky 1978). In other words, all human knowledge is of a social nature and is created by previous social participation (Wertsch 1985). Vygotsky (1978) documented this claim through the development of speech, which comes into existence as a tool for communication between children and the people around them. Speech transforms into inner speech and thus becomes the foundation of the child's thinking and further changes into an inner psychological function.

While other theories understand learning as a change in behavior or mental schemata, sociocultural theory sees it a change in participation in various activities (Sfard 2008). Vygotsky (1978) understood thinking and speech to be two sides of the same coin. This outlook has been accepted by a large number of authors who have agreed that speech not only expresses human thought but also enables and shapes it. For example, Sfard (2008) used the term *commognition* (a compound of the words communication and cognition) to stress the inseparable nature of the two terms.

Consequently, speech is a cultural tool, as it serves to share knowledge and ideas among members of a community, and a psychological tool, as it structures the processes and contents of people's thinking. Vygotsky (1978) claimed that our inner mental abilities come from the outside. In other words, a child's ability to speak becomes internalized and becomes a part of their thinking. It can be said that speech and communication connect individuals with their cultures. The relationship between inner mental processes and their expression is a dialectical one: interaction on leads to intra-action and vice versa (Neguerela-Azarola et al. 2015).

The aim of education is thus to support the internalization of desirable mental functions. Sfard (2008) recommended understanding education as participation in a certain discourse rather than the acquisition of information. Reznitskaya and Gregory (2013) thought of dialogic communication as an arena in which students can practice rational discussion. Students can then internalize the skills that they have honed in practice into individual psychological functions. For example, during a discussion, a student whose utterance was vague may be asked by the other students to clarify and elaborate on the statement as it was difficult to understand. If they do not ask, the student may not recognize that the utterance was vague. The student can later anticipate such reactions and mentally develop their statements before sharing them verbally. What started as a social interaction (a request for specification) becomes an intrapsychological cognitive habit (Reznitskaya and Wilkinson 2015).

According to Vygotsky (1978), the tools of intellectual adaptation are the key elements that connect the inner and outer spheres. These are psychological tools developed and used within a culture to master one's own psychological processes. Vygotsky likened these psychological tools to real-world tools that people use to transform the outer world. In his conception, however, people use psychological tools to transform their own psychological functions. Examples of psychological tools include various sets of signs, writing, calculations, sets of numbers, and maps. Language is thought of as the most important psychological tool and has been described as the tool of tools. Halliday (1993) claimed that when children start to learn language, their attempts are not an example of just one out of many types of learning. Instead, their attempts can be understood as creating the foundation for learning as such.

Therefore, learning can in essence be understood as the internalization of tools into one's thinking. As Vygotsky (1978) wrote, the use of psychological tools increases the number of ways in which we can behave and makes accessible the works of the genius few to the many. In addition, a tool that was created once can be used by other members of the given culture. Thus, as children mature psychologically, they widen their repertoire of tools, which they expand and transform into inner psychological functions.

1.3.2 Zone of Proximal Development and Scaffolding

Another concept by Vygotsky that influenced dialogic teaching theory is the *zone of proximal development*, the difference between a child's present developmental stage, meaning the level of tasks that the child can solve, and the child's potential, meaning the level of tasks that the child can solve with the assistance of an adult or someone more experienced. Vygotsky did not mean that this other person would complete the task for the child. More precisely, the zone of proximal development describes a situation in which the child has a chance to imitate activities that transcend their present abilities.

Consequently, Vygotsky (1978) claimed that only education that is ahead of the child's present abilities can be considered good. Such education creates a zone of proximal development since it creates and stimulates a set of inner processes, and these take place only via interaction with other people. After a certain time, the processes become internalized and become internal features of the given child. The first step in creating a zone of proximal development is thus placing the child in an interaction with someone whose abilities are more advanced and creating a situation in which said abilities can become apparent while solving a task.

It is noteworthy that zone of proximal development boundaries cannot be established by a rule of thumb because even the zones of proximal development of children in the same developmental stage can vary significantly. In fact, the scope of what they are able to achieve with assistance may differ radically (Vygotsky 1978). Thus, keeping such children in their respective zones of proximal development is not a simple task. To do so, Roehler and Cantlon (1997) suggested that a balance needs to be maintained between sufficient support and challenges: a task needs to be difficult enough that it is stimulating. At the same time, students need to be provided with support and clues so that their frustration remains low.

This brings us to the concept of *scaffolding* (Wood et al. 1976), which was formulated in connection with Vygotsky's concepts. Effective learning needs to occur in an interaction between a student and a more knowledgeable other (a parent, supervisor, or more experienced peer). The term "scaffolding" describes an interaction between these two sides that enables the student to solve a task that would be unsolvable without the support of the more knowledgeable other. The more knowledgeable other takes responsibility for elements that are beyond the student's current ability. By doing so, the other enables the student to solve the task. However, the aim is not to solve the task but to develop the skills necessary for solving the task.

Fading and an eventual transfer of responsibility (Van de Pol et al. 2010) are characteristic features of scaffolding. Since scaffolding is temporary, the support provided is decreased as the student's ability increases. The final point is the complete autonomy of the student who can generalize their competences and employ them in completing similar tasks. Scaffolding also needs to be contingent, i.e., tailored to the needs of students, for it to remain effective. This presumes that teachers can diagnose the needs of their students. They need to define the level of their students' current ability and to identify their misconceptions and potential sources of mistakes (see Palincsar and Brown 1984).

Based on a meta-analysis, Van de Pol et al. (2010) summarized that scaffolding can be motivated by several different intentions and executed through several different means. Scaffolding intentions include (a) support of students' meta-cognitive activities (direction maintenance), (b) support of students' cognitive activities (cognitive structuring, reduction of degrees of freedom), and (c) support of student affect (recruitment, frustration control). Scaffolding means, which are understood as tools for carrying out individual intentions, include (a) giving feedback, (b) hinting, (c) instructing, (d) explaining, (5) modeling, and (6) questioning. Specific scaffolding strategies come into existence—and are used in teaching—when teachers combine different scaffolding means with different scaffolding intentions (Van de Pol et al. 2010).

1.3.3 Dialogic Theory: Voices and Communicative Approaches

The theory of dialogic teaching was inspired not only by Vygotsky and those who followed in his footsteps but also by Bakhtin's (1981) theory of speech genres. Bakhtin differentiated between two speech genres: authoritative and dialogic discourse. The aim of the former is to persuade, mediate knowledge that is considered true, and ensure the reproduction of such knowledge. In essence, the aim of authoritative discourse is to convince its audience to accept the perspective of the speaker. Dialogic discourse opens up space for various perspectives, ideas, and aims to provide stimuli for thinking. Different voices, or perspectives, take turns in speaking in dialogic discourse.

Based on Bakhtin's theory of speech genres, Mortimer and Scott (2003) created a typology of four different communicative approaches. Apart from authoritative and dialogic discourse, their typology also includes interactive discourse, in which more than one person participates, and non-interactive discourse, in which only one person is allowed to speak. By combining these dimensions, Mortimer and Scott postulated the following four types of communicative approaches:

(a) *Non-interactive authoritative*: The teacher delivers a monolog on content that is considered true and presented to students for acquisition.
(b) *Interactive authoritative*: Speakers take turns, the teacher asks questions, and the students respond. The teacher evaluates whether the responses are correct.
(c) *Non-interactive dialogic*: Only one speaker talks, summarizing contrasting ideas and perspectives, comparing them, and offering stimuli for further thought.
(d) *Interactive dialogic*: Speakers take turns, and both the teacher and students present their ideas. The aim is to enable different speakers to express their opinions, which can then be compared and analyzed for converging and diverging points and their sources. Knowledge is understood not as set in stone but instead as something that eventually emerges out of the dialogue among the teacher and students.

Empirical research has repeatedly shown that the interactive authoritative approach is the most common approach found in schools. This approach has many similarities with the IRE structure (Mehan 1979), which comprises teacher initiation, student response, and teacher evaluation.

The interactive dialogic approach aligns with dialogic teaching. The necessary precondition for the occurrence of the interactive dialogic approach is the existence of various interrelated voices in one discourse. This phenomenon is known as *inter-animation* (Bakhtin 1981). If ideas are examined in parallel, the degree of inter-animation is low. However, if ideas are compared and participants look for their convergences and divergences, the degree of inter-animation is high.

Simply said, all these contemplations about voices inspired the dialogic teaching movement, which calls for student voices to be included in dialogue. Nonetheless, some authors have pointed out that not every call for student voices necessarily results

1.3 Theoretical Background

in authentic dialogue. For example, Alexander (2008) used the term *pseudo-inquiry* for a series of open questions seemingly inviting students to express their voices that are in fact vague and not stimulating for students. The student responses to such questions are routine and lacking in effort; they are followed by habitual evaluations from the teacher. The term "pseudo-inquiry" thus describes a situation in which student voices do not find authentic expression, although the surface conversation structure seems to be open and inclusive.

Segal et al. (2016) considered the conditions under which students would be able to authentically express themselves and assert their voices. They identified four necessary conditions: (a) students have the chance to speak, (b) they express their own ideas, (c) they do so in their own words, and finally (d) they attract the attention and interest of others. If these conditions are not met, classroom discourse might formally appear to be dialogic, but the common construction of meaning does not take place.

Segal and Lefstein (2016) emphasized that the key factor is whether students express their own thoughts and attract attention to them. There are situations—known as *exuberant voiceless participation*—in which students eagerly participate but instead of expressing new ideas and original voices they support the teacher's perspective and animate the teacher's voice. They repeat, variate, and imitate what was said by the teacher.

Matusov (2009) claims that education is essentially dialogic as students' meaning making is always unpredictable, undetermined, and never fully designed or controlled by the teacher. Despite this, conventional educational practices tend to distort dialogicity as the students are pushed to making themselves more similar to their more knowledgeable teacher. Therefore, Matusov suggests how to deepen dialogicity in the classroom: (a) to take the teacher as a co-learner who learns the subject matter with the students, (b) to regard knowledge as non-stable and continually transforming, and (c) to base instruction on genuine information-seeking questions that both the teacher and the students ask of each other.

Ideas regarding the expression of various voices seek to undermine the traditional asymmetry between a more knowledgeable teacher and a less knowledgeable student. In this regard, this stream seems to contradict to concepts like zone of proximal development or scaffolding (see above). Yet the dialogic and authoritative approaches do not stand in strict opposition to each other, nor are these approaches easily distinguishable. Instead, it is necessary to put the two approaches on a wide continuum. Bakhtin (1981) differentiated between two types of dialogue: Socratic and masterly. *Socratic dialogue* refers to the interactive dialogic approach in its purest form. The relationships between speakers are symmetrical, and the absence of a leading voice can result in confusion instead of a conclusion. *Masterly dialogue* includes a leading voice, the authority of which stems from some cultural necessity. For example, in the school environment this cultural necessity is represented by the curriculum. A dialogue then takes place among the voices of the teacher, the students, and the curriculum. This type of dialogue can in essence be likened to scaffolding (Cheyne and Tarulli 1999). Both kinds of dialogue are useful at school. Some authors (Scott 2008; Nurkka et al. 2014) have spoken of a rhythmization of discourse, referring to alternating between the two discourses: teaching proceeds most optimally when a phase of using the authoritative approach is alternated with a phase of using the dialogic approach.

While thinking about the nature of discourse and approaches to communication, one needs to bear in mind that both are applied in a specific context. In our case, the context at hand is the institution of a school. A school guarantees that culturally appreciated content will be transmitted to its students. The polyphony that accompanies this process of transmission is complex. As Maybin (2013) claimed, students at school enrich their own voices with many other voices (those of their teachers, peers, parents, and textbooks as well as those of other texts). Many of these voices (especially those of teachers and textbooks) already echo the voice of curriculum. In some cases, students reproduce these originally foreign voices and make them their own. In other cases, they adapt them or even signal their distance from them. In sum, dialogic interaction in a school environment is constructed both through repetition and voice imitation and by creative work with the many voices expressed by both students and teachers. Teachers paraphrase and translate student responses into the academic language of the school. Subsequently, students rephrase their responses and align them with the teachers' responses (Maybin 2013). In a school environment, this behavior cannot be understood as a violation of dialogic teaching; it is a mere consequence of the fact that the dialogue is situated in the specific context of the school institution.

1.3.4 Power Patterns—the Classroom as a Community of Learners

Both Vygotskian and Bakhtinian approaches are important in nurturing thinking about dialogic teaching. However, there is one noticeable incongruence between them. Sociocultural theory expects the teacher to be more knowledgeable and to show the students the path for their development. In contrast, dialogic theory supposes a polyphony of equally relevant voices. Thus, to combine both traditions, careful attention needs to be paid also to power dynamics in the classroom.

A number of authors have claimed that a change in power dynamics needs to take place before dialogic teaching can be implemented; the power relationships between teachers and students need to become more symmetrical (Chin 2006; Mortimer and Scott 2003). Patchen and Smithenry (2014) stated that when a teacher employs the monologic approach, that teacher is then considered to be the only epistemic and logistic authority in the classroom. *Epistemic authority* describes the ability to determine which ideas will be recognized as correct and which as incorrect. *Logistic authority* describes control over the rules of communication. In teaching practices, these authorities manifest in the teacher asking a question, deciding who will answer it (logistic authority), and evaluating whether the answer is correct (epistemic authority). This asymmetrical distribution of power is mirrored in the talk. One of the reasons for the prevalence of interactive authoritative discourse (Mortimer and Scott 2003) in classrooms is that it enables teachers to maintain their power. Interactive authoritative discourse makes students passive and reactive to the teacher, which in turn makes classroom management easier for the teacher (Sedova 2011).

Dialogic teaching requires a change on the level of power relationships. Put simply, a transformation of ordinary authoritative discourse into a discourse in which more voices are heard breaks down the common hierarchies between the teacher and students (Lyle 2008). In dialogic teaching, logistic authority is shared because students can influence who will speak and who will be addressed. The same applies to epistemic authority as students co-decide which responses are correct given that their correctness was not certain before the start of the discussion but is co-constructed in its progress (Patchen and Smithenry 2014).

These ideas have not yet been sufficiently addressed by research studies. One of the few exceptions is a study by Cornelius and Herrenkohl (2004), who observed a classroom in which the teacher's communicative approach transformed into one closer to the ideal presented by dialogic teaching. In the class, the nature of power relationships changed at the moment when the IRE structure (initiation from teacher—response from student—evaluation from teacher) stopped being the dominant talk pattern. The students started asking a greater number of questions and deducing more conclusions than the teacher did. They stopped referring to the teacher as the source of all knowledge and instead began to see themselves as the originators of the discussed ideas (Cornelius and Herrenkohl 2004). More recently, Cochran et al. (2017) studied power patterns in three elementary classrooms showing that a balance between teacher and student power empowers students in their learning. Candela (2005) investigated student participation in classroom dialogue and formulated the concept of *authorship* to describe situations in which students become responsible for deciding which educational content would be taught. Candela (2005) emphasized the importance of *collective authorship*, in which the weight of epistemic authority is not carried by a single person but is shared in the process of collective negotiation.

Collectivity is highly appreciated in dialogic teaching, as the classroom is understood as a *learning community* (Reznitskaya and Gregory 2013). All students work together on gaining new knowledge, they help each other learn, and the social structure of the classroom is set up in such a way that it supports relationships among students that intensify learning (Lyle 2008). Mercer (2000) used the term *interthinking* to claim that reciprocal communication leads to reciprocal thinking. When students are given a chance to interact, they are given a chance to pool their intellectual skills, enabling them to achieve more intellectually (Mercer and Littleton 2007).

Students in a classroom thus collectively formulate ideas, defend them, and evaluate their perspectives. As we stated above, we take learning to be a process of internalization: as students hone their skills of rational argumentation, their mental skills grow. However, the internalization process is reciprocal: as students gain new mental skills, they gain better argumentation skills, influence how the discussion will proceed, and thus bring new stimuli into the classroom. Reznitskaya and Gregory (2013) spoke of parallel cycles of individual and group transformation. In dialogic teaching, less advanced students benefit from the abilities of more advanced students because the former can observe the latter and try to eventually internalize their way of talking and thinking (Reznitskaya and Gregory 2013).

All the works cited above stress the positive effects of empowering students. However, the fact that students gain authority does not mean that the teacher loses it. The teacher still retains an important position in the structure of the learning community and is understood as a more experienced partner in the discussion. The teacher needs to provide students with more communicative space and vest them with greater epistemic authority than in the authoritative model of teaching. This does not mean, however, that the teacher would retreat into the role of a moderator or facilitator of student discussion, because dialogic education requires both student engagement and teacher intervention (Alexander 2017). This approach stems from Vygotsky's understanding of teachers as more competent adults who introduce children into the symbolic system of their culture (see above). According to Corden (2000), teachers should not suppress their role as experts—instead, they should use it to increase the expertise of students to the highest degree possible. Reznitskaya and Gregory (2013) claimed that students can recognize the teacher's knowledge of the subject from their participation in a different learning community (e.g., in the community of math and history teachers). Burbules (1993) noted that authority based in this way on the expert knowledge of its bearer does not necessarily have to question the symmetrical nature of interaction. The equality of participants is shown by the fact that they share similar roles: they ask questions, nominate the next speaker, and reply to responses from other speakers (Reznitskaya et al. 2012).

1.4 Summary

In this chapter, we introduced the basic theoretical concepts we work with in this book. We presented dialogic teaching as a part of the broader movement of dialogue-intensive pedagogies. All these pedagogies are based on the assumptions that there is a strong connection between speech and thought and that students learn through talk, especially when they are actively engaged and cognitively stimulated.

We further referred to inspirational sources of dialogic teaching, namely to Vygotsky's concepts of internalization, the zone of proximal development, and scaffolding, and to Bakhtin's concepts of voices and their inter-animation. We explored ideas concerning power patterns in the classroom and the vision of a classroom as a learning community with rather symmetrical relationships between teachers and students.

Through this, we revealed our notion of what dialogic teaching means. It is a style of teaching utilizing a connection between thinking and speech and aiming, through talk, to influence student thinking and understanding. Dialogic teaching operates in a zone of proximal development; the teacher is in the role of a more competent adult introducing students into the symbolic system of their culture and scaffolding student learning. But at the same time, an interactive dialogic discourse is established in the classroom; students are invited to express their voices, and their voices are heard. Power patterns are relaxed, and the students and the teacher are members of a learning community, thinking, and creating new knowledge together.

References

Alexander, R. J. (2001). *Culture and pedagogy: International comparisons in primary education.* London: Blackwell.

Alexander, R. J. (2008). *Essays on pedagogy.* New York: Routledge.

Alexander, R. J. (2017). *Towards dialogic teaching: Rethinking classroom talk* (5th ed.). Cambridge: Dialogos.

Alexander, R. J. (2018). Developing dialogic teaching: Genesis, process, trial. *Research Papers in Education, 33*(5), 561–598.

Alexander, R. J. (2020). *A dialogic teaching companion.* London: Routledge.

Applebee, A. N., Langer, J. A., Nystrand, M., et al. (2003). Discussion-based approaches to developing understanding: Classroom instruction and student performance in middle and high school English. *American Educational Research Journal, 40*(3), 685–730. https://doi.org/10.3102/00028312040003685

Bakhtin, M. M. (1981). *The dialogic imagination: Four essays.* Austin: University of Texas Press.

Barnes, D., & Todd, F. (1977). *Communication and Learning in Small Groups.* London: Routledge and Kegan Paul.

Burbules, N. C. (1993). *Dialogue in teaching: Theory and practice.* New York: Teachers College Press.

Burns, C., & Myhil, D. A. (2004). Interactive or inactive? A consideration of the nature of interaction in whole class teaching. *Cambridge Journal of Education, 34*(1), 35–49. https://doi.org/10.1080/0305764042000183115

Candela, A. (2005). Students' participation as co-authoring of school institutional practices. *Cult Psychol, 1*(3), 321–337. https://doi.org/10.1177/1354067X05055523

Chin, C. (2006). Classroom interaction in science: Teacher questioning and feedback to students' responses. *International Journal Science Education, 28*(11), 1315–1346. https://doi.org/10.1080/09500690600621100

Chinn, C. A., Anderson, R. C., & Waggoner, M. A. (2001). Patterns of discourse in two kinds of literature discussion. *Reading Research Quarterly, 36*(4), 378–411. https://doi.org/10.1598/RRQ.36.4.3

Cheyne, J. A., & Tarulli, D. (1999). Dialogue, difference and voice in the zone of proximal development. *Theoretical Psychology, 9*(1), 5–28. https://doi.org/10.1177/0959354399091001

Cochran, K. F., Reinsvold, L. A., & Hess, C. A. (2017). Giving students the power to engage with learning. *Research Science Ed, 47*(6), 1379–1401. https://doi.org/10.1007/s11165-016-9555-5

Corden, R. (2000). *Literacy and learning through talk: Strategies for the primary classroom.* Buckingham: Open University Press.

Cornelius, L. L., & Herrenkohl, L. R. (2004). Power in the classroom: How the classroom environment shapes students' relationships with each other and with concept. *Cognition Instructional, 22*(4), 467–498. https://doi.org/10.1207/s1532690Xci2204_4

Gutierrez, K. D. (1994). How talk, context, and script shape contexts for learning: A cross-case comparison of journal sharing. *Linguistics Education, 5*(3–4), 335–365. https://doi.org/10.1016/0898-5898(93)90005-U

Halliday, M. A. K. (1993). Towards a language-based theory of learning. *Linguistics Education, 5*(2), 93–116. https://doi.org/10.1016/0898-5898(93)90026-7

Howe, C., Hennessy, S., Mercer, N., et al. (2019). Teacher–student dialogue during classroom teaching: Does it really impact on student outcomes? *Journal Learning Science.* https://doi.org/10.1080/10508406.2019.1573730

Ing, M., Webb, N. M., Franke, M. L., et al. (2015). Student participation in elementary mathematics classrooms: The missing link between teacher practices and student achievement? *Education Studies Mathematical, 90*(3), 341–356. https://doi.org/10.1007/s10649-015-9625-z

Jones, P., & Hammond, J. (2016). Talking to learn: Dialogic teaching in conversation with educational linguistics. *Reseach Paper Education, 31*(1), 1–4. https://doi.org/10.1080/02671522.2016.1106691

Juzwik, M. M., Sherry, M. B., Caughlan, S., et al. (2012). Supporting dialogically organized instruction in an English teacher preparation program: A video-based, web 2.0-mediated response and revision pedagogy. *Teacher College Record, 114*(3), 1–42.

Kim, M. Y., & Wilkinson, I. A. G. (2019). What is dialogic teaching? Constructing, deconstructing, and reconstructing a pedagogy of classroom talk. *Learning, Culture and Social Interaction, 21,* 70–86. https://doi.org/10.1016/j.lcsi.2019.02.003

Kumpulainen, K., & Lipponen, L. (2010). Productive interaction as agentic participation in dialogic enquiry. In K. Littleto, & C. Howe. (Eds.). *Educational dialogues: Understanding and promoting productive interaction,* 1st edn. Routledge, Abingdon, New York.

Larraín, A., Freire, P., López, P., et al. (2019). Counter-arguing during curriculum-supported peer interaction facilitates middle-school students" science content knowledge. *Cognition Instruct, 37*(4), 453–482. https://doi.org/10.1080/07370008.2019.1627360

Lefstein, A., & Snell, J. (2014). *Better than best practice: Developing teaching and learning through dialogue.* Abingdon, New York: Routledge.

Lyle, S. (2008). Dialogic teaching: Discussing theoretical context and reviewing evidence from classroom practice. *Language Education, 22*(3), 222–240.

Matusov, E. (2009). *Journey into Dialogic Pedagogy.* New York: Nova Science Publishers.

Maybin, J. (2013). Towards a sociocultural understanding of children's voice. *Language Education, 27*(5), 383–397. https://doi.org/10.1080/09500782.2012.704048

Mehan, H. (1979). *Learning lessons: Social organisation in the classroom.* Cambridge: Harvard University Press.

Mercer, N. (2000). *Words and minds: How we use language to think together.* Abingdon, New York: Routledge.

Mercer, N., & Hodgkinson, S. (Eds.). (2008). *Exploring talk in school: Inspired by the work of Douglas Barnes.* London: SAGE.

Mercer, N., & Howe, C. (2012). Explaining the dialogic processes of teaching and learning: The value and potential of sociocultural theory. *Learning Cultural Society International, 1*(1), 12–21. https://doi.org/10.1016/j.lcsi.10.1016/j.lcsi.2012.03.001

Mercer, N., & Littleton, K. (2007). *Dialogue and the development of children's thinking: A sociocultural approach.* Abingdon, New York: Routledge.

Michaels, S., O'Connor, C., & Resnick, L. B. (2008). Deliberative discourse idealized and realized: Accountable talk in the classroom and in civic life. *Studies in Philosophy and Education, 27*(4), 283–297.

Mortimer, E. F., & Scott, P. H. (2003). *Meaning making in science classrooms.* Maidenhead, Philadelphia: Open University Press.

Muhonen, H., Pakarinen, E., Poikkeus, A.-M., et al. (2018). Quality of educational dialogue and association with students academic performance. *Learning Instruments, 55,* 67–79. https://doi.org/10.1016/j.learninstruc.2017.09.007

Neguerela-Azarola, E., García, P. N. & Buescher, K. (2015). From interaction to intra-action: The internalization of talk, gesture, and concepts in the second language classroom. In N. Markee (Ed) The handbook of classroom discourse and interaction, 1st edn. Wiley–Blackwell, Oxford.

Nurkka, N., Viiri, J., Littleton, K., et al. (2014). A methodological approach to exploring the rhythm of classroom discourse in a cumulative frame in science teaching. *Learning Culture Society International, 3*(1), 54–63. https://doi.org/10.1016/j.lcsi.2014.01.002

References

Nystrand, M., Gamoran, A., Kachur, R., & Prendergast, C. (1997). *Opening dialogue: Understanding the dynamics of language and learning in the English classroom*. New York: Teachers College Press.

O'Connor, C., Michaels, S. & Chapin, S. (2015). "Scaling down" to explore the role of talk in learning: From district intervention to controlled classroom study. In L. B. Resnick, C. S. C. Asterhan & S. N. Clarke (Eds.), *Socializing intelligence through academic talk and dialogue*. 1st edn. American Educational Research Association, Washington, D.C.

Palincsar, A. S., & Brown, A. L. (1984). Reciprocal Teaching of comprehension-fostering and comprehension-monitoring activities. *Cognition Instruct, 1*(2), 117–175. https://doi.org/10.1207/s1532690xci0102_1

Parker, M., & Hurry, J. (2007). Teachers' use of questioning and modelling comprehension skills in primary classrooms. *Education Review, 59*(3), 299–314. https://doi.org/10.1080/00131910701427298

Patchen, T., & Smithenry, D. W. (2014). Diversifying instruction and shifting authority: A cultural historical activity theory (CHAT) analysis of classroom participant structures. *Journal Research Science Teacher, 51*(5), 606–634. https://doi.org/10.1002/tea.21140

Phillipson, N., & Wegerif, R. (2016). *Dialogic education: Mastering core concepts through thinking together*. Abingdon, New York: Routledge.

Resnick, L. B., Asterhan, C. S. C. & Clarke SN (2015) Talk, learning, and teaching. In L. B. Resnick, C. S. C. Asterhan & S. N. Clarke (Eds.). *Socializing Intelligence Through Academic Talk and Dialogue*, 1st edn. American Educational Research Association, Washington, D.C.

Resnick, L. B., Asterhan, C. S. C., & Clarke S. N. et al. (2018). Next generation research in dialogic learning. In G. E. Hall, L. F. Quinn & D. M. Gollnick (Eds.). *The Wiley Handbook of Teaching and Learning*, 1st edn. Wiley, Hoboken.

Reznitskaya, A., Glina, M., Carolan, B., et al. (2012). Examining transfer effects from dialogic discussion to new tasks and contexts. *Contemporary Educational Psychology, 37*(4), 288–306. https://doi.org/10.1016/j.cedpsych.2012.02.003

Reznitskaya, A., & Gregory, M. R. (2013). Student thought and classroom language: Examining the mechanisms of change in dialogic teaching. *Educ Psychol, 48*(2), 114–133. https://doi.org/10.1080/00461520.2013.775898

Reznitskaya, A., Wilkinson, I. A. G. (2015). Professional development in dialogic teaching: Helping teachers promote argument literacy in their classrooms. In D. Scott & E. Hargreaves (Eds.). *The SAGE handbook of learning*. 1st ed. SAGE, London.

Roehler, L. R., Cantlon, D. J. (1997). Scaffolding: A powerful tool in social constructivist classrooms. In K. Hogan & M. Pressley (Eds.). *Scaffolding Student Learning: Institutional Approaches and Issues*. 1st Edn. Brookline Books, Cambridge.

Scott, P. (2008). Talking a way to understanding in science. In N. Mercer & S. Hodgkinson (Eds.). *Exploring Talk in Schools: Inspired by the Work of Douglas Barnes*. SAGE, London.

Sedova, K. (2011). Mocenské konstelace ve výukové komunikaci [Constellations of power in the classroom]. *Studia Paedagogica, 16*(1), 89–118.

Sedova, K., Salamounova, Z., & Svaricek, R. (2014). Troubles with dialogic teaching. *Learn Cult Soc Inter, 3*(4), 274–285. https://doi.org/10.1016/j.lcsi.2014.04.001

Sedova, K., Sedlacek, M., Svaricek, R., et al. (2019). Do those who talk more learn more? The relationship between student classroom talk and student achievement. *Learn Instr, 63*, 101217. https://doi.org/10.1016/j.learninstruc.2019.101217

Segal, A., & Lefstein, A. (2016). Exuberant, voiceless participation: An unintended consequence of dialogic sensibilities? L1-Educational Studies in Language and Literature 16:1–19. https://doi.org/10.17239/L1ESLL-2016.16.02.06

Segal, A., Pollak, I., & Lefstein, A. (2016). Democracy, voice and dialogic pedagogy: The struggle to be heard and heeded. *Lang Educ, 31*(1), 6–25. https://doi.org/10.1080/09500782.2016.1230124

Sfard, A. (2008). *Thinking as communicating: Human development, the growth of discourses, and mathematizing (Learning in doing: Social, cognitive and computational perspectives)*. New York: Cambridge University Press.

Van de Pol, J., Volman, M., & Beishuizen, J. (2010). Scaffolding in teacher-student interaction: A decade of research. *Education Psychology Review, 22*(3), 271–296. https://doi.org/10.1007/s10648-010-9127-6

Van der Veen, C., de Mey, L., van Kruistum, C., et al. (2017). The effect of productive classroom talk and metacommunication on young children"s oral communicative competence and subject matter knowledge: An intervention study in early childhood education. *Learning Instrument, 48*, 14–22. https://doi.org/10.1016/j.learninstruc.2016.06.001

Vygotsky, L. S. (1978). *Mind in society: The development of higher psychological processes*. Cambridge: Harvard University Press.

Webb, N. M., Franke, M. L., Ing, M., et al. (2014). Engaging with others mathematical ideas: Interrelationships among student participation, teachers instructional practices, and learning. *International Journal Education Research, 63*, 79–93. https://doi.org/10.1016/j.ijer.2013.02.001

Wells, G. (1999). *Dialogic Inquiry: Towards a Sociocultural Practice and Theory of Education*. Cambridge: Cambridge University Press.

Wells, G., & Arauz, R. M. (2006). Dialogue in the classroom. *J Learn Sci, 15*(3), 379–428.

Wertsch, J. V. (1985). *Vygotski and the social formation of mind*. Cambridge: Harvard University Press.

Wilkinson, I. A. G., Murphy, P. K., & Binici, S. (2015). Dialogue-intensive pedagogies for promoting reading comprehension: What we know, what we need to know. In L. B. Resnick, C. S. C. Asterhan, & S. N. Clarke (Eds.). *Socializing Intelligence Through Academic Talk and Dialogue*. 1st Edn. American Educational Research Association, Washington, D.C.

Wood, D., Bruner, J. S., & Ross, G. (1976). The role of tutoring in problem solving. *J Child Psychol Psyc, 17*(2), 89–100. https://doi.org/10.1111/j.1469-7610.1976.tb00381.x

Chapter 2
Elements of Dialogic Teaching and How to Get Them into Classrooms

Abstract In this chapter, we elaborate on components of dialogic teaching. We present repertoires of teaching talk, and indicators and principles as elements that together bring dialogic teaching to life. Further, we describe some initiatives aimed at getting dialogic teaching into the classroom through professional development programs for teachers. We evaluate the success of individual studies and consider what caused the very diverse outcomes of these studies. The diverse outcomes provide evidence that it is not easy to train teachers to implement dialogic teaching in their classrooms. With this notion in mind, in the last part of this chapter we analyze what obstacles teachers face when trying to teach dialogically.

2.1 Elements of Dialogic Teaching

Various concepts strive to capture the essence of dialogic teaching. Below, we will briefly present some of the most influential: repertoires of teaching talk, and indicators and principles of dialogic teaching. The concepts do not compete with each other. Rather, they represent different facets of dialogic teaching and are expected to work in synergy.

2.1.1 Repertoires of Teaching Talk

Alexander (2020) distinguished several repertoires of teaching talk: (a) *rote*—memorizing facts through repetition, (b) *recitation*—using IRE sequences to recall or test what is expected to be known already, (c) *instruction*—telling students what to do and how to do it, (d) *exposition*—the teacher imparting information and explaining things, (e) *discussion*—an open exchange of ideas aiming to share information and juxtapose opinions, (f) *deliberation*—weighing the merits of ideas, opinions, and evidence, (g) *argumentation*—reasoning and giving evidence, and (h) *dialogue*—structured questioning and elaborated responses intended to develop new student understanding; by using this repertoire, the teacher scaffolds student thinking.

Alexander (2020) thought that the last four teaching repertoires (discussion, deliberation, argumentation, and dialogue) could be considered as dialogic, as they emphasize working with language and talk to enhance student thinking and deepen understanding.

This is not to say that four dialogic talk repertoires should be employed all of the time. On the contrary, teachers should use a wide spectrum of communicative approaches, including authoritative ones (Reznitskaya and Wilkinson 2015). Teachers need to be aware of the functions of individual discourses and strategically balance the ratio of the usage of dialogic and non-dialogic repertoires. Some authors (Scott 2008; Nurkka et al. 2014) have spoken of a rhythmization of discourse—referring to alternating between dialogic and non-dialogic—that creates meaningful learning situations. However, it is necessary to bear in mind that the authoritative approach and related kinds of teaching talk (rote, recitation, instruction, and exposition) are very common in contemporary schools. As a result, the call for teachers to have a wide range of communicative patterns and repertoires and balance among them ultimately means that teachers should strengthen their dialogic approach (Mercer and Howe 2012).

2.1.2 Indicators of Dialogic Teaching

Indicators are observable phenomena that signal that dialogic teaching is taking place in the classroom. They can be understood as features of classroom talk from which dialogic teaching emerges. Different authors have used different indicators in their studies (see, e.g. Alexander 2020; Applebee et al. 2003; Molinari and Mameli 2013; Myhill and Warren 2005; Nystrand et al. 1997, 2001; Pimentel and McNeill 2013; Sotter et al. 2008). Recently, Hennessy et al. (2016) published an extensive system of codes to indicate dialogic teaching.

We see four indicators as crucial: teacher's open questions of high cognitive demand, uptake, student thoughts with reasoning, and open discussion. Each of these indicators represents a key element of dialogic teaching. Teacher's open questions of high cognitive demand enable students to go beyond the repetition of what they have already learned and use their thinking to construct new knowledge. Uptake calls on students to elaborate on emerging ideas and think them through on a deeper level. Student thoughts with reasoning most convincingly indicate that students are expressing their own voices and ideas. Finally, open discussion is evidence of polyphony and the inter-animation of voices. All of these elements combined create authentic classroom dialogue.

2.1.2.1 Teachers' Open Questions

Dialogic teaching uses questions that are fundamentally open and divergent because they enable a high degree of uncertainty in the process of establishing what a correct answer is (Burbules 1993). The role of questions in the authoritative approach is to control and evaluate what students know. The role of questions in dialogic teaching is different: they are supposed to help students construct new knowledge (Chin 2006) or inspire meaningful exploration that results in new knowledge (Reznitskaya et al. 2012). Questions thus work as scaffolding; they help identify and elaborate student concepts and construct an appropriate zone of proximal development for them. In other words, teachers use questions to make students think about the teaching content in a new way, one they would not employ without the teachers' assistance.

Multiple typologies of teacher questions have been identified by a number of researchers. For example, Nassaji and Wells (2000) differentiated questions based on the type of information they seek: (a) *known information questions*: one of the participants (typically the teacher) knows the correct answer, and (b) *negotiatory questions*: the answer is reached through discussion. Similarly, Boyd and Rubin (2006) divided questions into: (a) *display questions*: the teacher knows the answer and checks whether the student knows it, (b) *authentic questions*: open questions for which no correct answer exists prior to asking, and (c) *clarification requests*: these stem from a student's prior response that requires further clarification. A key factor for both typologies is the authenticity of the questions (see, e.g. Nystrand et al. 1997, 2001). Authentic questions are similar to real-world questions that speakers ask to acquire information that they do not have. This type of question enables students to express their voices. In contrast, display questions and questions leading to already acquired information can typically be found in the school environment and have little use outside of school (Mehan 1979). In dialogic teaching, authentic questions are preferred, or at least questions in response to which more than one answer could be regarded as correct (open questions).

After authenticity, the level of cognitive demand is the second criterion used to evaluate questions in dialogic teaching (Davis and Tinsley 1967; Gayle et al. 2006). If students do not carry out cognitively demanding operations, they can hardly construct new knowledge. Bloom's taxonomy, as revised by Anderson et al. (2001), is most often used to establish the level of questions. This taxonomy orders processes from the simplest to the most difficult. Remembering a fact is considered the easiest cognitive challenge; creating a new idea or an original product is considered to be the greatest cognitive challenge. The revised taxonomy is rather complex, and thus, its value is mostly theoretical. When it is used in real-world situations to evaluate the nature of teacher questions, the taxonomy is simplified to distinguish between two types of questions (Sedova et al. 2012): (a) questions of low cognitive demand that verify whether a previously taught fact is still remembered by students, and (b) questions of high cognitive demand that activate the higher categories of Bloom's taxonomy: understanding, application, analysis, evaluation, and creation. At the same time, it should hold that the answers that students seek are not available to them in textbooks or other material.

If we combine the dimensions of authenticity (openness) and cognitive demand, four types of questions emerge: (a) *closed questions of low cognitive demand*, which seek to check a fact previously learned by students, (b) *closed questions of high cognitive demand*, which ask students to apply a rule—as such, these questions do not rely on memorization since they presume student understanding, (c) *open questions of low cognitive demand*, which could be used to make students list examples from a broad range of possibilities—they would not need to perform any cognitively demanding tasks—examples include questions about aspects of students' lives that may be connected to the educational content currently being taught, and (d) *open question of high cognitive demand*, which lead to analysis, evaluation, or creation—no correct answers exist prior to the teacher's query. The theory of dialogic teaching considers the last type of questions to be the most valuable type for the development of student thinking.

2.1.2.2 Uptake

Uptake is just one of many types of feedback. According to Chin (2006), four types of teacher reactions to student responses can be distinguished: (a) the teacher receives a correct answer, validates it, and continues with a monologue or asks another question, (b) the teacher receives a correct answer and asks a follow-up question that elaborates on the previous idea, (c) the teacher receives an incorrect answer and corrects the student, and (d) the teacher receives an incorrect answer and asks a slightly revised or a guiding question.

Chin (2006) claimed that the second and fourth types of reaction are aligned with dialogic teaching. Such reactions can be described as uptake since they build upon what a student said by asking a follow-up question or providing a new stimulus. A key feature of teacher uptake is that it is connected to student responses. McElhone (2012) stated that teachers press students conceptually by providing them with uptake: the teachers make the students improve responses that were not complete, specific, or elaborate enough or that lacked support from evidence or example.

Teacher uptake disrupts the prevalent IRE pattern in which a teacher's question is followed by a student's response and then the teacher's evaluation that identifies the response as either correct or incorrect (Mehan 1979). Scott et al. (2010) claimed that uptake changes the structure of communication: instead of IRE, a new pattern of IRPR emerges in which the P stands for a prompt to be elaborated. The prompt merges feedback and a new question. This explains why the prompt is not followed by a new initiation (I) but instead by a new response (R). Classroom talk based on IRE is often considered to be rather unnatural because teachers ask a great number of questions and each question changes the course of the talk. If teachers provide students with uptake, they guarantee greater coherence in the conversation because the participants stay focused on one topic for a longer period of time. The topic is not abandoned for another once the first correct answer is provided; instead, it is elaborated further. Molinari and Mameli (2013) stated that this approach results in co-constructive sequences, which are a typical sign of the dialogic approach.

Knowledge is constructed by students with support from the teacher, who provides them with uptake and pressures them to elaborate on their responses.

Scott et al. (2010) stated that the aim of uptake is to suppress evaluation; evaluation always makes the teacher's voice more dominant since the teacher speaks both when approving an answer and when rejecting it. Nystrand et al. (1997) claimed that uptake validates student responses since by using it teachers express interest in student responses and give them the opportunity to make their answers more nuanced, emphasizing the students' voices.

2.1.2.3 Elaborated Student Thoughts with Reasoning

The nature of student utterances is an appropriate indicator for dialogic teaching. Teacher talk dominates most of the classroom time in traditionally conceived teaching. Student utterances are much shorter and less elaborated than teacher utterances. The aim of dialogic teaching is to empower student talk, which requires student utterances to be longer. For example, as a criterion of dialogicity Boyd and Rubin (2006) used *extended student talk* for an uninterrupted student speech on educational content lasting for at least 10 s.

Another criterion for considering student utterances is the cognitive processes that the students manifest in them. For example, Chinn et al. (2001) classified student responses in a language arts class based on the students' ability to: (a) interconnect ideas expressed in different parts of the assigned readings, (b) relate ideas found in the readings to content acquired outside of the school institution, (c) predict how the assigned reading would continue, (d) justify the causality of the read narrative, and (5) express a different opinion on the readings than the ones already voiced by their peers.

Pimentel and McNeill (2013) created a classification of student responses by combining the criteria of both length and cognitive level. Their classification distinguished four types of student utterances: (a) *no response*—a student does not reply even though asked to do so, (b) *word/phrase*, (c) *complete thought*—the response is structured as a sentence and includes no reasoning, and (d) *thought and reasoning*—the response describes a complete idea that includes either reasoning or argumentation.

Webb et al. (2014) noted that higher cognitive processes manifested in student utterances can arise when students elaborate on either their own ideas or ideas from their peers. Hennessy et al. (2016) took only those responses in which reasoning is made explicit as dialogic. These responses can include any of the following examples of reasoning: explanation, justification, providing an argument or counter-argument, analogy, categorization, making distinctions, and use of evidence.

2.1.2.4 Open Discussion

The most recurrent pattern of classroom talk is IRE: the initiation—response—evaluation pattern enacted between teacher and student (Mehan 1979). Open discussion disrupts the IRE pattern by opening up the common communicative dyad of teacher and student via the inclusion of more speakers. Nystrand et al. (1997) defined open discussion as a sequence that includes at least three participants and lasts at least thirty seconds. Wells and Arauz (2006) added that the teacher can (but does not have to) be one of the speakers in the open discussion. Molinari and Mameli (2013) labeled the same pattern as triadic interaction, as at least three participants interact together. From the perspective of dialogic teaching, the main advantage of open discussion is that it brings about polyphony and the inter-animation of voices.

Open discussion presents students with an opportunity to participate in the active construction of knowledge that they can influence and adjust (Mameli et al. 2015). This is done through speakers building upon one another's contributions. According to Asterhan and Schwarz (2016), three different types of discourse can arise: (a) *consensual co-construction*: speakers react to one another's verbal contributions by expanding, elaborating, or explaining ideas and do not challenge or criticize the ideas of others, (b) *disputative argumentation*: speakers defend their own viewpoint and undermine alternatives to convince an opponent to switch sides, thus aiming at winning at the expense of their opponent, and (c) *deliberative argumentation*: speakers listen to and critically examine the different ideas that are proposed in the course of a collaborative and respectful discussion and search for alternative perspectives that have not yet been considered. Even though Asterhan and Schwarz (2016) considered deliberative argumentation to be the most beneficial type of discourse, all three listed types have features of dialogic teaching and represent different types of open discussion.

2.1.3 Principles of Dialogic Teaching

In the previous chapter, we introduced individual elements of classroom talk that serve as indicators of dialogic teaching. Some academics have argued that the mere presence of indicators does not guarantee the presence of dialogic teaching. For example, Boyd and Markarian (2011, 2015) questioned the indicator of open questions, since their studies showed that teachers can motivate students to participate actively in open discussion even through the use of closed questions.

The reverse situation was described by Lefstein et al. (2015), who showed that a teacher can ask open questions to which students respond with short and abrupt replies. Apparently, the presence of the indicator of open questions does not in itself stimulate students to produce long and elaborated responses.

These findings open the possibility that these indicators cannot truly capture the nature of dialogic teaching. Boyd and Markarian (2011) used the term *dialogic stance*, which they did not relate to any specific discourse. They added that it is necessary to

2.1 Elements of Dialogic Teaching

observe function and not form. They further claimed that a group of students and a teacher enter a dialogic stance when students participate authentically and produce elaborate responses that build upon and relate to what has already been said by their peers. On a similar note, Lefstein and Snell (2014) used the term *dialogic moment* to describe a pedagogically rich sequence between a teacher and students that includes authentic student thinking and participation.

It is worth noting that both concepts are bound to specific situations. Lefstein and Snell (2014) claimed that dialogic moments can occur in a class for varying lengths of time. As such, their term does not describe a common feature of teaching nor an ability of teachers. Both Boyd and Markarian (2011) and Lefstein and Snell (2014) strove to avoid false (and largely formal) signs of dialogic teaching, and their concepts are suitable tools in such an endeavor. On the other hand, the terms are limited by being so vague that they are almost interchangeable with the common definition of dialogic teaching.

Another way to reconcile the fact that the mere presence of indicators does not equal dialogic teaching is Alexander's (2020) list of dialogic teaching principles. According to Alexander, these principles are complementary to repertoires and indicators as a gauge of the overall quality of teaching. Alexander conceived of the principles as general imperatives that need to be followed in dialogic teaching. According to Alexander, a dialogue has to be:

- *Collective*: The whole classroom (or all groups in the classroom) participates in the classroom talk. The learning tasks need to be directed toward all students; all participants take part in joint learning and enquiry.
- *Supportive*: The students feel supported by their teacher and peers in expressing their ideas. They are not worried about entering classroom communication, providing an incorrect answer, or potentially being ridiculed by their peers for an incorrect answer.
- *Reciprocal*: All participants listen to one another, share their ideas, and ponder the ideas of their peers. Any person can be in the position of the person who is asking or answering a question.
- *Deliberative*: Participants share and compare different points of view working toward a reasoned position.
- *Cumulative*: Talk progresses forward, individual responses build upon one another, and what has been said gets elaborated. Classroom talk takes into account its previous stages; a coherent line of thorough inquiry into the taught educational content is created.
- *Purposeful*: The teaching is aligned with specific teaching aims. Talk is a tool to be purposefully used in meeting curricular goals.

The principles are to be applied in parallel to repertoires and indicators. The principles play a corrective role and carry, perhaps, more significance than the indicators, as the indicators on their own do not guarantee dialogic teaching. At the same time, the principles in themselves are of a rather abstract nature and therefore more difficult to observe in the reality of the classroom than the indicators are. In addition, empirical studies researching the principles of dialogic teaching are far from common.

A study by Nurkka et al. (2014) is an exception as it examined the principle of cumulativity. The study operationalized cumulativity as an oscillation between the authoritative and dialogic approaches as it opens up and closes down discussions with different prevailing discourse types. A study by Van de Pol et al. (2017) examined the principles of collectivity, supportivity, reciprocity, and cumulativity. The study defined collectivity as a high degree of student talk that is enabled by a decrease in teacher talk. Supportivity was operationalized as the presence of authentic student and teacher questions. The authors of the study delineated reciprocity as situations in which one student reacts to what another student said. Finally, they defined cumulativity as identical with uptake. This approach by Van de Pol et al. (2017) slightly erodes the differences between the indicators and principles of dialogic teaching that are so clearly apparent in Alexander's (2006, 2017, 2020) seminal conception.

2.2 Teacher Professional Development Programs as a Tool for Delivering Dialogic Teaching to Classrooms

It is apparent that the concept of dialogic teaching as it is currently presented in the scholarly literature is enriched by complex and nuanced theory. Nonetheless, the empirical studies that map the current actual situation in classrooms can be summarized with a simple statement: dialogically conceived teaching is only very rarely seen (see Howe and Abedin 2013). There is a vast divide between theory and practice as the academic concepts of dialogic teaching clearly have little impact on what is going on in classrooms (Mercer and Howe 2012).

Not surprisingly, many intervention projects have been created that strive to introduce dialogic teaching into schools via teacher professional development (TPD) programs (e.g. Alexander 2018; Chinn et al. 2001; Hennessy et al. 2018; Lefstein and Snell 2014; Nystrand et al. 1997; Osborne et al. 2019; Reznitskaya et al. 2001; Schwarz et al. 2017). Some of these projects were successful; others reported only limited or no outcomes.

When designing TPD programs, researchers can learn from what has been discovered about effective TPD programs over the last two decades. Several influential reviews on the traits of effective TPD programs have been published (see, e.g. Borko et al. 2010; Darling-Hammond et al. 2017; Desimone 2009; Gaudin and Chaliès 2015) emphasizing traits like active experiential learning of participating teachers, using video recordings of teaching, reflections of teaching, peer collaboration and discussion during TPD, etc. Moreover, Wilkinson et al. (2015) summarized what proved to be effective in programs focused specifically on implementing dialogic teaching: (a) reflection on teaching practices through video recording and transcripts, (b) co-inquiry and co-planning of lessons, and (c) a dialogic approach to professional development. Below we will refer to studies sharing these traits.

However, even the projects that take these suggestions as guidelines are not necessarily successful in changing classroom talk patterns. What we want to show here is that even similarly designed projects have thus far produced very different outcomes. Our aim is not to present a comprehensive overview, as we include only studies based on measuring changes in classroom talk patterns as a result of an intervention. Simply said, we introduce here only studies that recorded and assessed the nature of classroom talk in participating classes, subsequently intervened in classroom talk through a TPD program, and then again recorded and assessed the classroom talk to evaluate changes in its nature. Below, we briefly describe the methodology of the projects and summarize their main findings.

Chinn et al. (2001) trained teachers in how to use collaborative reasoning, an approach to literature discussion intended to stimulate critical reading and thinking as well as personal engagement. Four teachers and their fourth-grade classes participated in the project. In the first step, each participating teacher had a class recorded on video. Subsequently, the teachers took part in a workshop focused on the use of collaborative reasoning. The teachers then prepared lessons using collaborative reasoning. Each teacher worked in tandem with one researcher, who followed the progress of the teaching and discussed it with the teacher. At the end of the project, two recordings of each teacher's lessons were made and compared with their first video from before the teachers had attended the workshop. This comparison revealed an increase in dialogic indicators—the students had begun to talk more in class, and the teachers talked less. The proportion of student responses to other students rose dramatically and the proportion of student-elaborated utterances providing evidence for a claim or offering alternative perspectives rose. The total number of teacher questions fell, but the proportion of authentic questions rose.

Wells and Arauz (2006) conducted a professional development program that lasted for seven years and had a fairly open structure. The participants were teachers interested in adopting an inquiry orientation to classroom discourse. The length of their involvement in the project varied. The group met over the years at workshops and discussion sessions. The nine teachers involved made regular video recordings of their own teaching. Researchers then divided the recorded episodes according to whether they were taken in the project's initial or final phase. These files were then compared to determine whether there had been a change in classroom discourse as a result of participation in the project. The researchers were primarily interested in instances of open discussion. They noted that there had been an increase in the number of discussion-type sequences, but the proportion of these sequences remained low.

Lefstein and Snell (2014) and Snell and Lefstein (2011) carried out a development program for teachers in which they monitored whether classroom talk became more dialogic. The program was conducted at a single elementary school and involved biweekly professional development workshops in which the researchers facilitated collaborative lesson planning and reflection on video excerpts of the classroom practices of seven teachers. Snell and Lefstein (2011) subsequently compared selected indicators (especially types of teacher questions and teacher feedback) across the sample in order to determine whether there had been a shift toward dialogic teaching. An increase in the openness of teacher questions was the only common pattern found.

Osborne et al. (2013) collaborated with eight teachers from four middle schools. Over the course of two years, the teachers attended five workshop days with the researchers and subsequently were supposed to disseminate the knowledge gained at their school through reflective meetings with other teachers. The workshops were mainly devoted to the question of how to engage students in discussion and how to get them to argue and model this argumentation. Between the workshops, the researchers visited the schools and collected data, including making video recordings, but did not provide the teachers with systematic feedback on their teaching. They relied on the expectation that the process of professional growth would stem from the teachers themselves. However, their subsequent evaluation of student performance revealed no changes.

Pimentel and McNeill (2013) surveyed the approach to discussion taken by five teachers in a professional development program focused on the implementation of urban ecology lessons in a middle school curriculum. The program included the question of how to promote active student participation in class discussions. All of the teachers in the program were asked to give two lessons that were recorded on video. A subsequent analysis showed that none of the teachers taught dialogically, the approach to teaching was authoritative, student-initiated interactions appeared only rarely, and most student utterances amounted to a single word or a simple phrase. There were few cases of students expressing more elaborate thoughts containing reasoning.

A group of researchers around Seidel and Gröschner are developing an ongoing *dialogic video cycle* program (see, e.g. Gröschner et al. 2015) using video as a reflective tool. In one of their studies (Pehmer et al. 2015), they involved six ninth-grade teachers in TPD with the aim of improving classroom dialogue. The core of the program lay in workshops that included group discussions of video recordings of the teaching of the participating teachers. Change was evaluated by comparing the teaching in the recordings made before the project to those from after its completion. In the analysis, the researchers focused on the types of teacher questions and feedback and the nature of student talk. They noted that the teacher questions and student talk remained unchanged, but the feedback changed; at the end of the project, feedback was less focused on tasks and more focused on student learning processes and self-regulation.

Since the 1990s, studies by O'Connor, Chapin, Michaels, and others have focused on the dialogic approach and "academically productive talk" from the perspective of research and further professional development. In their intervention program called *Project Challenge*, they focused on teaching mathematics in fourth through seventh grades. Only students who were identified as having potential talent in mathematics participated in the program. The program implemented change in the form of *talk moves*, which are "simple families of conversational moves intended to accomplish local goals" (Michaels and O'Connor 2015, p. 348). These simple formal tools serve teachers in eliciting responses in discussion and commenting on them (e.g. "What do you think of that?", "How would you explain it?", "Which ideas can you use to support your opinion?", "Based on what can you say so?"). The intervention included a choice of different tasks since the teachers were invited to rely on more challenging assignments. Additionally, the researchers assisted teachers in using certain discursive talk moves to open up discussion and facilitate academically productive talk. The students were taught using this approach for one to four years. The results showed that teachers' use of academically productive talk increased students' ability to argue in mathematics and that they performed significantly better than students who were not taught with this approach. Students taught with academically productive talk outperformed all of the other students in the district on standardized math tests (Chapin et al. 2009). Furthermore, their ability to listen to the teacher and explain their own ideas increased, as did their participation in complex mathematical discussion.

Wilkinson et al. (2017) created a professional development program to help elementary teachers use dialogic teaching to support students' argument literacy. Thirteen fifth-grade teachers were tasked with using text-based discussion to lead students to comprehend and formulate oral and written arguments. Their development program lasted eight months and comprised two intensive workshops, seven study group meetings, and four individual coaching sessions. The effects of the intervention were measured with pre- and post-intervention tests. The data were collected through several types of interviews and videotaping of classes. Teachers' leading of inquiry dialogue in text-based discussions was recorded on video so that any change could be observed and noted. The research team paid particular attention to the quality of recorded teacher facilitation and student participation. Pre- and post-intervention tests revealed a marked (and statistically significant) increase in both observed phenomena.

A large-scale intervention in English elementary schools across English, mathematics, and science classes was carried out by the foremost expert on dialogic teaching, Robin Alexander (Alexander 2018; Jay et al. 2017). Teachers from 38 schools along with 2492 fifth graders participated in the project. The teachers underwent a professional development program in which they presented recordings of their classes that showed how they attempted to implement dialogic teaching. The goal of the program was to teach teachers of various subjects to "deploy a variety of moves to probe, extend, and follow up pupil contributions on the principle that these would both improve engagement and yield cognitive gains" (Jay et al. 2017, p. 39). The teachers were provided with numerous sources on dialogic teaching and on how to obtain a quality recording of their lessons. They talked about their attempts at implementation with mentors, other teachers from their school, and university experts. They found discussions with mentors to be of the greatest value as this enabled them to talk about the relevant theoretical concepts. The effects of the intervention program were observed via recordings from both intervention and control classes: one recording was taken at the beginning of the trial and one at its end. The two recordings were subjected to qualitative and quantitative analysis. Quantitative analysis of the teachers' and students' selected verbal indicators revealed profound differences between the control and intervention groups. The participating teachers asked a higher number of open and follow-up questions and a smaller number of closed questions than teachers from the control group did. Furthermore, tests showed that students from the intervention classes had significantly better results than students from the non-intervention classes did (Jay et al. 2017).

This overview showed studies based on similar designs but resulting in divergent outcomes. Some of the programs can be considered very effective, having produced convincing changes in talk patterns in the classrooms (e.g. Chinn et al. 2001; Alexander 2018); others were substantially less effective. Even though all of the programs were well thought out, supported with the necessary theory, and carried out by experienced researchers, it does not hold that all of the original expectations were met. In most cases, only partial changes occurred.

From the observation of different impacts of similar projects, two important questions emerge to be considered. First, when thinking about the successful interventions, we have to ask what the underlying mechanisms of change are. The essence does not reside in design or in conformity with the guidelines of effective TPD projects. If this were the case, all the studies described above would have had comparable outcomes. As Walkoe and Luna (2020) stated, we have still a limited understanding of the process and mechanism of teacher learning in TPD, and thus we need a microgenetic analysis of how teachers are progressing to achieve TPD goals. This is what we attempt to offer in this book, primarily in Chaps 5, 6 and 7. Second, when thinking about the comparatively unsuccessful interventions, we have to ask what the obstacles causing the resistance to substantial change of talk patterns are. If so many projects fail to achieve their goals, there must be some common barriers impeding the changes. A careful analysis of the obstacles to dialogic teaching is thus needed.

2.3 Troubles with Dialogic Teaching

We have stated that the prevalent style of teaching is quite far from dialogic ideals. Teachers tend to teach in a traditional directive manner, using non-dialogic repertoires of teaching talk (rote, recitation, instruction, and exposition—see Sect. 2.1.1). Even when they take part in TPD focused on dialogic teaching, it is not always conducive to change. We can infer from this that there must be some obstacles for teachers who aspire to dialogic teaching. Few studies have carefully examined these obstacles—see Resnick et al. (2018), Hennessy and Davies (2020), and Sedova et al. (2014). However, many studies offer some partial reasons for the scarcity of dialogic teaching as the apparent divide between theory and practice provokes the search for an explanation. Below, we will summarize the most discussed sources of trouble with dialogic teaching.

2.3.1 Organizational Constraints

Some authors claim that the implementation of dialogic teaching is limited by the organizational constraints around teaching in schools. At school, conversation is different from in other settings. There is pre-defined content (curriculum), scheduled time and duration (lesson), and quite a high number of participants (students).

Concerning curriculum, Lefstein (2010) argued that the necessity to connect classroom talk to the curriculum prevents teachers from developing the ideas introduced by students. Sedova et al. (2014) conducted interviews with teachers and found that teachers perceive dialogue with students as desirable, but they see it as being in contradiction to their commitment to teach the subject matter. They see dialogue and discussion as something additional that does not contribute to building disciplinary knowledge in students. Dialogic teaching is thus perceived as an oxymoron of sorts. Resnick et al. (2018) added to this that testing plays an increasingly important role in schools, pushing teachers to focus on test preparation. This implies delivering facts and ready-made information rather than discussing different points of view.

According to Michaels and O'Connor (2015), teachers experience fear about the content of their discussions and worry that they will not be able to keep the discussions within the boundaries staked by the curriculum. They are anxious that discussions may require them to possess knowledge that they do not have.

Simply said, curriculum is firmly determined at school. In contrast, authentic dialogue is not fully predictable and kept under control. Twiner et al. (2014) noted that flexible interplay is needed between a teacher's intended meaning-making trajectory and the meaning-making trajectories that are instantiated in interaction with students through dialogic interaction. This means that teachers enter the classroom with certain plans that pursue educational goals. The teachers need to ensure that their students' spontaneous conversations will not digress from the pursuit of the goals or discourage the students from achieving them. However, to keep this balance between what is intended (curriculum) and what is spontaneous (dialogic interaction) is not an easy task for teachers.

Time pressure goes hand in hand with curricular concerns. As Michaels and O'Connor (2015) claimed, teachers feel a constant lack of time to deliver the content prescribed by the curriculum and to achieve the assessment goals. Similar findings were reported by Lefstein (2010) and Sedova et al. (2014). The time pressure can cause teachers to give little space to student contributions and their elaboration. Leading students to construct the knowledge on their own is much more time consuming than when the teacher gives them the correct answer straight away. Thus, the limited time available for a given curricular unit means a challenge for the dialogic approach.

Further, there are many students in the classroom, some of whom are keen to talk while others prefer to stay silent (Sedova and Navratilova 2020). In dialogic teaching, all students are expected to talk and to be heard, as the dialogue is to be collective (Alexander 2020). Again, the intention to let all students express their voices is contradicted by the limited time in a lesson (see Lefstein and Snell 2014). Moreover, most classes are rather heterogeneous. Student abilities are not equally developed; student family backgrounds can also vary significantly. It is an accepted fact that family background and cognitive aptitude play a decisive role in a student's learning motivation and academic achievement (Hattie and Yates 2013). In such a situation, it is difficult for a teacher to plan and create meaningful scaffolding because it presumes a more or less individual diagnosis of the skills and abilities that a given student has already acquired. In dialogic teaching, the teacher should give students tasks that are located in their zone of proximal development (Vygotsky 1978). However, this is not easy to do in a collective classroom setting when the zones of individual students differ.

Finally, teachers at school have to deal with classroom management. Dialogic teaching is founded on symmetrical relationships between a teacher and students in the sense that the students are free to express their voices (Mortimer and Scott 2003). This is closely connected to the idea that power relationships in dialogic teaching should be democratic (Lyle 2008). However, case studies have clearly shown that it is difficult for teachers to maintain a positive working atmosphere enabling focused teaching and learning in their classrooms without relying on traditional authoritative methods of classroom management (Lefstein 2002; Pace 2003; Sedova 2011; Winograd 2002). These studies demonstrated that teachers who strive for democratic relationships in the classroom based on student empowerment often face disruptions and resistance from the students. Consequently, a lack of dialogue in the classroom can be the result of the teacher's fears of student misbehavior.

2.3.2 Teacher Mindset

There is an agreement among scholars in the field that deep change in teaching cannot happen without a shift in teachers' conceptual knowledge and beliefs (Butler et al. 2004). Hennessy and Davies (2020) claim that a non-trivial shift in teacher mindsets is needed for the implementation of dialogic teaching.

Resnick et al. (2018) claim that many teachers believe that students must learn facts before they can engage in meaningful dialogue. This approach to learning as accumulating bits of information through drill and practice is incompatible with dialogic teaching. According to Hennessy and Davies (2020), teachers' epistemological orientation toward genuine commitment to student ideas and agency are necessary prerequisites for dialogic teaching. As we have outlined above, teachers feel committed to the curriculum, making them less sensitive to student voices and agency. Mercer et al. (2019) asserted that there is no unavoidable conflict between curriculum and the dialogic approach, as dialogue develops learning and thinking skills in students and thus supports the curricular aims. However, to recognize this requires abandoning the traditional view of what learning at school means.

One more category of teacher beliefs obstructs dialogic teaching: their conception of students. Many authors claim that this is the critical point, since many teachers believe that not all students are capable of engaging in challenging dialogue (e.g. Pimentel and McNeill 2013; Snell and Lefstein 2018). As Hofmann (2020) wrote, teachers' understanding of their students' capabilities is often a barrier to change toward more dialogic practices. Dialogic teaching is based on challenging students thinking. To do so, teachers have to expect all student in the classroom to be able to think and reason at high levels. According to Resnick et al. (2018), belief that differences in inherited intelligence explain most differences in learning success, is reversive to dialogic teaching.

Teachers believing in different dispositions of students to take part in productive dialogue tend to exclude low-achieving or silent students from communication (Jackson 2011), or engage them in non-challenging interactions (Black 2004; Sedova and Salamounova 2016) addressing them only if the task is simple. This strategy violates the principle of collectivity (Alexander 2020) and inflicts that not all student in the classroom can benefit from classroom talk the same way.

2.3.3 Unbearable Complexity of Change

Hennessy and Davies (2020) hypothesized that one reason that TPD on dialogic teaching may have a limited impact is that the change it requires in teaching style is too complex and demanding for the teachers. The notion about the complexity of the change is shown in Sect. 2.1, introducing various elements that together define dialogic teaching. Teachers should simultaneously use the appropriate repertoire of teaching talk, implement adequate indicators of dialogic teaching, and maintain all of the principles of dialogic teaching. Moreover, they have to do all this while being limited in time and curriculum (see above). According to Resnick et al. (2018), dialogic teaching requires a set of complex skills that must be hard-developed during TPD and require continuous support to be sustained. Otherwise, teachers tend to regress to "safe" forms of classroom talk.

Thus, even when teachers favor dialogic teaching and strive to implement it in their classrooms, they often fail. There are some valuable case studies of teachers who adopted only partial or superficial features of dialogic teaching, and who—despite their efforts—failed to preserve meaningful classroom dialogue (see, e.g. Billings and Fitzgerald 2002; Lefstein 2008; Emanuelsson and Sahlström 2008; Nystrand et al. 1997). Simply said, it is difficult for teachers to put dialogic teaching into practice (Lefstein 2010; Resnick et al. 2018) and this might be an explanation for why dialogic teaching is so rare.

The transition toward dialogic teaching is extremely challenging as it requires changing teacher-student interaction patterns (Juzwik et al. 2012). Lefstein (2008) stated that teachers find implementing dialogic teaching difficult since it takes place on the micro-level of interaction between teachers and students, which is typically outside of teachers' conscious control and so is ruled by ingrained habits and routines. Therefore, even when teachers agree with the main ideas of dialogic teaching, they find it difficult to adapt their behavior and classroom practices accordingly.

More than teacher education or intentional decisions, an important role is played by the experiences that a teacher had as a student. Teachers often imitate what they observed from their teachers and mentors who were powerful role models (Lortie 1975; Gröschner et al. 2020). Therefore, as Gröschner et al. (2020) argued, reflecting on their own school experiences is an important aspect of a teacher's adapting to dialogic teaching. More generally, to get one's own interaction behavior under conscious control requires explicit effort in changing well-established norms (Hofmann 2020).

2.4 Summary

In this chapter, we presented various elements of dialogic teaching: repertoires of teaching talk with an emphasis on the dialogic ones: discussion, deliberation, argumentation, and dialogue. Further, we introduced indicators of dialogic teaching stressing four of them as essential: open questions of high cognitive demand, uptake, elaborated student thoughts with reasoning, and open discussion. Finally, we presented the six principles of dialogic teaching: that it should be collective, reciprocal, deliberative, supportive, cumulative, and purposeful. We take dialogic teaching as an intersection of these three dimensions: it takes place in dialogic repertoires, the dialogic indicators are present, and the dialogic principles are followed.

We have described several intervention programs focused on implementation of dialogic teaching. We showed that despite having similar designs, these programs have produced heterogeneous results, with some of them not producing any convincing change. We discussed why it is hard for teachers to transform their teaching into dialogic teaching. We introduced three main sources of troubles with dialogic teaching—organizational constraints, teacher mindset, and the complexity of change. We argued that when interpreting outcomes of successful intervention programs, it is necessary to look in detail into how teachers learned in these programs.

References

Alexander, R. J. (2006). *Towards dialogic teaching: Rethinking classroom talk* (3rd ed.). Cambridge: Dialogos.
Alexander, R. J. (2017). *Towards dialogic teaching: Rethinking classroom talk* (5th ed.). Cambridge: Dialogos.
Alexander, R. J. (2018). Developing dialogic teaching: Genesis, process, trial. *Research Papers in Education, 33*(5), 561–598.
Alexander, R. J. (2020). *A dialogic teaching companion*. London: Routledge.
Anderson, L. W., Krathwohl, D. R., Airasian, P. W., et al. (Eds.). (2001). *A taxonomy for learning, teaching and assessing: A revision of Bloom's taxonomy of educational objectives* (1st ed.). New York: Longman.
Applebee, A. N., Langer, J. A., Nystrand, M., et al. (2003). Discussion-based approaches to developing understanding: Classroom instruction and student performance in middle and high school English. *American Educational Research Journal, 40*(3), 685–730. https://doi.org/10.3102/00028312040003685
Asterhan, C. S. C., & Schwarz, B. B. (2016). Argumentation for learning: Well-trodden paths and unexplored territories. *Education Psychology, 51*(2), 164–187. https://doi.org/10.1080/00461520.2016.1155458
Billings, L., & Fitzgerald, J. (2002). Dialogic discussion and the Paideia Seminar. *American Educational Research Journal, 39*(4), 907–941. https://doi.org/10.3102/00028312039004905
Black, L. (2004). Differential participation in whole-class discussions and the construction of marginalised identities. *Journal of Educational Enquiry, 5*(1), 34–54.
Borko, H., Jacobs, H. & Koellner, K. (2010). Contemporary approaches to teacher professional development. In E. Baker, B. McGaw & P. Peterson (Eds.). *International Encyclopedia of Education*. Elsevier, Oxford

References

Boyd, M. P., & Markarian, W. C. (2011). Dialogic teaching: Talk in service of a dialogic stance. *Language Education, 25*(6), 515–534. https://doi.org/10.1080/09500782.2011.597861

Boyd, M. P., & Markarian, W. C. (2015). Dialogic teaching and dialogic stance: Moving beyond interactional form. *Research Teacher English, 49*(3), 272–296.

Boyd, M. P., & Rubin, D. (2006). How contingent questioning promotes extended student talk: A function of display questions. *Journal Literature Research, 38*(2), 141–169. https://doi.org/10.1207/s15548430jlr3802_2

Burbules, N. C. (1993). *Dialogue in teaching: Theory and practice*. New York: Teachers College Press.

Butler, D. L., Novak Lauscher, H., Jarvis-Selinger, S., et al. (2004). Collaboration and self-regulation in teachers' professional development. *Teacher Teacher Education, 20*(5), 435–455. https://doi.org/10.1016/j.tate.2004.04.003

Chapin, S. H., O'Connor, C., & Anderson, N. C. (2009). *Classroom discussions: Using math talk to help students learn, Grades K-6*. Sausalito: Math Solutions.

Chin, C. (2006). Classroom interaction in science: Teacher questioning and feedback to students' responses. *International Journal of Science Education, 28*(11), 1315–1346. https://doi.org/10.1080/09500690600621100

Chinn, C. A., Anderson, R. C., & Waggoner, M. A. (2001). Patterns of discourse in two kinds of literature discussion. *Reading Research Quarterly, 36*(4), 378–411. https://doi.org/10.1598/RRQ.36.4.3

Darling-Hammond, L., Hyler, M. E., & Gardner, M. (2017). *Effective teacher professional development*. Palo Alto: Learning Policy Institute.

Davis, O. L., & Tinsley, D. C. (1967). Cognitive objectives revealed by classroom questions asked by social studies student teachers and their pupils. *Peabody Journal of Education, 45*, 21–26.

Desimone, L. M. (2009). Improving impact studies of teachers' professional development: Toward better conceptualizations and measures. *Educational Researcher, 38*(3), 181–199.

Emanuelsson, J., & Sahlström, F. (2008). The price of participation: Teacher control versus student participation in classroom interaction. *Scandinavian Journal Education Research, 52*(2), 205–223. https://doi.org/10.1080/00313830801915853

Gaudin, C., & Chaliès, S. (2015). Video viewing in teacher education and professional development: A literature review. *Educational Research Review, 16*(1), 41–67.

Gayle, B. M., Preiss, R. W. & Allen, M. (2006). How effective are teacher-initiated classroom questions in enhancing student learning? In B. M. Gayle, R. W. Preiss, & N. Burrell et al. (Eds.). *Classroom communication and instructional processes: Advances through meta-analysis*. 1st edn. Erlbaum, Mahwah.

Gröschner, A., Jähne, M. F., & Klass, S. (2020). Attitudes towards dialogic teaching and the choice to teach: The role of preservice teachers' perception on their own school experience. In N. Mercer, R. Wegerif & L. Major (Eds.). *The Routledge international handbook of research on dialogic education*. Routledge, Abingdon.

Gröschner, A., Seidel, T., Kiemer, K., & Pehmer, A.-K. (2015). Through the lens of teacher professional development components: The 'Dialogic Video Cycle' as an innovative program to foster classroom dialogue. *Professional Development in Education, 41*(4), 729–756.

Hattie, J., & Yates, G. C. R. (2013). *Visible learning and the science of how we learn*. Abingdon, New York: Routledge.

Hennessy, S., & Davies, M. (2020). Teacher professional development to support classroom dialogue: Challenges and promisses. In N. Mercer, R. Wegerif & L. Major (Eds.). *The Routledge international handbook of research on dialogic education*. Routledge, Abingdon.

Hennessy, S., Dragovic, T., & Warwick, P. (2018). A research-informed, school-based professional development workshop programme to promote dialogic teaching with interactive technologies. *Professional Development in Education, 44*(2), 145–168. https://doi.org/10.1080/19415257.2016.1258653

Hennessy, S., Rojas-Drummond, S., Higham, R., et al. (2016). Developing a coding scheme for analysing classroom dialogue across educational contexts. *Learning Culture Social Interaction, 9*, 16–44. https://doi.org/10.1016/j.lcsi.2015.12.001

Hofmann, R. (2020). Dialogue, teachers and professional development. In N. Mercer, R. Wegerif & L. Major (Eds.). *The Routledge international handbook of research on dialogic education.* Routledge, Abingdon.

Howe, C., & Abedin, M. (2013). Classroom dialogue: A systematic review accross four decades of research. *Cambridge Journal of Education, 43*(3), 325–356. https://doi.org/10.1080/0305764X.2013.786024

Jackson, K. (2011). Approaching participation in school-based mathematics as a cross-setting phenomenon. *Journal of the Learning Sciences, 20*(1), 115–150.

Jay, T., Willis, B., Thomas, P., et al. (2017). *Dialogic teaching: Evaluation report and executive summary.* London: Education Endowment Foundation.

Juzwik, M. M., Sherry, M. B. & Caughlan, S. et al. (2012). Supporting dialogically organized instruction in an English teacher preparation program: A video-based, web 2.0-mediated response and revision pedagogy. *Teachers College Record 114*(3), 1–42.

Lefstein, A. (2002). Thinking power and pedagogy apart—Coping with discipline in progressivist school reform. *Teachers College Record, 104*(8), 1627–1655. https://doi.org/10.1111/1467-9620.00215

Lefstein, A. (2008). Changing classroom practice through the english national literacy strategy: A micro-interactional perspective. *American Educational Research Journal, 45*(3), 701–737. https://doi.org/10.3102/0002831208316256

Lefstein A (2010) More helpful as problem than solution: Some implications of situating dialogue in classrooms. In K. Littleton & C. Howe (Eds.). *Educational dialogues: Understanding and promoting productive interaction.* 1st edn. Routledge, Abingdon, New York.

Lefstein, A., & Snell, J. (2014). *Better than best practice: Developing teaching and learning through dialogue.* Abingdon, New York: Routledge.

Lefstein, A., Snell, J., & Israeli, M. (2015). From moves to sequences: Expanding the unit of analysis in the study of classroom discourse. *British Educational Research Journal, 41*(5), 866–885. https://doi.org/10.1002/berj.3164

Lortie, D. C. (1975). *Schoolteacher: A sociological study.* Chicago: The University of Chicago Press.

Lyle, S. (2008). Dialogic teaching: Discussing theoretical context and reviewing evidence from classroom practice. *Language and Education, 22*(3), 222–240.

Mameli, C., Mazzoni, E., & Molinari, L. (2015). Patterns of discursive interactions in primary classrooms: An application of social network analysis. *Research Papers Education, 30*(5), 546–566. https://doi.org/10.1080/02671522.2015.1027727

McElhone, D. (2012). Tell us more: Reading comprehension, engagement, and conceptual press discourse. *Read Psychol, 33*(6), 525–561. https://doi.org/10.1080/02702711.2011.561655

Mehan, H. (1979). *Learning lessons: Social organisation in the classroom.* Cambridge: Harvard University Press.

Mercer, N., Hennessy, S., & Warwick, P. (2019). Dialogue, thinking together and digital technology in the classroom: Some educational implications of a continuing line of inquiry. *International Journal of Educational Research, 97*, 187–199.

Mercer, N., & Howe, C. (2012). Explaining the dialogic processes of teaching and learning: The value and potential of sociocultural theory. *Learning Culture and Social Interaction, 1*(1), 12–21. https://doi.org/10.1016/j.lcsi.10.1016/j.lcsi.2012.03.001

Michaels, S., & O'Connor, C. (2015). Conceptualizing talk moves as tools: Professional development approaches for academically productive discussions. In L. B. Resnick, C. S. C. Asterhan & S. N. Clarke (Eds.). *Socializing intelligence through academic talk and dialogue,* 1st Edn. American Educational Research Association, Washington, D.C.

References

Molinari, L., & Mameli, C. (2013). Process quality of classroom discourse: Pupil participation and learning opportunities. *International Journal of Educational Research, 62,* 249–258. https://doi.org/10.1016/j.ijer.2013.05.003

Mortimer, E. F., & Scott, P. H. (2003). *Meaning making in science classrooms.* Maidenhead, Philadelphia: Open University Press.

Myhill, D. A., & Warren, P. (2005). Scaffolds or straitjackets? Critical moments in classroom discourse. *Educational Review, 57*(1), 55–69. https://doi.org/10.1080/0013191042000274187

Nassaji, H., & Wells, G. (2000). What's the use of "triadic dialogue"? An investigation of teacher–student interaction. *Application Linguist, 21*(3), 376–406. https://doi.org/10.1093/applin/21.3.376

Nurkka, N., Viiri, J., Littleton, K., et al. (2014). A methodological approach to exploring the rhythm of classroom discourse in a cumulative frame in science teaching. *Learning Culture Society International, 3*(1), 54–63. https://doi.org/10.1016/j.lcsi.2014.01.002

Nystrand, M., Gamoran, A., Kachur, R., & Prendergast, C. (1997). *Opening dialogue: Understanding the dynamics of language and learning in the English classroom.* New York: Teachers College Press.

Nystrand, M., Wu, L. L., & Gamoran, A. et al. (2001). Questions in time: Investigating the structure and dynamics of unfolding classroom discourse. CELA research report. The National Research Center on English Learning and Achievement, Albany.

Osborne, J. F., Borko, H., Fishman, E., Gomez Zaccarelli, F., Berson, E., Busch, K. C., et al. (2019). Impacts of a practice-based professional development program on elementary teachers' facilitation of and student engagement with scientific argumentation. *American Educational Research Journal, 56*(4), 1067–1112.

Osborne, J., Simon, S., Christodoulou, A., et al. (2013). Learning to argue: A study of four schools and their attempt to develop the use of argumentation as a common instructional practice and its impact on students. *Journal Research Science Teaching, 50*(3), 315–347. https://doi.org/10.1002/tea.21073

Pace, J. L. (2003). Using ambiguity and entertainment to win compliance in a lower-level US History class. *Journal Curriculum Studies, 35*(1), 83–110. https://doi.org/10.1080/00220270210157597

Pehmer, A.-K., Gröschner, A., & Seidel, T. (2015). Fostering and scaffolding student engagement in productive classroom discourse: Teachers' practice changes and reflections in light of teachers professional development. *Learning Culture Social International, 7,* 12–27. https://doi.org/10.1016/j.lcsi.2015.05.001

Pimentel, D. S., & McNeill, K. L. (2013). Conducting talk in secondary science classrooms: Investigating instructional moves and teachers' beliefs. *Science and Education, 97*(3), 367–394. https://doi.org/10.1002/sce.21061

Resnick, L. B., Asterhan, C. S. C., & Clarke, S. N. et al. (2018). Next generation research in dialogic learning. In G. E. Hall, L. F. Quinn & D. M. Gollnick (Eds.). *The Wiley handbook of teaching and learning.* 1st ed. Wiley, Hoboken.

Reznitskaya, A., Anderson, R. C., McNurlen, B., Nguyen-Jahiel, K., Archodidou, A., & Kim, S.-Y. (2001). Influence of oral discussion on written argument. *Discourse Processes, 32*(2–3), 155–175. https://doi.org/10.1080/0163853X.2001.9651596

Reznitskaya, A., Glina, M., Carolan, B., et al. (2012). Examining transfer effects from dialogic discussion to new tasks and contexts. *Contemporary Educational Psychology, 37*(4), 288–306. https://doi.org/10.1016/j.cedpsych.2012.02.003

Reznitskaya, A., & Wilkinson, I. A. G. (2015). Professional development in dialogic teaching: Helping teachers promote argument literacy in their classrooms. In D. Scott & E. Hargreaves (Eds.). *The SAGE handbook of learning.* 1st ed. SAGE, London.

Scott, P. (2008). Talking a way to understanding in science. In N. Mercer & S. Hodgkinson (Eds.), *Exploring talk in schools: Inspired by the work of Douglas Barnes.* SAGE, London.

Scott, P., Ametller, J., & Mortimer, E. et al. (2010). Teaching and learning disciplinary knowledge: Developing the dialogic space for an answer when there isn't even a question. In K. Littleton &

C. Howe (Eds.), *Educational dialogues: Understanding and promoting productive interaction*. 1st edn. Routledge, London, New York.

Sedova, K. (2011). Mocenské konstelace ve výukové komunikaci [Constellations of power in the classroom]. *Studia Paedagogica, 16*(1), 89–118.

Sedova, K., & Navratilova, J. (2020). Silent students and the patterns of their participation in classroom talk. *Journal of the Learning Sciences*. https://doi.org/10.1080/10508406.2020.1794878

Sedova, K., & Salamounova, Z. (2016). Teacher expectancies, teacher behaviour and students' participation in classroom discourse. *The Journal of Educational Enquiry, 15*(1), 44–61.

Sedova, K., Salamounova, Z., & Svaricek, R. (2014). Troubles with dialogic teaching. *Learning Culture Society International, 3*(4), 274–285. https://doi.org/10.1016/j.lcsi.2014.04.001

Sedova, K., Svaricek, R., & Salamounova, Z. (2012). *Komunikace ve školní třídě [Communication in the classroom]*. Praha: Portál.

Schwarz, B. B., Cohen, I. & Ophir, Y. (2017). The epidemic effect of scaffolding argumentation in small groups to whole-class teacher-led argumentation. In F. Arcidiacono, & A. Bova (Eds.), *Interpersonal argumentation in educational and professional contexts*. Springer, Cham.

Snell, J., & Lefstein, A. (2011). *Computer-assisted systematic observation of classroom discourse and interaction: Technical report on the systematic discourse analysis component of the Towards Dialogue study*. London: King's College London.

Snell, J., & Lefstein, A. (2018). "Low ability", participation, and identity in dialogic pedagogy. *American Educational Research Journal, 55*(1), 40–78.

Sotter, A. O., Wilkinson, I. A. G., Murphy, P. K., et al. (2008). What the discourse tells us: Talk and indicators of high-level comprehention. *International Journal Education Research, 47*(6), 372–391. https://doi.org/10.1016/j.ijer.2009.01.001

Twiner, A., Littleton, K., Coffin, C., et al. (2014). Meaning making as an interactional accomplishment: A temporal analysis of intentionality and improvisation in classroom dialogue. *International Journal Education Research, 63*, 94–106. https://doi.org/10.1016/j.ijer.2013.02.009

Van de Pol, J., Brindley, S., & Higham, R. J. E. (2017). Two secondary teachers' understanding and classroom practice of dialogic teaching: A case study. *Education Studies, 43*(5), 497–515. https://doi.org/10.1080/03055698.2017.1293508

Vygotsky, L. S. (1978). *Mind in society: The development of higher psychological processes*. Cambridge: Harvard University Press.

Walkoe, J. D. K., & Luna, M. J. (2020). What we are missing in studies of teacher learning: A call for microgenetic, interactional analyses to examine teacher learning processes. *Journal of the Learning Sciences, 29*(2), 285–307. https://doi.org/10.1080/10508406.2019.1681998

Webb, N. M., Franke, M. L., Ing, M., et al. (2014). Engaging with others" mathematical ideas: Interrelationships among student participation, teachers" instructional practices, and learning. *International Journal of Educational Research, 63*, 79–93. https://doi.org/10.1016/j.ijer.2013.02.001

Wells, G., & Arauz, R. M. (2006). Dialogue in the classroom. *Journal Learning Science, 15*(3), 379–428.

Wilkinson, I. A. G., Murphy, P. K. & Binici, S. (2015). Dialogue-intensive pedagogies for promoting reading comprehension: What we know, what we need to know. In L. B. Resnick, C. S. C. Asterhan & S. N. Clarke (Eds.), *Socializing intelligence through academic talk and dialogue*. 1st edn. American Educational Research Association, Washington, D.C.

Wilkinson, I. A. G., Reznitskaya, A., Bourdage, K., et al. (2017). Toward a more dialogic pedagogy: Changing teachers beliefs and practices through professional development in language arts classrooms. *Language and Education, 31*(1), 65–82. https://doi.org/10.1080/09500782.2016.1230129

Winograd, K. (2002). The negotiative dimension of teaching: Teachers sharing power with the less powerful. *Teaching and Teacher Education, 18*(3), 343–362. https://doi.org/10.1016/S0742-051X(01)00073-7

Chapter 3
How to Change Classroom Talk: TPD Program Design and Research Methods

Abstract This chapter introduces the methodology used in an intervention project we conducted with the aim of getting dialogic teaching into Czech classrooms. First, we describe the TPD program entitled "Effective Classroom Dialogue" that we conducted with two groups of teachers between 2013 and 2015. The aim was to induce a change toward dialogic teaching in participating classrooms and at the same time to study the processes of teacher development and learning during the TPD program. In the second part of this chapter, we present our methods of data collection during the TPD program. In the third part of the chapter, we present how we analyzed the data. Finally, we discuss the ethical aspects and research limits of the intervention.

3.1 The "Effective Classroom Dialogue" TPD Program

The idea to invite teachers to take part in a TPD program was influenced by our previous research findings. We knew that the nature of classroom discourse in ordinary Czech classrooms is very different from the ideal prescribed by dialogic teaching. At the same time, we knew that Czech teachers like the concept of dialogic teaching: they value both dialogue and discussion in the classroom, although they often state that such teaching is demanding time-wise and not all students are able to meaningfully participate in classroom communication. Finally, we knew that even though Czech teachers do not apply the methods of dialogic teaching, they often believe that their teaching is dialogic (Sedova et al. 2012). We therefore started thinking of ways to change the teaching practices of Czech teachers at lower-secondary schools.

The nature of the change we wanted to implement was determined by the theory we presented in Chaps 1 and 2. We wanted to establish authentic interaction between teachers and students with students being verbally engaged, expressing their voices and at the same time being cognitively stimulated. We decided to apply the indicators of dialogic teaching (see Sect. 2.1.2) and the principles of dialogic teaching (see Sect. 2.1.3) as the guidelines for the transformation. In the program, we presented the indicators and principles of dialogic teaching to teachers and supported them in implementing them in their lessons.

The TPD design was inspired by what is currently known to be effective in TPD programs (see Sect. 2.2). We wanted the TPD program to include active experiential learning of participating teachers, the use of video recordings of teaching, reflections on the teaching, peer collaboration and discussion during TPD, etc. We decided to employ a reflective approach, which is currently a key concept in teacher education (Korthagen and Vasalos 2005). The reflective approach contradicts the widely disseminated idea that teacher participation in short-term seminars is effective (Boyle et al. 2004), instead upholding the concept that regular activities done within the school are the most beneficial for teacher development (Whitehead 1989). We therefore saw long-term cooperation with teachers in their own environments as a vital element to our TPD program. We wanted to enable teachers to continually reflect on their teaching and experiment with new methods while at the same time maintain responsibility for the actions in their classrooms. The change we wanted to implement was meant to be driven by a lively dialogue between researcher and teacher; the change was to be collaborative (Somekh 2006).

3.1.1 The TPD Program Design

We registered the educational program "Effective Classroom Dialogue" at the Ministry of Education, Youth and Sports of the Czech Republic in the category of further professional development for teachers and requested its accreditation. Once the program received accreditation, it was offered by Masaryk University as a course in its lifelong education program. We conducted two rounds of the TPD program, one in the 2013/2014 academic year and the other one in the 2014/2015 academic year. There were four participating teachers per round. Consequently, we have data from eight teachers and their classes. We—the four researchers who authored this book—met with the four participating teachers at workshops. Each one of us guided one teacher throughout the duration of the program: we attended their classes, recorded their lessons on video, and had discussions with them in follow-up reflective interviews.

The program had three steps that were repeated in a spiral: (1) workshops for teachers that featured group discussions between teachers and researchers, (2) teaching and recording of lessons on video, and (3) reflective interviews between a researcher and a teacher that were stimulated by a video-recorded lesson.

We presumed that our workshops would provide teachers with stimuli for implementing a particular change and that its consequences would be reflected in the interviews, which in turn would enable teachers to change their practices even further.

The spiral nature of our program was inspired by Korthagen's ALACT model (Korthagen and Kessels 1999; Korthagen et al. 2001), which comprises five steps: (1) a teacher's action, (2) a look back at the action, (3) awareness of the essential aspects, (4) creation of alternative methods of action, and (5) trial of alternative

3.1 The "Effective Classroom Dialogue" TPD Program

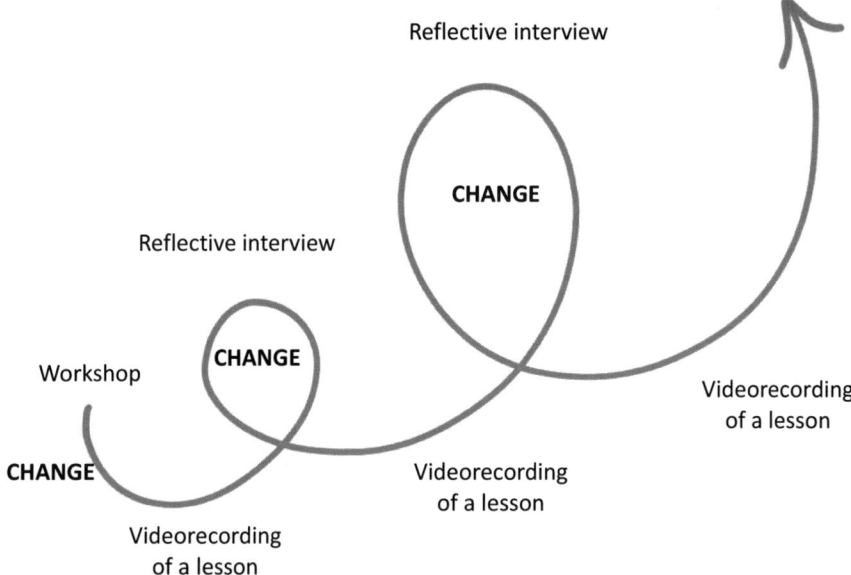

Fig. 3.1 Form of the development program

methods (see Fig. 3.1). Step 1, which is also Step 5 in our program, entails recording a teacher delivering their lesson. Steps 2 and 3 include reflective interviews based on the recording. Step 4 comprises the planning of the next lesson by the teacher (in collaboration with a researcher), and Step 5 is the teaching of the next lesson.

3.1.2 The TPD Curriculum

Figure 3.2 shows how the three key components of our TPD program—workshops, video recordings, and reflective interviews—were sequenced in time. We describe each component below.

3.1.2.1 Workshops for Teachers

During the first three workshops, we presented the theory and individual concepts of dialogic teaching (in approximately 45 min) and then discussed with the teachers the ways in which it could be implemented in everyday teaching practice (45–90 min). We discussed the value of individual principles and indicators of dialogic teaching, brainstormed relevant methods for their implementation, and pondered the limits of the suggested approaches. The fourth and final workshop differed from this structure,

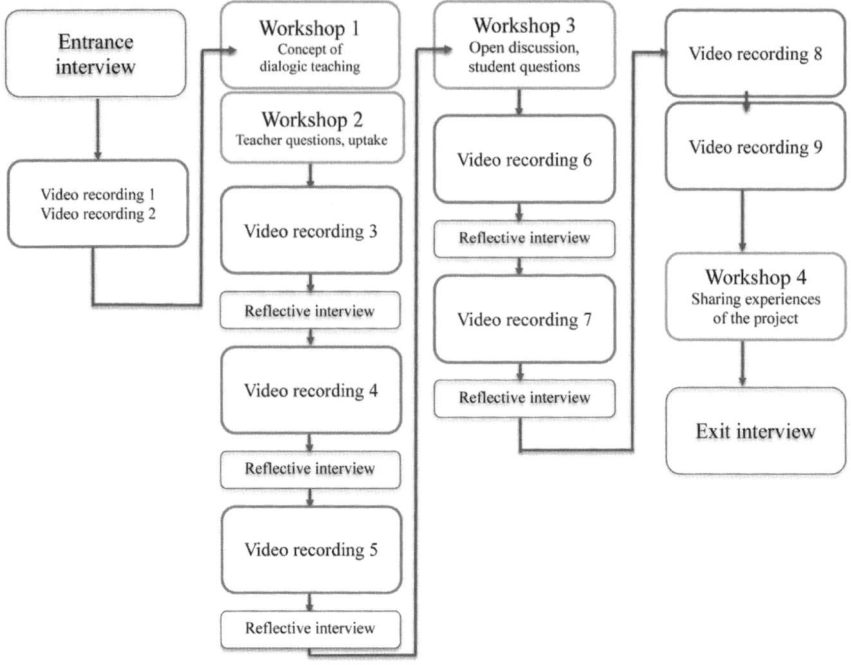

Fig. 3.2 An outline of the TPD

as it focused solely on sharing and evaluating the teachers' experience with TPD and its impact on their classroom practices.

The workshops all took place at Masaryk University. All participating teachers and researchers were present at each workshop, which provided the chance for collegial discussions to arise. The following paragraphs describe the content of the individual workshops.

In the first workshop, the teachers were acquainted with the TPD program and the research project. We briefly introduced the nature of ordinary classroom talk and contrasted it with dialogic teaching. We then described the principles of dialogic teaching as defined by Alexander (see Chap. 2). We introduced the key indicator that we would be observing in the project: student thoughts with reasoning (see Chap. 2). The teachers described how they perceived their teaching practices and the extent to which they could be considered dialogic. We stressed during the first workshop that leading meaningful dialogue with students is desirable and, at the same time, very difficult. Each teacher left the workshop with a handout on dialogic teaching and its aims and principles.

The second workshop took place only a week after the first so that we could follow up on our discussion. Regarding theory, in the second workshop the teachers were acquainted with two indicators of dialogic teaching: open questions of high cognitive demand (see Chap. 2) and uptake. We illustrated both indicators with examples from teaching practices recorded in our previous projects. Since we had found it useful to provide teachers with transcripts of video recordings, we gave the teachers very detailed transcripts during the second workshop. We asked them to identify open and closed questions, divide them into categories based on the level of their cognitive demand, and brainstorm questions of their own. At this point, it became apparent that even though the teachers understood the concept of open questions of high cognitive demand, they could identify them in transcripts only with difficulty. The teachers discussed how they could implement more open questions of high cognitive demand and uptake in their teaching. The teachers were then given a handout that included examples of the discussed indicators of dialogic teaching.

We opened the third workshop, which took place six weeks after the second one, with a group reflection on what had changed in the participating teachers' practices since the TPD program had started. The teachers talked about aspects of dialogic teaching that they had managed to implement and about aspects with which they had struggled. The researchers appreciated the progress achieved to that point. The aim of this group reflection was to enable the teachers to understand that all of the challenges that they had faced were natural parts of their learning process. The teachers reported that they were having the greatest difficulty with recognizing which student responses were productive and could be developed with uptake. They also noted that it was demanding to make all students participate, including those with lower academic achievement. The theory presented in the third workshop focused on the indicators of open discussion (see Chap. 2). As in the previous two workshops, we did not provide the teachers with step-by-step instructions for implementing open discussion. Instead, we gave them handouts with some model examples. The teachers worked with transcripts as they tried to identify the right conditions to enable students to interact with each other.

The fourth workshop took place approximately one month after the third and did not present the teachers with any new inputs: its nature was purely reflective. In the workshop, the teachers discussed the extent to which they had managed to implement dialogic teaching, which elements they had included successfully, and the elements with which they still struggled. The researchers appreciated the progress achieved by the teachers and added some new points to the discussion. Positive emotions and a feeling of work well done were experienced by both the teachers and the researchers.

3.1.2.2 Lessons and Recordings

The teachers left the second and third workshops with the task of implementing the discussed indicators: open questions of high cognitive demand and uptake (after the second workshop) and open discussion (after the third workshop). The researchers continually emphasized the importance of keeping the principles of dialogic teaching in mind and implementing them as well. During the project, the teachers taught their classes as they would normally, and the researchers visited them on pre-arranged dates to record their teaching on video.

The first two recordings were obtained even before the first workshop as a document of teaching prior to the TPD program. The researchers then recorded lessons five or six times during the TPD program and two times after its end to record the final state of achieved change. All of the lessons lasted 45 min, which is the standard duration in Czech lower-secondary schools. Two cameras were used to obtain the recordings: one situated at the back of the classroom capturing the teacher and one at the front of the classroom recording the students. The researchers never interrupted the lessons: they operated the camera so that it would always record the teachers even when they moved around the classroom.

Each recording was processed within a week and changed into a transcription. Each researcher worked on transcribing the recordings of their teacher. The transcripts then served as the basis for reflective interviews with the teachers.

3.1.2.3 Reflective Interviews

At the beginning of each round of the TPD program (2013/2014 and 2014/2015), stable pairs were created that comprised a teacher and a researcher. Each teacher was assigned a researcher who recorded their lessons, transcribed the video recordings, talked about their teaching in the workshops, and, most importantly, discussed their practices with them in reflective interviews.

Reflective interviews took place within a week of each recording and lasted 45–90 min. The choice of meeting place was up to the teachers. Some pairs met in the schools, some in cafés, and others in the teachers' homes. The interviews were stimulated by the teacher and researcher observing a segment of a video recording (approximately a few minutes long), which they then discussed. The interviews focused on how the teachers managed to implement indicators and principles of dialogic teaching as seen from the very detailed perspective of recordings and transcriptions. At the beginning, the teachers found it difficult to examine their teaching in such a detailed manner. Nevertheless, because the reflections repeated in cycles, the teachers become more sensitive to actions in their classrooms and were more and more able to reflect on them critically.

During the interviews, the teachers and researchers paid attention to problematic moments in which the dialogic teaching indicators were not implemented or the principles were violated. The researchers and the teachers discussed the factors that inhibited the implementation of both indicators and principles and how they could be overcome. They discussed what could be done in the next lesson so that apparent deficits could be reduced.

3.1.3 Teachers Participating in the Teacher Development Program

We cooperated with eight lower-secondary school (ISCED 2A) teachers and their classes during the two rounds of intensive data collection. We sent an invitation to the program to all the schools in South Moravia. We specified in the invitation that we were looking for teachers qualified to teach Czech language and literature and civics who would be willing to test new dialogic methods in teaching. In return for their time, the teachers would be compensated financially and would receive a certificate confirming they had passed the TPD program issued by the Ministry of Education, Youth and Sports.

We chose only teachers with at least five years of teaching experience to participate in our program. According to Measor (1985), such teachers have passed the first critical phase of the teaching profession. They have decided to continue working as teachers, can focus on things other than their own actions in teaching, have mastered the elements of classroom organization, and have gained a certain self-confidence that is not limited by the boundaries of their classrooms (Sikes 1985). Table 3.1 briefly describes the basic characteristics of the chosen teachers.

Table 3.1 Research participants

Teacher	Teaching experience (years)	Subject	Grade	Number of students in class	School	Cooperating researcher
Jonas	6	Czech language and literature	7	21	School A	Zuzana
Radek	8	Civics	9	22	School A	Roman
Hana	20	Czech language and literature	7	18	School B	Klara
Vaclav	3	Civics	9	20	School C	Martin
Marcela	22	Civics	8	26	School C	Martin
Daniela	11	Czech language and literature	7	20	School D	Klara
Marek	12	Czech language and literature	7	19	School E	Zuzana
Martina	5	Civics	7	19	School E	Roman

All of the participants were given pseudonyms

3.2 Research Aims and Data Collection Methods

We set two research aims at the beginning of the project. First, we wanted to determine whether carrying out the TPD program was effective in changing classroom talk at the level of dialogic teaching indicators and principles. This question is answered in detail in Chap. 4. Second, we wanted to examine carefully how the transformation took place and what the underlying mechanisms of change were. Our wish was to look in detail into how teachers learned and developed their teaching during the TPD program and thereby to fill a significant knowledge gap in the field (see Sect. 2.2). Chapters 5, 6 and 7 present our findings concerning this.

3.2.1 Data Collection Methods

We used a large number of data collection methods during the research project. First, we conducted two in-depth interviews with each teacher to ascertain how they perceived teaching and classroom talk, one before the start of the program and one after its end. Second, we obtained either nine or ten video recordings for each teacher: two before the start of the TPD program, five or six during its run, and two after its end. Third, we recorded at least five reflective interviews with the teachers discussing the video recording transcripts. Fourth, we recorded the group discussions of the teachers and researchers during workshops. We had access to the teachers' lesson plans and filled in our own research logs. In addition, we interviewed some students.

3.2.1.1 In-Depth Teacher Interviews

We interviewed each teacher at the beginning of our research project before we entered their classrooms as researchers. We intended to map their opinions on classroom talk and their teaching methods. These interviews were focused on three specific areas: how teachers perceived their students, how they reflected on themselves and their own teaching, and what their teaching goals and preferred methods are.

The individual in-depth interviews lasted 45–80 min and took place either in the school (e.g., in a teacher's office) or outside it, in cafés or parks, depending on the given teacher's preference. Only one teacher and one researcher took part in each interview, which helped establish a confidential atmosphere. All of the initial in-depth interviews were audio-recorded with the teachers' consent and then transcribed word-for-word.

The second in-depth interview took place after the end of the TPD program. The areas discussed included: evaluation of the program and the teachers' participation, suggestions for further improvement of the program, the limitations of dialogic

3.2 Research Aims and Data Collection Methods

teaching, and predictions for the future. The interviews lasted between 45 and 60 min, and their recordings were then transcribed.

3.2.1.2 Video Recordings of Lessons

All lessons were recorded with two cameras: one directed at the teacher and the other at the students. The first captured the actions of the teacher throughout the lesson. Its placement was influenced by the specific design of each classroom, but it was typically situated at the back or to the side of the classroom. The second camera was typically placed in a corner of the classroom or near a wall so that it could record student actions. All of the recordings were digital, which enabled their easy transfer to the researchers' computers and immediate analysis.

We planned to record the teachers twice before the start of the program, twice after its end, and five times during its run. Four teachers, however, felt that one more video recording would help them achieve better results and so these teachers (Jonas, Hana, Daniela, and Martin) were recorded six times during the program. This is why some teachers were recorded nine times and others ten times. Our qualitative analyses made use of all of the recordings; our quantitative analyses worked with a set of nine recordings for each teacher.

3.2.1.3 Reflective Interviews

The reflective interviews were the most essential component of the TPD program and took place during its run. They focused on establishing how the teachers understood the indicators and principles of dialogic teaching and how they approached their implementation in the recorded lessons.

The interviews were stimulated by watching the recordings in pairs of one teacher and one researcher. The interviews were similar in content: the researchers always chose two or three significant episodes from the previously recorded lesson delivered by their teacher. These episodes were transcribed and analyzed (for the presence or lack of indicators and principles) prior to the interview. The researcher then observed the episodes with the teacher; both of them were equipped with transcripts of the episodes. The teacher could stop the recording and comment on it at any moment, which became common practice. In the subsequent discussion, the teacher typically evaluated the episode and their own actions in the classroom. The researcher commented on the same but from the perspective of dialogic teaching theory and knowing the results of the initial analyses of the episode. However, the aim was not to look into the past; our intention was for the teachers to change their future behavior. The discussions therefore also included talking about plans for subsequent lessons.

3.2.1.4 Group Discussions

Group discussions among the teachers and researchers took place during the four workshops. The researchers first introduced the theory of dialogic teaching in the first three workshops and explained to the teachers the nature of the planned change. Subsequently, the teachers freely expressed their opinions on which methods would be particularly useful and what, on the other hand, could turn out to be a factor limiting the implementation of dialogic teaching. They reacted to the responses of their colleagues by either furthering or critiquing their arguments. The fourth workshop focused entirely on the teachers' evaluation of their participation in the project. All of the group discussions took place in a relaxed and pleasant atmosphere. The discussions were recorded on video and then transcribed verbatim.

3.3 Analytical Procedures

We analyzed data from the video recordings, interviews, and group discussions both quantitatively and qualitatively. The quantitative analysis was to determine whether the TPD program was effective in inducing change; the qualitative analysis was to explore how the change took place and what the development trajectories of individual teachers were.

3.3.1 *Quantitative Analysis*

The quantitative analysis was based on coding the indicators and principles of dialogic teaching (see Sects. 2.1.2 and 2.1.3). Subsequently, we compared the degree to which they were present before the program started, during the program, and after the program ended. We analyzed the relationships among various dialogic teaching principles and indicators—we examined whether they tended to co-occur or rather to counter each other.

3.3.1.1 Coding Based on Indicators

All teaching episodes from the video recordings were coded with a set of codes identical to the dialogic teaching indicators that we discussed with the teachers during the program. The codes included: student thoughts with reasoning, teacher's open questions of high cognitive demand, teacher uptake, and open discussion. All of the indicators were labeled with proper codes. This enabled us to know the specific number of examples of each indicator in the individual episodes, lessons, and all video files. We measured the length of the indicator of open discussion. All coding

3.3 Analytical Procedures

was done in pairs of two researchers. For information about reliability control, see Sedova et al. (2016).

Student thoughts with reasoning

Student thoughts with reasoning were a key indicator that we coded according to Pimentel and McNeill's (2013) classification, which distinguishes the following types: (a) no response, (b) a response comprising one word or one phrase, (c) a response that includes a complete idea (the response is structured as a sentence but does not include an argument or explanation), and (d) a thought with reasoning (the response is structured as a sentence and includes either reasoning or argumentation).

We selected only examples of the fourth type for our analyses. We think that only complete ideas with reasoning or argumentation represent a state in which students productively participate in mutual construction of knowledge, think, and present their thoughts to their peers.

An example of student thoughts with reasoning (line 2):

1 **Teacher:** So, tell me, why do you think that Aragorn is a hero?
2 **Student:** Well, I think Aragorn was afraid at first. But he overcame his fear and led his army into battle. It was a victorious battle, so he simply decided to take on the burden of responsibility and by doing so helped everybody to succeed.

Teacher's open questions of high cognitive demand

We coded the teachers' questions, distinguishing four types: (a) closed questions of low cognitive demand (e.g., test questions with given answers that are memorized by students), (b) closed questions of high cognitive demand (e.g., a test question that students answer by thinking), (c) open questions of low cognitive demand (e.g., an authentic question with many possible answers that does not require thinking in which students answer based on their opinions, feelings, or experience), and (d) open questions of high cognitive demand (e.g., an authentic question with many possible answers that requires high-level thinking to be answered).

Only examples of the last type were selected for analyses. This is because the theory of dialogic teaching only considers open questions of high cognitive demand to be productive tools for dialogue creation.

An example of a teacher's open question of high cognitive demand

1 **Teacher**: So, tell me, why do you think that Aragorn is a hero?

Teacher uptake

In accordance with Nystrand (Nystrand et al. 1997, 2001), we operationalized uptake to be a situation in which a teacher elaborates a response provided by a student. The teacher typically presents the student with a new question based on the student's response.

An example of teacher uptake (lines 3 and 5):

1 **Teacher**: So, would you go to a bullfight?
2 **Students**: Yes. No. No.
3 **Teacher**: Why yes?
4 **Students**: Umm, because (.) it's nice.
5 **Students**: ((*laughing*))
6 **Teacher**: How exactly? Could you explain how exactly it's nice?

Open discussion

In accordance with Nystrand (Nystrand et al. 1997, 2001), we coded only sequences that included at least three participants who reacted to one another's responses for at least 30 s as examples of open discussion. The teacher can participate in such a triadic interaction but does not have to.

An example of an open discussion (the entire sequence):

1 **Teacher**: Why do you think that Don Quixote's behavior is crazy?
2 **Student 1**: Well, some guy has been building a mill for a half a year so he could mill flour and a knight comes and starts thrashing the place. Does that make any sense?
3 **Student 2**: No.
4 **Student 3**: He's paranoid.
5 **Student 2**: Yeah, exactly.
6 **Student 4**: I think every action or behavior has some sort of meaning.
7 **Student 1**: Just because somebody thinks what they do is meaningful doesn't actually make it meaningful.
8 **Student 4**: But it's meaningful for that one person.

3.3.1.2 Coding Based on Principles

We expected to measure the indicators from the very beginning of the project; the need to measure some principles arose only gradually. Two principles were discussed the most in the reflective interviews and group discussions: collectivity and purposefulness. These two principles were apparently challenging to implement. Implementing the other principles appeared to be non-problematic. We therefore decided to focus on these two principles in our analyses. For information about reliability control, see Sedlacek and Sedova (2017).

We decided to operationalize collectivity as the number of students making any utterance in a single episode. We therefore established the number of students talking in each teaching episode—the higher the number of students, the more collective the episode.

Measuring the implementation of purposefulness was markedly more difficult. A purposeful passage is one that is aligned with the educational aims of the teacher for the given lesson or in line with the subject or curricular aims. This is an important distinction as sometimes a particular teacher's aims were not met, but school or curricular aims were. We coded such passages as purposeful. On the other hand, sometimes an activity that was planned by the teacher lacked purpose and was at the same time not aligned with either school or curricular aims. Such teaching activities were coded as purposeless.

Entire episodes or parts of episodes could be purposeless. A teacher could suddenly transition to organizational matters, the teacher and students might start joking around, or the course of communication could simply veer away from educational content. Thus, episodes could not be coded as a whole for purposefulness; instead, we coded individual talk moves. Any interaction that was not related to educational content was coded as purposeless. The same fate befell even passages that were only seemingly related to educational content. In the end, we divided our data into purposeful and purposeless passages and then measured their lengths in seconds.

3.3.1.3 Statistical Procedures

To assess the impact of the TPD program, we compared the measured values for indicators and principles in teaching episodes recorded in pre- and post-program lessons (see Chap. 4). We examined the 51 episodes from pre-lessons and the 43 episodes from post-program lessons. Our comparison was based on a Wilcoxon signed-rank *t* test, which is used when the sample data are not necessarily normally distributed.

We also examined the relationships among various dialogic teaching principles and indicators. The data sample was created from the interactive whole-class teaching episodes recorded during the entire program in all of the classrooms. The complete data corpus included 220 episodes. We used multiple hierarchical linear regression to establish the nature of the relationships among principles and indicators. We used SPSS and R to analyze the data. The results of the quantitative analysis are described in Chap. 4.

3.3.2 Qualitative Analysis

The primary sources for the qualitative analysis were the video recordings and their transcripts. The data from the lessons, which at this point had already been divided into teaching episodes in which indicators and principles were labeled, were subjected to subtle qualitative analytical procedures, as we wanted to study what was going on in the classrooms before the program started, during the program, and after the program ended in the most detailed manner possible. To do so, we used linguistic ethnography as analytic lens.

Linguistic ethnography combines linguistic and ethnographic approaches to study how language and its context (i.e., situations in which it is used) influence each other (cf. Duranti and Goodwin 1992). This body of research claims that specific situations call for specific uses of language (Lemke 1990) and that this specific use of language affects the situation and its occurrence. A detailed analysis of language is the starting point of analysis in linguistic ethnography. It is used to describe the nature and function of a given language situation and understand its values and norms (He 2000, p. 120; Maybin and Tusting 2011, p. 1; Rampton et al. 2004, p. 2). This influences the specific analytical approaches that are used within linguistic ethnography. While analyzing classroom discourse, we used open coding, conversation analysis, and multimodal analysis. For a thorough description of the procedures, see Sedova (2017a, b) and Sedova et al. (2017).

The purpose of open coding was to create codes as units of analysis with the smallest level of abstraction (Strauss and Corbin 1990). Therefore, the transcripts of the video recordings were coded to be as close to the collected data as possible. At the same time, we also employed conversation analysis. We did not consider individual responses to be isolated. Instead, we saw them as connected to previous responses and as causes for subsequent ones. Therefore, we used conversation analysis to see the utterances of both the teachers and students as gears in a machine in which the movement of one gear caused another gear to move as well. We applied multimodal analysis in order to capture everything that was going on, not relying solely on verbal data from transcripts. Therefore, we worked first solely with the transcripts and examined the nature of the verbal communication, including its language features and specifics. We then analyzed the data in its visual form working with the video recordings. Lastly, we compared the results of the analyses of verbal data with the findings from the analyses of visual data.

Other essential sources of data, apart from the video recordings of lessons, were audio recordings of the interviews that we led with the teachers. The analysis enabled us to understand the subjective views of teachers regarding what was happening in individual lessons. The interviews and their analysis allowed us to understand why the teachers had behaved as they did, how they currently evaluated their actions, and how they had felt while delivering the lessons and undergoing the TPD program. To analyze teacher interviews, we used open coding and conversation analysis. We also employed thematic coding along with the constant comparative method (Strauss and Corbin 1990).

The lesson plans that we were given by the teachers were valuable sources of information, albeit of a supplemental nature. The lesson plans helped us identify the parts of lessons that teachers had planned to be dialogic. In a way, they guided us toward segments that we could discuss in our reflective interviews with the teachers and analyze for further insights. Such parts of teaching were always good material for discussion. Lesson plans, like all of the other sources of our data, were open coded.

Transcripts of group discussions became another source of supplemental information. When they were introduced to selected theory on dialogic teaching, the teachers expressed their opinions on which parts of dialogic teaching could be used in practice and which could not. Transcripts of their discussions helped us understand how the teachers thought about the characteristics of dialogic teaching and how they understood them. The transcripts functioned as another type of reflection since in the discussions the teachers expressed how they evaluated the process of change in their teaching to that point. The transcripts of the group discussions were not coded in their entirety due to their size. Nevertheless, we coded parts of the discussions related to a particular phenomenon or process examined in our analyses of the video recordings or reflective interviews.

3.3.2.1 Case Studies

As we wanted to explore in detail how teachers learned and developed their teaching during the TPD program, we applied individual case studies of participating teachers as one of our methodological tools. We used multiple sources of evidence to study the particularity and complexity of a single case (Stake 1995) to closely examine the data within a real-life context (Yin 2003).

To document the step-by-step change in teacher classroom practices during the TPD program, we combined evidence of what a teacher did (data from the video recordings of lessons) with how the teacher thought about it (data from interviews and group discussions). This interconnection of data sources made it possible to demonstrate the logic of the development and to discuss causes, conditions, and underlying mechanisms.

For each teacher, we first created a developmental trajectory based on the measurement of the indicators (see Figs. 5.1 and 6.1 in chaps 5 and 6). Through the qualitative analysis of the video recordings and interviews, we strove to understand what happened in and between individual lessons and what had worked to enhance or inhibit the implementation of dialogic teaching elements and their coordination.

For this book we chose only two teachers (see chaps 5 and 6), but their case studies represent phenomena that we observed across our sample. These two teachers therefore serve as models to comprehend how all the participating teachers approached the stimuli from the TPD program, what challenges they faced when trying to implement them in their classrooms, and what helped them in progressing to achieve the goals of the TPD program.

3.4 Ethical Aspects of the Research

The research methods were planned so as to uphold three ethical principles: informed consent, confidentiality, and availability of the research to its participants (Tracy 2010; Economics and Social Research Council 2015). The ethical principle that paved our way into school classrooms was the requirement for teachers' informed consent to participate in the project (Hammersley and Atkinson 2007, pp. 210–212). First, we explained the aims of the research and the intervention to the teachers so that they would understand both as fully as possible. Only then could they relevantly express whether they agreed to participate. Having explained the aims of the research to teachers, we decided—in cooperation with the teachers and their head teachers—to inform the parents of the involved students about the planned research. Each student from the classrooms to be observed was given a form including information about the project. These students were asked to give the form to their parents, who were asked to indicate in the form whether they agreed to the student's participation. The parents were also to indicate whether they agreed to their child being recorded on video. Although we were apprehensive about the parents' choices, in the end almost all of them consented to participation and video recording. Only a minority of parents preferred that their children not participate; these students were situated outside of the focus of camera so that they would not be recorded and at the same time could still be involved in education.

Real names were exchanged for pseudonyms even before the recorded data were to be transcribed. Thus, no subsequent handling of the data (coding, analysis, interpretation) could reveal the real identity of the participating teachers. Our data were not given to any third parties or people.

We provided the teachers with the analytic outcomes throughout the TPD program since we discussed the results of partial analyses with the teachers during the reflective interviews. If a change were to take place, it was necessary to continually analyze the data and discuss the provisional findings in the tandem of teacher and researcher. Once the research was concluded, we presented the teachers with the complete research findings.

3.5 Limits of the Research

Like all research, this study has some limitations. The first limiting factor is certainly the size of our data sample, which makes no claims to be representative. We cooperated with only eight experienced teachers who voluntarily decided to join the project. They were obviously highly motivated to work on transforming their teaching. They were self-confident enough to give permission to have their teaching recorded multiple times by the research team. The certificate and financial compensation, both of which the teachers were to receive at the end of the program, were important motivating factors. We believe that these two elements played a role not in the process of implementing change but rather in the decision to remain involved in the TPD program. None of the teachers left the program although the option was explicitly mentioned at the beginning. The findings are therefore only applicable to motivated and self-confident teachers who enter development programs of their own volition.

The second limitation to our research lies in our use of camera and other recording technologies. There is a wide consensus that the presence of a camera influences the behavior of the recorded participants. By recording a video file, we intruded into the delicate balance of the classroom. Both the recorded teacher and the students may have altered their behavior. Nevertheless, the longer a camera is present in a classroom, the less it affects the behavior of students (Kress et al. 2005). Even though researchers agree that the presence of a camera influences the behavior of individuals, Heath et al. (2010) claimed that its influence is exaggerated because both teachers and students get used to its presence quickly. In our project, we tried to lower the influence of the camera by having the same researcher observe the classes prior to the recording, sit at a desk in the back, and take notes. Thus, at the start of the recording, the researcher was already quite familiar to both the teacher and the students.

The third important limitation is the fact that we as researchers strongly (and subjectively) influenced the researched reality. This is, however, an essential part of any intervention research. We agree with Kuhn (1962) that researchers do not possess knowledge that could be said to be neutral. Any research is always influenced by the subjective values held by its researchers. We intentionally wanted to change the communication patterns of the teachers and students in the given classrooms. To do so, we needed to activate the teachers and make them enthusiastic about changing their teaching practices (Somekh 2006). Teachers do not learn by acquiring abstract ideas from unknown sources—they need to fully understand the methodology behind a change (Schön 1983; Hennessy et al. 2011). Furthermore, we were aware of the gap between the worlds of theory (which we represented as researchers) and practice (which was represented by the participating teachers). We made use of intervention research to overcome this gap (Zeichner 2010). While considering the many possible forms that our intervention research could take, we chose not to define goals for our teachers or to give them prescriptive descriptions of what works. We opted for intervention research based on cooperation between researchers and teachers so as not to force the teachers to adopt methods that they would discard after the end of the program. In addition, we did not want to dismiss the possibility that our own understanding of the theory and practice of dialogic teaching would develop. We were aware of the hierarchical imbalance between university-based researchers and schoolteachers that could prevent us from achieving completely equal cooperation (Wells 2011) despite our efforts.

These limitations led us to listen to the teachers more in both the reflective interviews and the group discussions. We decided to record all of our interventions, whether we were explaining dialogic teaching principles and indicators or discussing the lessons taught by the teachers. At all such times, our cameras and audio recorders were on. All of the recorded data were then subjected to thorough qualitative and quantitative analysis.

3.6 Summary

This chapter introduced an intervention project we conducted with the aim of getting dialogic teaching into Czech classrooms. First, we described the TPD program entitled "Effective Classroom Dialogue" that we conducted for two groups of teachers between 2013 and 2015. The aim was to induce change toward dialogic teaching in participating classrooms and at the same time to study the processes of teacher development and learning during the TPD program. Therefore, in the second part of this chapter we present the methods of data collection during the TPD program; in the third part of the chapter, we present how we analyzed the data. Finally, we discuss ethical aspects and research limits of the intervention.

References

Boyle, B., While, D., & Boyle, T. (2004). A longitudinal study of teacher change: What makes professional development effective? *Curric Journal, 15*(1), 45–68. https://doi.org/10.1080/1026716032000189471

Duranti, A., & Goodwin, Ch. (1992). *Rethinking kontext: Language as an interactive phenomenon.* Great Britain: Cambridge University Press.

Economics and Social Research Council (2015). ESRC framework for research ethics. https://esrc.ukri.org/files/funding/guidance-for-applicants/esrc-framework-for-research-ethics-2015/.

Hammersley, M., & Atkinson, P. (2007). *Ethnography: Principles in practice.* Abingdon: Routledge.

He, A. W. (2000). Grammatical and sequential organization of teachers' directives. *Linguistics and Education, 1*(1–2), 119–140.

Heath, C., Hindmarsh, J., & Luff, P. (2010). *Video in qualitative research: Analysing social interaction in everyday life.* London: SAGE.

Hennessy, S., Warwick, P., & Mercer, N. (2011). A dialogic inquiry approach to working with teachers in developing classroom dialogue. *Teaching College Record, 113*(9), 1906–1959.

Korthagen, F. A. J., & Kessels, J. P. A. M. (1999). Linking theory and practice: Changing the pedagogy of teacher education. *Education Research, 28*(4), 4–17. https://doi.org/10.3102/0013189X028004004

Korthagen, F. A. J., Kessels, J. P. A. M., Koster, B., et al. (2001). *Linking practice and theory: The pedagogy of realistic teacher education.* Mahwah: Erlbaum.

Korthagen, F. A. J., & Vasalos, A. (2005). Levels in reflection: Core reflection as a means to enhance professional growth. *Teaching and Teaching, 11*(1), 47–71. https://doi.org/10.1080/1354060042000337093

Kress, G. R., Jewitt, C., Bourne, J., et al. (2005). *English in urban classrooms: A multimodal perspective on teaching and learning.* New York, London: Routledge/Falmer.

Kuhn, T. (1962). *The structure of scientific revolutions.* Chicago: University of Chicago Press.

Lemke, J. L. (1990). *Talking Science: Language.* Learning, and Values. Ablex Publishing.

Maybin, J., & Tusting, K. (2011). Linguistic ethnography. In J. Simpson (Ed.), *The Routledge Handbook of Applied Linguistics.* Routledge, London.

Measor, L. (1985). Critical incidents in the classroom: Identities, choices and careers. In S. J. Ball & I. F. Goodson (Eds.), *Teachers' lives and careers.* Falmer, Lewes.

Nystrand, M., Gamoran, A., Kachur, R., et al. (1997). *Opening dialogue: Understanding the dynamics of language and learning in the English classroom.* New York: Teachers College Press.

Nystrand, M., Wu, L. L., Gamoran, A. et al. (2001). Questions in time: Investigating the structure and dynamics of unfolding classroom discourse. CELA research report. The National Research Center on English Learning and Achievement, Albany

Pimentel, D. S., & McNeill, K. L. (2013). Conducting talk in secondary science classrooms: Investigating instructional moves and teachers' beliefs. *Science and Education, 97*(3), 367–394. https://doi.org/10.1002/sce.21061

Rampton, B., Maybin, J., & Roberts, C. (2004). Introduction: Explorations and encounters in linguistic ethnography. Draft chapter for Linguistic ehnopraphy: Interdisciplinary explorations.

Schön, D. A. (1983). *The reflective practitioner: How professionals think in action.* New York: Basic Books.

References

Sedlacek, M., & Sedova, K. (2017). How many are talking? The role of collectivity in dialogic teaching. *International Journal of Educational Research, 85,* 99–108. https://doi.org/10.1016/j.ijer.2017.07.001

Sedova, K., Sedlacek, M., & Svaricek, R. (2016). Teacher professional development as a means of transforming student classroom talk. *Teaching and Teacher Education, 57,* 14–25. https://doi.org/10.1016/j.tate.2016.03.005

Sedova, K., Svaricek, R., & Salamounova, Z. (2012). *Komunikace ve školní třídě [Communication in the classroom].* Praha: Portál.

Sedova, K. (2017a). A case study of a transition to dialogic teaching as a process of gradual change. *Teaching and Teacher Education, 67,* 278–290. https://doi.org/10.1016/j.tate.2017.06.018

Sedova, K. (2017b). Transforming teacher behaviour to increase student participation in classroom discourse. *Teacher Development, 21*(2), 225–242. https://doi.org/10.1080/13664530.2016.1224775

Sedova, K., Salamounova, Z., Svaricek, R., & Sedlacek, M. (2017). Teachers' Emotions in Teacher Development: Do They Matter? *Studia Paedagogica, 22*(4), 77–110. https://doi.org/10.5817/sp2017-4-5

Sikes, P. J. (1985). The life cycle of the teacher. In S. J. Ball & I. F. Goodson (Eds.), *Teachers' lives and careers.* Falmer, Lewes.

Somekh, B. (2006). *Action research: A methodology for change and development.* Maidenhead: Open University Press.

Stake, R. E. (1995). *The art of case study research.* Thousand Oaks: Sage.

Strauss, A. L., & Corbin, J. M. (1990). *Basics of qualitative research: Grounded theory procedures and techniques.* Newbury Park, California: Sage.

Tracy, S. J. (2010). Qualitative quality: Eight "big-tent" criteria for excellent qualitative research. *Quality Inquiry, 16*(10), 837–851. https://doi.org/10.1177/1077800410383121

Wells, G. (2011). Integrating CHAT and action research. *Mind Culture Act, 18*(2), 161–180. https://doi.org/10.1080/10749039.2010.493594

Whitehead, J. (1989). Creating a living educational theory from questions of the kind, "how do I improve my practice?" *Cambridge Journal of Education, 19*(1), 41–52. https://doi.org/10.1080/0305764890190106

Yin, R. K. (2003). *Case stude research: Design and methods.* Thousand Oaks: Sage.

Zeichner, K. (2010). Rethinking the connections between campus courses and field experiences in college and university-based teacher education. *Journal Teaching and Education, 61*(1–2), 89–99. https://doi.org/10.1177/0022487109347671

Chapter 4
Did Transformation Happen? The Effects of the TPD Program on Classroom Talk

Abstract In this chapter, we present the most important results of the quantitative analysis. We have two basic aims. First, we want to show any changes in the values of the measured indicators and principles between the lessons before and after the TPD program. Positive changes in the values offer evidence of the effects of the TPD program. Second, we analyze mutual relationships between the measured indicators and principles, taking student thoughts with reasoning as the dependent variable. Simply said, we determine the necessary appropriate conditions for this valuable kind of talk to occur.

4.1 Research Questions and Procedure

We conducted a TPD program focused on dialogic teaching, and we wanted to assess its impact. To evaluate the effectiveness of the program, we compared pre- and post-intervention lessons and looked for differences in the presence of dialogic indicators and principles (see Sects. 3.3.1.1 and 3.3.1.2). The following questions guided the analysis:

(1) Was the frequency of dialogic teaching indicators different in the pre- and post-intervention lessons?
(2) Was the extent of the implementation of dialogic teaching principles different in the pre- and post-intervention lessons?

Apart from evaluating the effectiveness of the program, we also wanted to acquire a deeper understanding of the interconnected changes triggered by the implementation of dialogic teaching. Thus, in the next step, we examined a key parameter of dialogic teaching: student thoughts with reasoning. We wanted to establish which indicators or principles correlate with an increase in the occurrence of student thoughts with reasoning and to what extent. Our aim was to further the current theoretical understanding of how dialogic teaching works and how it can be applied in teaching practice. To do so, we asked the following questions:

(3) *To what extent do open questions of high cognitive demand, uptake, and open discussion influence student thoughts with reasoning?*
(4) *To what extent are the principles of collectivity and purposefulness related to student thoughts with reasoning and other indicators of dialogic teaching?*

In order to answer the first two research questions, which seek to analyze the effects of intervention, we studied video recordings of lessons taught by the participating teachers. For each teacher, we recorded two pre- and two post-intervention lessons. Each lesson was divided into episodes; the average was 4.5 episodes per lesson. As was mentioned in Chap. 3, an episode is defined by one specific teaching activity that is coherent and pursues a didactic aim that is formulated either explicitly or implicitly. To answer the first two research questions, we examined 51 pre- and 43 post-intervention lessons. In the first step, we conducted a descriptive analysis. In the next step, we examined whether the results of the descriptive analysis can be considered significant and attributable to participation in our intervention program using a Wilcoxon signed-rank t test.

Our remaining two research questions aim to establish which indicators or principles correlate with the highest increase in the frequency of student thoughts with reasoning. To answer these questions, we relied on our data corpus, which included all the interactive whole-class teaching episodes recorded during the program. A total of 220 episodes met these criteria. Multiple linear regression was used to answer our third and fourth research questions. We tested several causal models that defined the basic possibilities of relationship configurations among the variables. For a detailed description of the analytical procedures, see Sedova et al. (2016), and Sedlacek and Sedova (2017).

4.2 Changes in Dialogic Teaching Indicators

Below, we summarize the changes in the measured indicators for the participating teachers before and after the TPD program. In the series of Tables 4.1, 4.2, 4.3, and 4.4, we show the values of the individual indicators for each teacher in pre- and post-TPD episodes and the difference between them. We also present the average pre- and post-TPD values and the difference. Positive numbers in the Difference column indicate change in a desirable direction.

4.2.1 Open Questions of High Cognitive Demand

A significant increase is apparent if we compare the aggregate occurrence of teacher's open questions of high cognitive demand in pre- and post-TPD episodes. Table 4.1 gives the occurrence values for the individual teachers and for all of them combined.

4.2 Changes in Dialogic Teaching Indicators

Table 4.1 Distribution of open questions of high cognitive demand in pre- and post-TPD episodes

	Pre			Post			
	Mean	N	Standard deviation	Mean	N	s. o.	Standard deviation
Jonas	7.40	5	11.84	14.00	2	4.00	6.60
Radek	3.13	8	3.18	20.67	3	17.55	17.54
Hana	6.67	6	8.55	4.17	6	5.27	−2.50
Vaclav	7.33	7	6.59	15.67	6	3.77	8.34
Marcela	5.14	5	4.44	9.00	7	7.33	3.86
Daniela	2.00	11	2.00	4.64	8	4.94	2.64
Marek	0	2	0	1.87	6	1.67	1.87
Martina	1.57	7	1.11	9.20	5	8.64	7.63
All	**4.15**	**51**	**4.71**	**9.91**	**43**	**6.64**	**5.75**

Table 4.2 Distribution of uptake in pre- and post-TPD episodes

	Pre			Post			Difference
	Mean	N	Standard deviation	Mean	N	Standard deviation	
Jonas	9.60	5	4.88	12.50	2	9.50	2.90
Radek	0.67	8	1.11	8.67	3	5.77	8.00
Hana	3.55	6	4.16	2.67	6	1.66	−0.88
Vaclav	6.22	7	4.86	6.83	6	3.50	0.61
Marcela	2.57	5	1.38	2.00	7	1.2	−0.57
Daniela	1.82	11	1.76	2.55	8	2.33	0.73
Marek	1.00	2	0.00	2.50	6	2.22	1.50
Martina	1.29	7	1.46	0.67	5	0.88	−0.62
All	**3.34**	**51**	**2.45**	**4.80**	**43**	**3.38**	**1.47**

Table 4.3 Length of open discussion in seconds in pre- and post-TPD episodes (in seconds)

	Pre			Post			Difference
	Mean	N	Standard deviation	Mean	N	Standard deviation	
Jonas	7.40	5	11.84	789.00	2	166.00	781.60
Radek	29.88	8	29.87	70.67	3	68.88	40.79
Hana	0.00	6	0.00	93.50	6	62.33	93.50
Vaclav	3.56	7	6.32	374.67	6	372.66	371.11
Marcela	46.13	5	65.91	295.86	7	363.46	249.73
Daniela	0.00	11	0.00	124.91	8	166.23	124.91
Marek	0.00	2	0.00	299.71	6	224.81	299.71
Martina	184.86	7	107.83	451.80	5	468.96	266.94
All	**33.97**	**51**	**27.72**	**312.52**	**43**	**236.66**	**278.53**

Table 4.4 Distribution of student thoughts with reasoning in pre- and post-TPD episodes

	Pre			Post			Difference
	Mean	N	Standard deviation	Mean	N	Standard deviation	
Jonas	2.00	5	2.82	27.00	2	1.41	25.00
Radek	1.75	8	1.75	4.00	3	3.61	1.86
Hana	3.33	6	5.20	3.33	6	3.61	0
Vaclav	3.57	7	3.31	13.83	6	14.99	10.26
Marcela	3.00	5	3.16	6.14	7	6.81	3.81
Daniela	1.36	11	1.56	8.63	8	10.04	8.68
Marek	0	2	0	8.66	6	6.62	8.66
Martina	3.43	7	3.95	10.20	5	10.37	6.94
All	**2.41**	**51**	**3.04**	**8.93**	**43**	**9.72**	**6.52**

Table 4.1 shows that all teachers but one (Hana) increased the frequency of open questions of high cognitive demand after the TPD program. The difference between pre- and post-TPD episodes is statistically significant; i.e., it repeats with such regularity that it cannot be considered random. We can understand the difference by observing that in 79% of the post-TPD episodes, teachers asked more open questions of high cognitive demand than their mean pre-TPD frequency.

4.2.2 Uptake

The frequency of each individual teacher's use of uptake in pre- and post-TPD episodes can be found in Table 4.2. This indicator increased, albeit only slightly (there was a mean of 1.47 more uptakes in post-TPD episodes). The results for individual teachers are quite varied. A slight decrease in uptake frequency occurred in the lessons taught by Hana, Marcela, and Martina, and a slight increase took place in lessons taught by Vaclav, Daniela, and Marek. A substantial improvement was observed in the lessons of Radek and Jonas, in which the former provided eight more uptakes in his episodes.

The visible small difference was not confirmed as a statistically significant change.[1]

4.2.3 Open Discussion

A significant increase between pre- and post-TPD episodes in the length of open discussion is apparent (Table 4.3). There was a mean of 34 s of open discussion in

---

[1] Detailed results of statistical testing are given in Table 2 in Appendix.

pre-intervention episodes and 312 s in post-intervention episodes of similar duration (i.e., it amounted to more than five minutes). While Hana, Daniela, and Marek did not employ any open discussion at all in their pre-intervention episodes, it became a common technique in the teaching repertoire of all teachers after the intervention. Jonas used open discussion the most. He was also the teacher who progressed the most in its use. The least progress was observed in Hana's classes; even in her case, there was 1.5 min more of open discussion after the intervention.

The difference is statistically significant,[2] meaning that in approximately 84% of the post-TPD episodes, we measure a longer time of open discussion than the average in the episodes before the intervention.

4.2.4 Student Thoughts with Reasoning

As Table 4.4 shows, there was an increase in student thoughts with reasoning for almost all the teachers. Hana was the only exception: despite the intervention, the frequency of student thoughts with reasoning remained the same in her classes. Other than that, the changes were substantial among the individual teachers. The last row of Table 4.4 shows that there was a mean of six more examples of student thoughts with reasoning in all post-TPD episodes than there were in all pre-TPD episodes.

The measured difference can be evaluated as significant,[3] which means that in approximately 70% of post-TPD episodes, there will be a higher number of student thoughts with reasoning than the average in the pre-TPD episodes.

4.3 Changes in Dialogic Teaching Principles

Below, we summarize changes in the measured principles in the pre- and post-TPD episodes of the participating teachers. In Tables 4.5 and 4.6, we show the values of the two principles for each teacher in pre- and post-TPD episodes and the differences between them. We also state the average pre- and post-TPD values and the difference. Positive numbers in the Difference column indicate a change in a desirable direction.

4.3.1 Collectivity

We operationalized collectivity as the number of students speaking in a given episode.

The results of the descriptive analysis show an increase in the mean (Table 4.5). Across the sample, there is a gain of two more verbally participating students in

---

[2]Detailed results of statistical testing are given in Table 3 in Appendix.
[3]Detailed results of statistical testing are given in Table 4 in Appendix.

Table 4.5 Number of verbally participating students in pre- and post-TPD episodes

	Pre			Post			Difference
	Mean	N	Standard deviation	Mean	N	Standard deviation	
Jonas	6.80	5	3.03	14.50	2	2.12	7.70
Radek	5.20	8	3.66	10.33	3	4.16	5.13
Hana	11.50	6	4.37	8.83	6	4.62	−2.67
Vaclav	6.78	7	3.15	11.83	6	1.72	5.05
Marcela	8.80	5	4.21	8.86	7	5.28	0.06
Daniela	5.55	11	3.07	5.36	8	3.72	−0.19
Marek	6.50	2	2.12	7.14	6	4.01	0.64
Martina	9.00	7	4.79	8.00	5	3.16	−1
All	**7.51**	**51**	**3.97**	**9.36**	**43**	**4.35**	**1.85**

Table 4.6 Distribution of time spent purposefully in teaching episodes (in seconds)

	Pre			Post			Difference
	Mean	N	Standard deviation	Mean	N	Standard deviation	
Jonas	286.60	5	266.17	722.00	2	190.91	435.40
Radek	76.33	8	160.31	465.00	3	555.88	388.67
Hana	173.67	6	274.36	323.67	6	311.52	150.00
Vaclav	339.33	7	360.06	397.50	6	176.32	58.17
Marcela	220.14	5	111.41	270.71	7	244.85	50.57
Daniela	190.81	11	186.29	217.55	8	196.17	26.74
Marek	46.50	2	65.76	207.14	6	273.28	160.64
Martina	230.29	7	179.84	419.60	5	376.15	189.31
All	**195.45**	**51**	**200.52**	**377.89**	**43**	**290.63**	**182.44**

an episode. However, not all teachers increased collectivity—Hana, Daniela, and Martina decreased it.

As with the indicators of dialogical teaching, we verified the statistical significance[4] of the principles. The difference in the numbers of actively participating students in pre- and post-TPD episodes was not statistically significant.

4.3.2 Purposefulness

We measured the amount of time in individual episodes in which classroom talk was clearly determined by curriculum and educational goals (see Sect. 3.3.1.2).

---

[4]Detailed results of statistical testing are given in Table 5 in Appendix.

Table 4.6 provides evidence that post-TPD episodes were more purposeful than pre-TPD episodes; the principle of purposefulness increased among all teachers by 180 s in aggregate.

The tests of significance[5] confirmed that there was a statistically significant increase in the length of purposeful passages in episodes after the TPD program, as compared to in the pre-TPD episodes. This means that teachers organized their lessons more purposefully in more than 79% of post-intervention episodes in comparison with the pre-intervention values.

4.4 Student Thoughts with Reasoning in Relation to Other Indicators and Principles

This chapter examines whether certain elements of dialogic teaching, specifically indicators and principles, operated in coordination during the TPD program or rather countered each other. We use student thoughts with reasoning as a dependent variable, as we knew we were not able to influence this indicator directly. We did not work with students who were responsible for the nature of their talk. We worked only with teachers and expected that the changed talk patterns of the teachers would influence the talk patterns of students. In other words, we thought that the implementation of open questions of high cognitive demand, uptake, and open discussion would result in an increase in student thoughts with reasoning. This assumption was tested through careful statistical analysis.

We were also interested in whether keeping the principles of collectivity and purposefulness made implementing the indicators of dialogic teaching easier or worked against the indicators (e.g., whether the more students are talking, the lower the probability that their utterances will be long and elaborate and contain reasoning). Simply said, we wanted to know whether all the elements of dialogic teaching have the potential to create synergy and whether implementing the indicators could go hand in hand with maintaining principles, or whether the dominance of some elements could cause a lowering of other elements.

4.4.1 Student Thoughts with Reasoning in Relation to Other Indicators

During the TPD program, we worked with teachers and trained them in implementing open questions of high cognitive demand, uptake, and open discussion. We were not able to directly influence student talk with reasoning, but we expected it to increase as a consequence of the changed talk patterns of the teachers. This expectation was positively proven by statistical analysis.

---

[5]See Footnote 4.

The regression models (Table 4.7) showed that the occurrence of student thoughts with reasoning can best be explained by a model including all the observed indicators of dialogic teaching: teacher's open questions of high cognitive demand, uptake, and the length of open discussion. In short, increasing the other indicators contributes to increasing student thoughts with reasoning. An analysis of variance (F-test) confirmed that all of the indicators explain 55% of the variance of student thoughts with reasoning. Hence, all three indicators can be considered significant and help explain the variability of student thoughts with reasoning. Table 4.7 summarizes the data on the regression coefficients.

To summarize, we wanted to establish the extent to which open questions of high cognitive demand, uptake, and open discussion explain the occurrence of student thoughts with reasoning. Our analysis showed that all the indicators that the participating teachers attempted to include in their practices significantly influenced the frequency of the occurrence of student thoughts with reasoning. Once the effect of the three indicators is combined, it explains 55% of the variance of student thoughts with reasoning. This finding has a considerable application overlap because it proves that

Table 4.7 Regression coefficients

	Model	Unstandardized coefficients		Standardized coefficients			Tolerance	VIF
		B	Std. error	Beta	t	Sig.		
1	Constant	2.37	0.39		5.99	0.00		
	Open discussion	0.02	0.00	0.68	13.91	0.00	1.00	1.00
2	Constant	0.97	0.46		2.11	0.03		
	Open discussion	0.02	0.01	0.69	14.86	0.00	0.99	1.00
	Uptake	0.31	0.06	0.24	5.21	0.00	0.99	1.00
3	Constant	0.47	0.46		1.04	0.14		
	Open discussion	0.01	0.00	0.60	12.28	0.00	0.85	1.91
	Uptake	0.22	0.07	0.18	2.91	0.00	0.49	2.03
	Questions of high cognitive demand	0.14	0.06	0.15	2.28	0.02	0.43	2.27

VIF variance inflation factor
Dependent variable: the amount of student thoughts with reasoning in the episodes
The final regression equation takes the form:
$Y = 0.47 + 0.01 * x_1 + 0.22 * x_2 + 0.15 * x_3$
Y = the number of student thoughts with reasoning
X_1 = time of open discussion (second)
X_2 = amount of uptake
X_3 = number of open questions of high cognitive demand

teachers can change the talk behavior of their students with their own talk behavior. More specifically, the higher the frequency of open questions of high cognitive demand, uptake, and open discussion in a teacher's practice, the more thoughts with reasoning their students produce. We consider this to be a crucial finding.

4.4.2 Complex Model of Relationships Among Dialogic Teaching Indicators and Principles

In this section, we want to include all the indicators and principles we measured in one complex model. The question is, as we stated above, whether all the elements of dialogic teaching have the potential to create synergy or whether they counter each other.

The final model is depicted in Fig. 4.1. The model implies positive relationships between all elements. Put simply, all of the indicators and principles of dialogic teaching observed in the project worked in synergy. Moreover, it is important to note that particular principles work in synergy with particular indicators. By asking open questions of high cognitive demand, teachers can strengthen the purposefulness of their teaching, which then increases the number of student thoughts with reasoning. Hence, if a teacher asks a sufficient number of open cognitively demanding questions in a teaching episode, they ensure that their teaching meets its goal and its effectivity increases. If the teacher keeps the episode within the bounds of planned content and aims, and thereby satisfies the principle of purposefulness, then their students are more capable of producing thoughts with reasoning. Further, an increase in the length of open discussion leads to strengthening collectivity in the classroom. We maintain that if a teacher keeps communication in the open discussion mode, then the number of actively participating students increases and so does the number of student thoughts with reasoning. Hence, student learning becomes more intense.

To explain the final model in detail: First, the model shows that the most explained variable is the indicator of student thoughts with reasoning, as we are able to explain 55% of the variability in the frequency of this type of utterance in an episode. This frequency of occurrence is significantly influenced by the three indicators of dialogic teaching that the teachers can control: open questions of high cognitive demand, uptake, and open discussion. We found that the presence of student thoughts with reasoning was explained the most by the length of open discussion in an episode ($\beta = 0.60$). Teachers' open questions of high cognitive demand were shown to have medium strength ($\beta = 0.29$). Both of these indicators influenced the relationship between student talk and the principles of purposefulness and collectivity. These indirect and positive relationships are symbolized in the model by dashed lines.

In the final comprehensive model, the principle of collectivity is predicted by the length of open discussion. This part of the model enabled us to explain roughly 33% of the dispersion in the number of students who communicated actively per episode. This is a strong relationship ($\beta = 0.57$), which means that if a teacher maintains

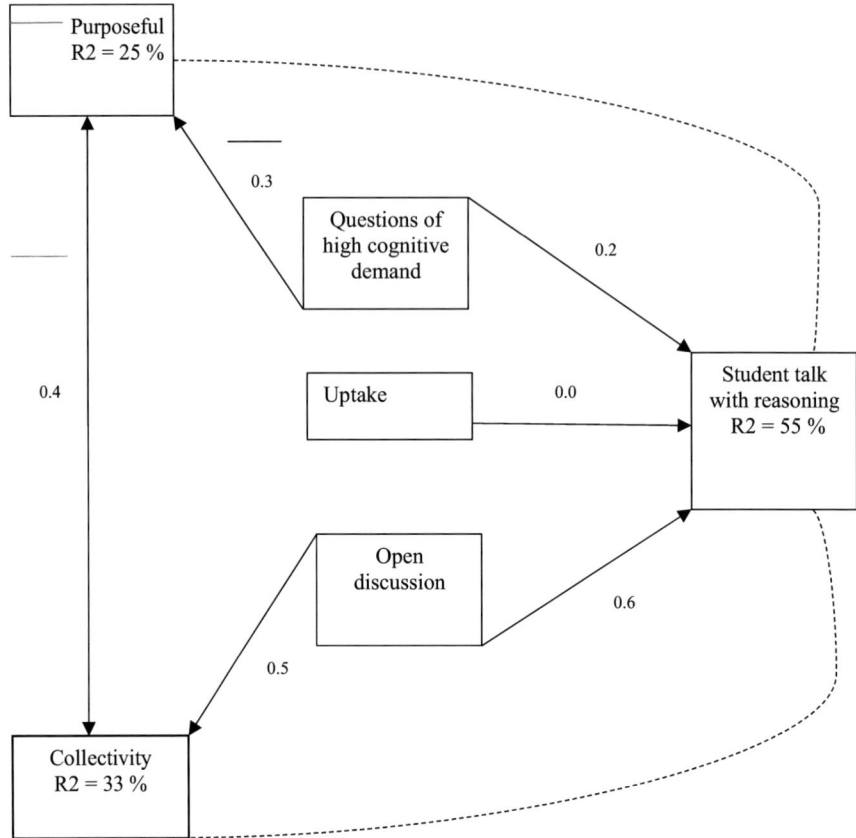

Fig. 4.1 Final model of the relationships among indicators and principles of dialogic teaching

communication in open discussion mode, more students can communicate actively. The other indicators of dialogic teaching were not significant in terms of effect size, and we could not explain more of the variability by including them in the final model.

It appears that teachers could influence the purposefulness of a teaching episode with open questions of high cognitive demand. Such questions were shown to be a medium-strength predictor ($\beta = 0.33$). If a teacher asked open questions of high cognitive demand, the frequency of student thoughts with reasoning increased in the given teaching episode as did the length of time spent methodologically effectively. As in the previous case, the other indicators did not help explain more of the variability in the length of time spent effectively per episode. Overall, this is the least explained part of the final model; the coefficient of determination for the purposefulness variable is only 25%.

4.5 Summary

This chapter was intended to test whether the TPD program was successful. We investigated differences in the frequency of all the observed parameters comparing episodes in the lessons that participating teachers taught before the TPD program and after its completion.

During the course of the TPD program, teachers were trained to ask open questions of high cognitive demand, to provide students with uptake, and to invoke open discussions. Because of this change in the talk behavior of teachers, we expected that a change would also take place in the talk behavior of students in the form of an increase in student thoughts with reasoning. The TPD program significantly increased the frequency of three indicators out of four: the values for open questions of high cognitive demand, open discussion, and student thoughts with reasoning were significantly higher at the end of the program than at its beginning. We consider the increase in student thoughts with reasoning as especially important since student talk mirrors student understanding and learning (see Chap. 1). The frequency of uptake did not increase in a significant way after the program. Nonetheless, because of the increase in the three indicators, we can consider the program effective in strengthening the features of dialogic teaching.

In terms of the principles of dialogic teaching, both collectiveness and purposefulness increased. However, only the change in purposefulness was statistically significant. These results imply that teachers were able to solve the challenges of curricular constraints (see Sect. 2.3.1); they are able to be dialogic and at the same time to focus on subject matters and educational goals. Also, in shifting to dialogic teaching, they engaged slightly more students, which means they did not prove the belief that only a few students are able to participate in challenging dialogue (see Sect. 2.3.2).

Finally, we examined the relationships between individual indicators and principles of dialogic teaching, and we found that there was mutual support between them and that they worked in synergy. We view this discovery as positive, as it signals a full-blown realization of dialogic teaching.

References

Sedlacek, M., & Sedova, K. (2017). How many are talking? The role of collectivity in dialogic teaching. *International Journal of Educational Research, 85,* 99–108. https://doi.org/10.1016/j.ijer.2017.07.001

Sedova, K., Sedlacek, M., & Svaricek, R. (2016). Teacher professional development as a means of transforming student classroom talk. *Teaching and Teacher Education, 57,* 14–25. https://doi.org/10.1016/j.tate.2016.03.005

Chapter 5
The Case of Daniela: The Nonlinear Development of Change

Abstract This chapter focuses on the teacher Daniela. What we want to show through her case is most importantly the fact that the change toward dialogic teaching was not straightforward. It was not a case of gradually increasing individual indicators and principles, with every subsequent lesson being better than previous one. On the contrary, the development took place through alternating phases of progress and of regression. We label this as a nonlinear development of change.

In the following two chapters, we present case studies of two teachers undergoing our TPD program. In Chap. 4, we assessed the TPD program as effective in invoking increases in dialogic teaching indicators and principles. The analysis was based on a comparison of averaged values from all of the participating teachers' lessons before and at the end of the TPD program. This approach is useful for providing evidence that a change happened. On the other hand, it cannot reveal how the process of transformation proceeded. This is what we want to offer in this chapter and Chap. 6 through detailed and contextualized examinations of two teachers. We monitored how they went through TPD program; we use their stories to illustrate and interpret some phenomena that were common across our sample of teachers.

This chapter focuses on the teacher Daniela. What we want to show through her case is most importantly the fact that the change toward dialogic teaching was not straightforward. It was not a case of gradually increasing individual indicators and principles, with every subsequent lesson being better than previous one. On the contrary, the development took place through alternating phases of progress and of regression. We label this as a nonlinear development of change.

At the beginning of this chapter, we present some contextual information about teacher Daniela. Next, we describe individual lessons she taught during the TPD program to show how her teaching practices were successively changing. The data from the lessons are complemented by data from the reflective interviews to demonstrate how Daniela was thinking about the transformation process. Finally, we offer some interpretations for why the development of the change was nonlinear. In other words, we examine what was behind the switch between success and lack of success in applying dialogic teaching indicators and principles.

5.1 About Daniela

Daniela participated in the TPD program during the 2014/2015 school year. She was an experienced teacher with 12 years of teaching experience and a habit of continually improving her teaching practices. She was a favorite among students because of her friendly and optimistic nature. Daniela taught Czech language and literature along with history. She also served as an educational counselor at her school.

The school at which Daniela taught was situated on the periphery of a large city and was an ordinary lower-secondary school. The school had a good reputation because of its efforts to provide quality education and care for its students. We observed Daniela teaching Czech language and literature in the seventh grade, which she did four times per week for 45 min each time. Three of these classes were devoted to language and grammar and one to language arts—it was in the latter that our observations took place. The class consisted of 11 girls and 9 boys whose socioeconomic background was either middle or working class. All of the students had Czech as their home language. One of the students was integrated with autism spectrum disorder, and a teaching assistant consequently was present during the observations. Daniela had taught the students even the year prior to our observations, and she described the students' cooperation with her as excellent.

5.2 The Series of Lessons that Daniela Taught During the TPD Program

As we noted earlier, this case study follows the nonlinear development of change. The observed indicators did not increase steadily over consecutive lessons. On the contrary, phases of clear progress were followed by phases of regression. Figure 5.1 shows the indicators for individual lessons. There were three distinct peaks: Lesson 3, Lesson 6, and the last two lessons, 9 and 10. These peaks relate to several indicators. There were also phases of descent, most particularly in Lessons 4, 7, and 8. This development is described in detail and interpreted below.

Lessons 1 And 2: Before entering The TPD program

Daniela entered the program as a competent and professional teacher. She was always well prepared and had no problems with classroom management. Both lessons recorded before the start of the TPD program were well structured and had clear aims that Daniela managed to accomplish. We can illustrate this claim with the example of the first lesson focused on the topic of modern fairy tales. Daniela first asked her students to brainstorm the features of traditional fairy tales, which she put on the whiteboard. All of them then proceeded to read the modern fairy tale "The Dragon from Vojtěšská Street" by Karel Čapek.[1] Daniela and the students then looked for

---

[1] Karel Čapek was a significant Czech writer who lived from 1890 to 1938.

5.2 The Series of Lessons that Daniela Taught During the TPD Program

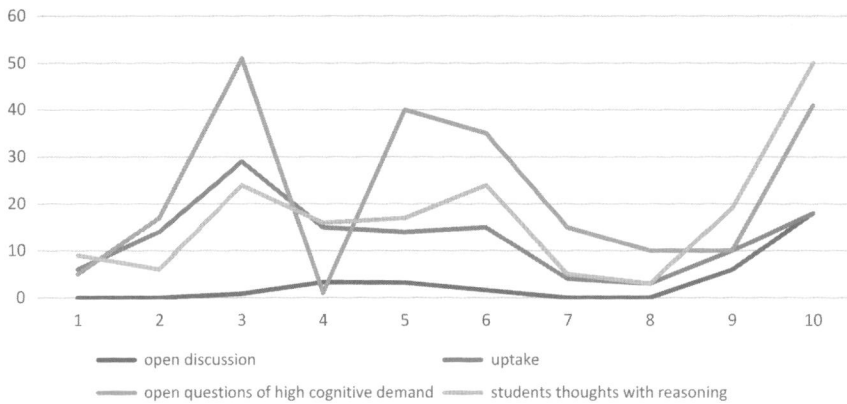

Consecutive lessons are on the horizontal axis; individual indicators are on the vertical axis. The indicator of open discussion was measured in minutes. The values for all of the other indicators are absolute and represent their total frequency in individual lessons.

Fig. 5.1 Development of indicators over consecutive lessons

differences between Čapek's fairy tale and the features of traditional fairy tales. The lesson ended with a summary of the differences and a mini-lecture on Karel Čapek and several other modern Czech fairy tales and their authors. The following extract shows the nature of the classroom discourse.

Extract 5.1: Lesson 1

Daniela and her students analyzed "The Dragon from Vojtěšská Street" in which Mr. Trutina, a member of an animal protection society, finds an abandoned dragon egg and raises Amina, a female dragon with seven heads who hatched from the egg. Naturally, Mr. Trutina faces certain challenges from the authorities and agencies, his neighbors, and his employer. In the end, it is revealed that Amina was a cursed princess.

1. **Teacher:** So, we were just discussing that good and evil are always clearly present in a traditional fairy tale. And we said that those who are good end up well and those who aren't good don't end up well, right? We were saying that it isn't really possible to improve oneself in such fairy tales, that fate is given, and things are black and white. Is this also the case for "The Dragon from Vojtěšská Street"?
2. **Students:** Uh huh. ((*agreeing*))
3. **Teacher:** Uh huh. ((*agreeing*)) And who was the good one here?
4. **Klara:** That Mr. Trutina.
5. **Katka:** The dragon.
6. **Teacher:** That Mr. Trutina. ((*nodding her head approvingly*)). Of course. The dragon also might have been good as a cursed princess. And who was the bad one?
7. **Vitek:** Everybody else.
8. **Teacher:** Everybody else? Well, there was Mr. Pour, the patrolman, but he wasn't so bad, I guess.

   [**Jana:** He was neutral.]

9 **Teacher:** He was neutral, right. Vitek ((*pointing at Vitek with a marker*)), try to specify what you said.
10 **Vitek:** Everybody who didn't understand that he wanted to keep the dragon and (.) Like, his employer and his landlord.
11 **Teacher:** Uh huh. ((*agreeing*)) Perfect. So who is bad in an ordinary fairy tale ((*pointing at the words "GOOD AND EVIL" written on the board*))? Who represents evil?
12 **Students:** A witch. An evil queen.
13 **Teacher:** Yes, a witch or an evil queen, for example.
14 **Viky:** A dragon.
15 **Teacher:** Perfect – a dragon who eats princesses. It's often a dragon who is bad in traditional fairy tales. And suddenly, we have a dragon who is good ((*pointing at "GOOD"*)), which is strange. And evil ((*pointing at "EVIL"*)) is what Vitek described ((*pointing at Vitek*)). So (.) some officials for the authorities and their rules they won't budge from. Do you know who else is good in this fairy tale? I've already given you a clue. It's the dragon who doesn't behave like a traditional fairy tale dragon. So how does the dragon from Vojtěšská Street actually behave?
16 **Klara:** Like a dog.
17 **Aneta:** Like a baby.
18 **Teacher:** ((*pointing at Klara*)) Like a dog, right? Like an ordinary animal or a child. ((*pointing at Aneta*)) Like somebody who needs to be taken care of and isn't in fact evil at all. And this is typical of modern fairy tales ((*erasing the white board*)). The rules for traditional fairy tales are turned on their head, and that's what makes the modern fairy tale modern.

It is obvious from the excerpt that Daniela's teaching included some dialogic features even before the start of the TPD program. Extract 1 shows that Daniela had lively interactions with her students and asked many questions that the students willingly answered. Her students performed mental work: they needed to decide which characters in the story could be considered positive and which negative. All of these features can be labeled dialogic.

On the other hand, the lesson included aspects that are not associated with dialogic teaching. First, Daniela's question was not very cognitively demanding. The students were asked to divide the characters into positive and negative (line 1) or describe what a dragon typically does in a fairy tale. Daniela did not ask them to explain their answers. This type of teacher question combined with a lack of uptake results in very short student answers that only rarely contain reasoning (as can be seen in lines 4, 5, 7, 12, 14, 16, and 17). The only exception was Vitek's response (in line 10). All of the important conclusions were presented by the teacher herself (lines 15 and 18), and so a shared construction of knowledge did not take place. It would be more accurate to say that students assisted the teacher in constructing knowledge and only animated her voice (see Sect. 1.3.3). Also, interaction was channeled into the dyadic form of a student and a teacher. The students did not react to one another; it was apparent they wanted to interact with the teacher and follow the instructions they were given.

5.2 The Series of Lessons that Daniela Taught During the TPD Program

Lesson 3: Rapid increase in indicators

Lesson 3 was the first lesson recorded after the TPD program started. It was recorded after the first workshop on the concept of dialogic teaching and its aims and principles and the second workshop on teacher's open questions of high cognitive demand and uptake. Figure 5.1 shows that there was a rapid increase in both indicators. At the same time, there was also a marked increase in the degree of student thoughts with reasoning. Lesson 3 focused on fables in general and on Ivan Krylov's fable about a wolf and a lamb in particular. The lesson included a discussion of fables as a literary genre and their features and functions. The final activity of the lesson was the role play of a trial between the wolf and the lamb in which the students took on the role of the jury to decide whose side the law was on.

Extract 5.2: Lesson 3

Having read and analyzed the fable, the students were drawn into a communication sequence with Daniela on the nature of fables as a literary genre.

1. **Teacher:** So <u>fairy tales</u> were created for children (.) to substitute for school (.), OK? To teach them what's right and wrong ((*gestures freely with her hands and moves away from the middle row to the one next to the door*)). (1) But what about fables?
2. **Tereza:** They were created for adults.
3. **Teacher:** ((*nods at her*)) Why do you think so, Tereza?
4. **Tereza:** ((*mumbling something unintelligibly*))
5. **Teacher:** ((*scanning the classroom*)) So, any ideas? You seem to have a consensus going, you seem to agree ((*Klara raises her hand*)) … so, Klara?
6. **Klara:** Well, adults have more power than children, so when adults would then, like, I don't know, maybe the wolf represents … some man, the man would get angry and he could harm them ((*the teacher is nodding her head and her hands are connected in front of her chest*))
7. **Teacher:** You think this is a good explanation? I'll try to translate it … ((*looking at Klara*))
8. **Klara:** Yep.
9. **Teacher:** …So, let's assume that there is a king and this king (.) is behaving badly toward his servants. And (.) the servants want to let him know about that. (.) So, what can they do to let the king know that he is behaving badly? ((*glancing across the classroom to where a student is saying "They can write a book…"*)) They can write it down, can't they? They can write: "We have a king, but he is behaving badly, he is always proud, he doesn't think about his subjects …" ((*entering the space between the middle row and the row next to the windows*)) (.) Do you have any idea what would happen, say in the Middle Ages, to a person who wrote this down?
10. **Patrik:** They would execute him.
11. **Teacher:** Of course they would. And if he weren't executed, he'd be put into prison. So what did the clever servants do?
12. **Students:** ((*offering answers in very quiet voices*))
13. **Veronika:** ((*in a whisper*)) They would write it anonymously.
14. **Teacher:** ((*pointing at Veronika to draw attention to her answer*)) Excellent. Yes, the first option is to write it anonymously. ((*Vitek is raising his hand*)) And the second

solution? I think I already heard it somewhere here ... ((*walking into the space between the middle row and the row next to the windows and gesturing to Vitek to speak*))

15　**Vitek:** They could change the people into animals and put those animals into a fairy tale or a fable.

16　**Teacher:** And ... (.) if such a servant were caught, one who'd written such a fable, and the king wanted to question him, what would happen next?

17　**Klara:** He'd say that it's just a wolf and definitely not a king and that's all that he meant.

Extract 5.2 shows that student responses became longer (lines 6, 15, and 17) and took the form of exploratory talk in which students explained their own thoughts and not an acquired piece of information. This also explains why their answers were tentative and imperfect. Still, unlike in Extract 5.1, here the students formulated the key findings relevant to the fable genre (line 15) and its social functions (lines 6 and 17). In so doing, they were assisted by the teacher and they all constructed new knowledge together.

The change in classroom discourse was that Daniela asked many open questions of high cognitive demand, such as why fables were created in the first place (line 1), how servants could express their discontent without being punished (line 11), and how servants could protect themselves when facing possible sanctions (line 17). It is important to note that Daniela provided her students with enough time to develop their ideas and she helped them by giving them uptake (line 3) or revoicing (line 9). In Extract 2, Daniela animated the voices of her students; she was not trying to formulate the key findings.

Still, the lesson was not very coherent in comparison with the two previous lessons. It included well-managed talk sequences (Extract 5.2), but also parts that were not purposeful and can be labeled as purposeless. This was specifically the case of the first activity in the lesson, which was meant to warm the students up to the topic of fables. Daniela asked her students to imagine the animals that they liked the most and the least and talk about them. The resulting interaction was superficial, was not fueled forward by reasoning or argumentation, and was not connected to the content of the lessons or its aims.

Extract 5.3: Lesson 3

The teacher asked the students to think about their favorite animal. She then asked the students to state which animal they had thought about.

1　**Tereza:** So I thought of my dog, Alvin, because he is, like, totally (.) like, totally cute and obeys commands.

2　**Teacher:** Hmmm, a doggie. What's typical for dogs? Tereza, please tell us again why you thought of a dog. (1) And what features he has.

3　**Tereza:** My dog is cute ... (1) [**T:** Hmm. ((*nodding her head in approval*)).] He is also a good dog ...((*nodding again*)) (1) and (.) he obeys commands.

4　**Teacher:** He obeys, excellent. ((*pointing at Jarda who is sitting two benches away from Tereza*)) Jarda, what about you? ((*smiling*))

5　**Jarda:** I don't know. Nothing came to me. ((*shrugging his shoulders*))

6　**Teacher:** Risa. ((*asking the student next to Jarda to speak*))

5.2 The Series of Lessons that Daniela Taught During the TPD Program

7   **Risa:** I thought of a hamster.
8   **Teacher:** ((*approaching him*)) Why?
9   **Risa:** Because I've wanted one ever since I was six and my mom has never let me have one.
10 **Teacher:** So (.) That was kinda good. (1) What is typical for hamsters (.)?
11 **Risa:** They have those tiny arms and tiny legs and are really tiny and (.) cute ((*jokingly spreading his arms*))

Extract 5.3 clearly shows that the teacher tried to involve students in talk by offering them a potentially attractive topic. She also tried to prolong their answers by providing them with uptake (lines 2, 8, and 10). However, cognitive activation did not occur since the students only listed the animals they liked and justified doing so because the animals are "cute" (lines 3 and 11). The activity came to a close when Daniela asked her students whether they understood what the topic of their lesson would be. The students answered that they would talk about animals and Daniela praised them for doing so. Yet, there was no connection to the lesson's aim, which was to understand the literary mechanisms of fables and their social functions. This means that the principle of purposefulness was violated. Neither the teacher nor the students returned to this activity later in the lesson or linked back to it. Simply said, it was wasted time.

The first reflective interview between a researcher and Daniela happened after this lesson. In the interview, the researcher spoke highly of the manner in which Daniela had asked her questions.

Extract 5.4: Interview after Lesson 3

1   **Researcher**: So, I think a lot of things went really well in the lesson.
2   **Teacher:** Really? Well, I'm happy about that.
3   **Researcher:** Your questions, I mean, you ask lots of cognitively demanding questions. And they're even open.
4   **Teacher:** Well, I'm glad about it. I really am.
5   **Researcher:** Those questions, I think, are perfectly OK. There's nothing to improve there.

Extract 5.4 shows simple praise from the researcher and its non-problematic acceptance from the teacher. Extract 5.5 shows how Daniela's first activity was critiqued as ineffective:

Extract 5.5: Interview after Lesson 3

1   **Researcher**: During the first workshop, we discussed several principles and one them was the principle of purposefulness. Because it sometimes happens that some activities are included in teaching because the teacher wants them to be dialogic. But those activities often have no real purpose. Like from the perspective of …
2   **Teacher:** Lesson aims.
3   **Researcher:** Lesson aims. Which is not your case. But the connection of some of your activities to your aims is not entirely 100 percent. And we could think about how to increase this rate so that all of the activities would be connected to your aims. You asked

them two questions at the beginning of your lesson. What their favorite animal is. And what did they actually do?
4. **Teacher:** They just talked about the animals they have at home.
5. **Researcher:** And they all said that they are cute. And then you asked them which animals they are afraid of. And they said they fear spiders and ants. It was interesting when they mentioned that ants are treacherous. Somebody mentioned earthworms. Others suggested spiders, ants, and earthworms. It was rather long (.) but it wasn't later connected to fables.
6. **Teacher:** They talked about insects, how they fear them, about spiders and how they fear them, but this isn't the role that insects have in fables, as something ominous.
7. **Researcher:** Yes, I understand. You thought they would mention different animals, right?
8. **Teacher:** Yes, that's what I expected. I thought they would mention some type of beast (.) and I could connect it later to the wolf.

The interview indicated that the teacher had expected the students to list favorite animals that often feature in fables. She had also expected her students to justify their choices by mentioning characteristics that also feature in fables. These expectations were not met. She also allowed her students to talk about animals in their preferred way. By doing so, she enabled them to voice their opinions. At the same time, the whole activity shifted from its planned course and became purposeless from the perspective of the subject matter.

To sum up, there was a rapid increase in the indicators of dialogic teaching immediately after the second workshop took place. On the other hand, this increase was accompanied by a partial decrease in purposefulness.

Lesson 4: Absence of open questions of high cognitive demand

In the next lesson, Daniela's students analyzed Karel Čapek's travel writings about his visit to a bullfight in Spain. After a short introduction, the students read the text aloud, the meanings of some difficult words were explained, and then the students scanned the text for evidence to establish Čapek's opinion of bullfighting. The students then expressed their own opinions regarding bullfighting. Daniela invited them to brainstorm Czech customs that—like bullfighting—include cruel behavior toward animals. The lesson ended with a discussion of this topic. The lesson itself was purposeful and coherent, and individual activities built upon one another. Extract 5.6 captures the nature of the classroom discourse in this particular lesson.

Extract 5.6: Lesson 4

1. **Teacher:** So, would you go to a bullfight?
2. **Students:** Yes. No. No.
3. **Teacher:** Why yes?
4. **Vitek:** Mmm, because (.) it's nice.
5. **Teacher:** How exactly? Could you explain how exactly it's nice?
6. **Vitek:** Well, you can see t– (.) the courage (.) of all those (.) who enter the bullfight and (.),
7.   [**Tereza:** An experience.]
8. the atmosphere is, the audience is cheering, that is amazing, and I'd like to go.

5.2 The Series of Lessons that Daniela Taught During the TPD Program

9 **Teacher:** Mmm ((*agreeing*)), of course. Franta, do you want to add anything?
10 **Franta:** Well, it could be quite an experience if–
11 **Teacher:** Totally, right? ((*nodding approvingly*)) Anybody else would– would like to go? Risa? ((*Risa is raising his hand*))
12 **Risa:** Well, I would like to go because I think it is traditional there.
13 **Teacher:** Uh huh ((*agreeing*)), well said.
14 **Tereza:** I wouldn't mind peeking in if the bull just ran around. Like, they wouldn't kill it, if it were just like a rodeo, then why not? Yep, if it were like a rodeo, but I wouldn't go to a bullfight.
15 **Viky:** Only a masochist would go.
16 **Teacher:** ((*laughing*))
17 **Tereza:** Or I could stay till it got serious, till the point when– then I'd probably leave.
18 **Teacher:** Uh huh ((*agreeing*)).
19 **Tereza:** Because I wouldn't be able to watch.

This entire interaction was driven by the question of whether students would visit a bullfight, which the teacher asked in line 1. Although the question is open, it is a question of lower cognitive demand since students could offer their opinions without more precise argumentation, and they did so for most of the duration of the extract. There were exceptions: Daniela used double uptake (lines 3 and 5) to influence Vitek to produce a more nuanced response in line 6. Additionally, Risa's response in line 12 can be considered productive. Yet, the other students only expressed whether they would like to be spectators at a bullfight. With the exception of Daniela's communicative sequence with Vitek (lines 3–6), the teacher did not strive to increase the cognitive demand of the classroom talk. She invited students to join the talk (lines 9 and 11), approved of what they said, and appreciated their utterances (lines 9, 11, 13, 16, and 18). The communication consistently focused on the topics of bullfighting and travel writing and the students willingly talked, but Daniela's questions were not very cognitively challenging. This lesson was similar to others that Daniela taught before the program: it was well structured, and it included many interactions between the teacher and the students who were willing to talk. Nonetheless, their utterances were short and lacked argumentation because Daniela did not ask them to elaborate their utterances. In sum, Daniela to a great extent returned to her original ways of teaching.

During the subsequent interview, the researcher appreciated that the lesson was well structured and purposeful and that activities built upon one another. The teacher responded by saying that she had planned the sequence of activities so that they would gradually build upon one another and climax when the central aim of the lesson had been accomplished. Nevertheless, Daniela had the following to say on the topic of asking questions:

Extract 5.7: Interview after Lesson 4

1 **Teacher:** Those questions of high cognitive demand, I (.) tried to (.) ask them, because I think I ask them almost automatically in most of my lessons, so in this one, I (.) didn't (.) really (.) prepare them in advance.

It is likely that Daniela emphasized the purposefulness of the activities in her fourth recorded lesson because purposelessness was discussed during the previous interview after her third recorded lesson. There was not a problem with purposefulness in her fourth lesson. However, open questions of high cognitive demand—the presence of which the researcher had praised after the previous lesson—were completely absent in the fourth lesson. Therefore, although asking open questions of high cognitive demand had been unproblematic for Daniela in Lesson 3, she in fact regressed in this regard in Lesson 4.

It can be understood that even when a teacher changes their behavior (e.g., in the area of asking questions, as was seen in Daniela's third recorded lesson), such a change might not be sustainable since this new pattern has not become a habit. A visible regression followed when Daniela stopped focusing on asking open questions of high cognitive demand.

Many of the questions that she asked were too easy for her students. She often asked them to locate a piece of information in the text or produce factual information from memory (related to, for example, habits in the Czech Republic and abroad). This led the researcher to emphasize the possibility of increasing the level of cognitive challenge in the next lesson.

Extract 5.8: Interview after Lesson 4

1. **Researcher:** And I want to ask you now if you think there was anything challenging for your students in this lesson.
2. **Teacher:** I think, not really, in this particular lesson. I think the lesson was friendly; even the text was sort of friendly. Maybe those few words in Spanish, those might've been new to them, but other than that, no, I don't think there was anything especially challenging for them.
3. **Researcher:** [I think the same.]
4. **Teacher:** [And they even worked independently.] They didn't get stuck, they got it. Yeah, it was a chill lesson.
5. **Researcher:** Hmm ((*approvingly*)). I think the same. Well, maybe it seems to me now as if it were too easy. That it was perhaps too [nice (.) nice]
6. **Teacher:** [Like too easy. ((*laughing*))]
7. **Researcher:** Perhaps you could do an experiment and raise the bar a little. Perhaps you could think of a question that would be challenging for them, but it also has to be meaningful, so it would be meaningful to pay attention to it, so they would not, like, (.) lose lots of time on something not really important. And it's also good to think in advance about how you could help them with it.
8. **Teacher:** We'll focus on travel writing again in our next lesson. I think it'd be interesting to connect this literary topic with history and the theme of overseas discoveries. So it's going to be interesting to put these things in a historical context and that could be difficult for them. So I guess I should want them to do it. So I'll divide them into two or three groups, and each will write their own travelogue and they'll send it to the others as a Word file. And they could work on their own texts, I think that's good. But I can't have too many groups because we wouldn't have enough time.
9. **Researcher:** So which key questions could you ask them?
10. **Teacher:** I'll see what they come up with and I'll work with that. (.) They'll probably start as a boat crew and will be exploring a new continent or a new island and will

probably meet some natives they'll start trading with, so (.) those are the questions that come to me now (.) and that I could ask (.), like, what could they gain from meeting the natives or to develop the text further (.) hmmm (.) I'll have to think about it.

In the extract, the researcher emphasized that Daniela's questions were not situated far enough in the students' zone of proximal development. This was confirmed by Daniela who considered her lesson to be "friendly" for the students, which she understood as not challenging. Since the researcher noticed that Daniela was successful with the activities that she had prepared, the researcher highlighted that Daniela's questions need to be both challenging and purposeful. The researcher also emphasized that Daniela needs to know in advance how she will scaffold her activity for her students.

Lesson 5: Overly difficult questions

The next lesson was also dedicated to travel writing. The students first presented their homework from the previous lesson in which they created a fictional travelogue describing a voyage to an imaginary island called Goldalusia. The other students were asked to identify passages that represented the genre of travel writing. The students were then instructed to modify the text so that it would become a fairy tale, a legend, and a piece of fantasy literature. The students spent a short amount of time in group work. The longest activity in the lesson consisted of a dialogue between the teacher and the students discussing the possibilities of changing the travelogue into a fairy tale, a legend, or an example of fantasy literature. This was a cognitively challenging task in accordance with the researcher's suggestion from the interview after the previous lesson. According to Bloom's taxonomy, the students were working on the level of creation because they were suggesting and creating changes in the text.

Extract 5.9: Lesson 5

The students were thinking about ways to change the travelogue into a fairy tale.

1. **Teacher:** So, how can you change this travelogue into a fairy tale? I will ask (.) Vitek and Karel to answer. ((*points at the boys*))
2. **Vitek:** So at the start, we begin with the classic "once upon a time."
3. **Teacher:** ((*nodding*)) Certainly. Did you think of anything else? Would it still be a fairy tale if we just added "once upon a time" and then left it as it is?
4. **Vitek:** No.
5. **Teacher:** Nope, so we have to do something with it.
6. **Karel:** Those natives were evil.
7. **Teacher:** So you would add evil? (.) That's what's missing? Hmm ((*nodding*)).
8. **Vitek:** And because this is a fairy tale, good needs to win and so those who arrived there need to beat the natives. ((*nodding*))
9. **Teacher:** OK, and then?
10. **Monika:** There should be a moral for little children, no?

11 **Teacher:** Of course, a moral for little children. So what would you add there? The boys have already given you a clue ((*pointing at Vitek and Karel*)) by saying that there should be good and evil ((*using her hands to show the existence of the two counterpoints*))

12 **Monika:** Something like good triumphs over evil.

Extract 5.9 captures a part of the interaction regarding transforming a text into a fairy tale. In this part of the lesson, the students were able to react promptly and managed to incorporate fairy tale features into the already existing text. This concerned the phrase "once upon a time" (line 2), the triumph of good over evil (lines 6, 8, and 12), and a moral (line 10). However, they were less successful when they were supposed to apply the same procedure to the remaining two genres, legends and fantasy.

Extract 5.10: Lesson 5

The students were thinking of ways to change the travelogue into a legend.

1 **Klara:** I was thinking that the legend could tell us how Goldalusia got its name. Or something. Like it could be the story of someone who came there, saw the gold, and called it Goldalusia.

2 **Teacher:** Perfect. Did you also have an idea ((*pointing at Aneta, Eliska, and Alzbeta*)) for how to change this into a legend?

3 **Aneta:** I have nothing. ((*shaking her head*))

4 **Teacher:** Well?

5 **Risa:** There'd have to be a hero.

6 **Teacher:** (((*pointing at Risa*)) A hero, you think there'd have to be a hero? ((*nodding*)) I guess it would read better. Michal, ((*pointing at Michal on the last bench*)) how would you make this a legend?

7 **Michal:** Yes, into a legend, well, I have no idea.

8 **Teacher:** No idea? And you boys? (.) Vitek and Karel?

9 **Vitek:** ((*shaking his head*)) I have nothing.

10 **Teacher:** So you have nothing. What about you, Johanka and Adelka?

11 **Johanka:** Nothing as well.

12 **Teacher:** Nothing? Not (.) a single idea? Alright then. Klara, you started well. A legend tells about (.) how something (.) came into existence. So it has some basis in reality. So the real part would be that it's called Goldalusia, and that is true, it is called Goldalusia. And then you try to explain why it's called that. So we could come up with a story about sailors and natives, and then something would happen to them and they'd call the island Goldalusia.

The difference between Extracts 5.9 and 5.10 lies in the degree of students' competence to solve the task. While all of their utterances in Extract 5.9 attempted to solve the task at hand, only Klara's utterance in line 1 is relevant in Extract 5.10. After that, the students only expressed confusion and did not even try to answer the question (lines 3, 7, 9, and 11). As Fig. 5.1 shows, Daniela asked a substantially higher number of open questions of high cognitive demand in this lesson in comparison with the previous recorded lesson. At the same time, the figure also shows that student thoughts with reasoning rose only slightly since they were not always capable of

5.2 The Series of Lessons that Daniela Taught During the TPD Program

following the instructions of their teacher. While open questions of high cognitive demand did increase in this particular lesson—probably due to the input provided by the researcher—they did not stimulate the students to produce sophisticated thoughts with reasoning.

As the next interview revealed, Daniela was not content with the lesson. She stated that the students did not respond eagerly enough, she had had to restate her questions several times, and she was not successful in eliciting the responses she had hoped for. Daniela explained the lack of productive student engagement as a result of the difficulty of her tasks.

Extract 5.11: Interview after Lesson 5

1 **Teacher:** Well, I had (.) this feeling that I really worked so hard and that (1) I had to talk so much. When we were talking about the travelogues, I felt I had to force them to answer and make them think.
2 **Researcher:** Why do you think this was the case?
3 **Teacher:** It was clear that they managed the transformation into a fairy tale well, that we'd talked about fairy tales not long ago so they understood them, but with the legend, we (.) I don't know, the last time we talked about that was in the sixth grade and so they couldn't really apply the rule that the story has to have some basis in reality. You know how we talked about it last time, that I don't have to worry about raising the bar for them and giving them a more challenging task, so I thought of this task and then I was surprised that it was really difficult for them. ((*laughter*))

Later in the interview, the researcher suggested that the students could have managed the task if Daniela had provided them with scaffolding. The researcher said that the students could have received summaries of the main features of fantasy and legends, which might have enabled them to complete the task. It was apparent during the lesson that the students could not proceed with the task since they could not remember the features of these literary genres. In contrast, they transformed the text into a fairy tale with ease since these features were still in their memory (from Lesson 3). Daniela agreed that the encountered problem could have been solved in this way. In summary, the indicator of open questions of high cognitive demand was met in Lesson 5. On the other hand, the teacher could not provide her students with the necessary scaffolding. The teacher stated that she saw the difficulty of her questions as a significant problem that prevented the students from spontaneous participation in communication. Having reflected on this, Daniela crafted her next lesson so that her students would like it and their eagerness to communicate with her would be reinstated.

Lesson 6: Attempts to include open discussion, violation of purposefulness

Between Lessons 5 and 6 for Daniela, she and the other teachers participated in the third workshop, which focused on open discussion and various examples of its applications in teaching. In her next recorded lesson, Daniela decided to attempt to include open discussion through an activity that she had devised: the students were to ask questions based on a picture of a boy on a horse.

The lesson examined the short story "The Summer of the Beautiful White Horse" by William Saroyan, and it was divided into three parts. Daniela gave her students a picture of a boy on a horse with the instructions to paste the picture into their notebooks and create a question of their choice related to the picture. Individual students read their questions aloud, and the whole classroom answered spontaneously (see Extract 5.12). In the second part, all of the students read the short story aloud. In the final part, they all interpreted the short story focusing on the motives of the characters in the short story.

As can be seen in Fig. 5.1, the length of open discussion in this lesson decreased in comparison with the previous two lessons in which it had appeared spontaneously, even before the teachers had been presented with the task of including this indicator in their teaching. The indicator of student thoughts with reasoning increased, as did the indicator of open questions of high cognitive demand. These increases were caused by the third part of the lesson in which Daniela led the interpretation of the story in an exemplary way. She asked truly well-formulated questions and provided her students with both uptake and scaffolding. In this lesson, Daniela made good use of the feedback on her previous recorded lesson. This can be seen in Extract 5.12, which shows how the students interpreted a part of the short story in which two boys who loved horses, Mourad and Aram, stole a horse from a farmer named John Byro and took care of it and rode it. When the farmer met the boys with the horse, he stated that he used to have a similar horse. He also said that he knew their family and that it is honest.

Extract 5.12: Lesson 6

Daniela asked the students questions to interpret the horse owner's behavior.

1 **Teacher:** And then there is this strange scene when the farmer whose horse is missing meets Mourad and Aram with the horse (1). Do you remember it?
2 **Students:** Uh huh ((*agreeing*)).
3 **Teacher:** And I would be interested in knowing how John Byro actually acted in that scene. He clearly recognized his horse. (1) Well, Risa? ((*pointing at Risa who is raising his head*))
4 **Risa:** He was certain that it was his horse but he also knew that their family is too honest to steal a horse. So he thought the horse was his but said it wasn't.
5 **Teacher:** So why (.) why did he say (.) this wasn't his horse? Because he really thought the boys didn't steal the horse?
6 **Viky:** Because their family had a reputation for being honest people who don't steal.
7 **Teacher:** And do you think that John Byro knew that this was his horse or that he didn't know it?
8 **Viky:** Well, I think he suspected that the horse was his but (.) he just wanted (.)
9 **Johanka:** He wanted to test them.
10 **Students:** ((*murmuring*))
11 **Teacher:** Test them? Like to see whether they'd return the horse or not? And what about the boys?
12 **Students:** ((*murmuring*))

5.2 The Series of Lessons that Daniela Taught During the TPD Program

13 **Teacher:** They returned the horse. And what do you think actually made them return the horse?
14 **Tereza:** Because the farmer recognized the horse.
15 **Klara:** They realized their family is honest and that at that moment they weren't and they were shaming their family.
16 **Teacher:** Yes, shaming their entire family. That was well said by the farmer when he pointed out that the family is honest.

The teacher wanted her students to discover why the farmer did not say that the horse was his. Furthermore, she wanted them to discuss why such a move by the farmer was effective. These questions were not easy for the students to answer, and the solution was only brought up by Klara in line 15. Up until that moment, the students showed hesitation (lines 8, 10, and 12) or proposed that the farmer was uncertain about whether the horse was his because the boys came from an honest family (lines 4 and 6) or expressed the opinion that the boys had returned the horse because the farmer recognized it as his (line 14). Yet, the teacher skillfully asked questions (lines 5, 7, 11, and 13) that enabled the students to formulate the right conclusion. In this part of the lesson, the teacher clearly made use of the feedback on asking questions and scaffolding student answers.

Daniela decided to implement an open discussion in the first part of the lesson in which students worked with the picture of a boy riding a horse. At the same time, she considered the activity described in Extract 5.13 to be the lesson's key segment. In addition to striving to meet the indicator of open discussion, she wanted to correct what she perceived as a failure in her previous session: students' inadequate participation in classroom talk.

Extract 5.13: Lesson 6
Students asked the questions they had created and the whole class answered.

1 **Aneta:** Is the boy happy?
2 **Teacher:** That's a good question if he's (.) happy. Would you be able to answer this question, Aneta? Can you tell from the picture? If he is happy?
3 **Johanka:** I don't think he is because he's constantly running away from something.
4 **Teacher:** So you think he is escaping from something?
5 **Klara:** Probably because he's sad.
6 **Teacher:** So you think he's sad? So, a kid in Armenia ((*pointing at the picture projected on the board*)) or somewhere in the countryside, when he wants to be in a better mood, he just jumps on a horse and takes it for a ride.
7 **Klara:** Well, maybe the horse is his best friend.
8 **Jana:** But that doesn't actually tell us if he's happy or not.
9 **Teacher:** Uh huh. ((*nodding approvingly and pointing at Viky*))
10 **Viky:** Well, if the theory that the horse is his best friend is correct than maybe he is happy.
11 **Teacher:** Hmmm. ((*nodding approvingly*)) So even if he were sad a moment ago, now that he managed to jump on his horse and ride in the countryside maybe his mood is getting better.

12 **Jitka:** Well, I was thinking about whether he's too small to ride a horse.
13 **Teacher:** Ehm ((*pointing at Jitka*)), great. What do you think? Is he too small to ride a horse?
14 **Students:** Nope. ((*murmuring*))
15 **Klara:** Well, if that horse is his best bud and if he's been riding it since childhood and trusts him, then–
16 **Teacher:** Hmmm. ((*thoughtful*))
17 **Vitek:** The horse is controlling where they're going.
18 **Teacher:** ((*nodding approvingly*)) So who is actually in control when you ride a horse? The rider or the horse?
19 **Students:** The rider. The horse. Both of them.
20 **Teacher:** Who thinks it's the horse?
21 **Students:** ((*approximately five students raise their hands*))
22 **Teacher:** Who thinks it's the rider?
23 **Students:** ((*approximately two students raise their hands, some murmuring follows*))
24 **Teacher:** And who thinks it's both of them?
25 **Students:** ((*all of them raise their hands*))
26 **Teacher:** And why do you think both of them are in control?
27 **Viky:** Well because– if the horse wanted to get rid of him, then he would get rid of him, but then the boy
28 **Teacher:** [Yes, Viky.] ((*pointing at Viky*))
29 **Viky:** [controls where the horse is running.]
30 **Aneta:** Well, when I'm riding a horse there is this unity as if (.) we were one body.
31 **Teacher:** ((*nodding approvingly*)) You said that very nicely. Do you think that if you wanted to improve your mood and took a really strong motorcycle into the countryside, do you think it would be similar to riding that horse? ((*pointing at the picture*))
32 **Vitek:** Well, if you rode that horse hard into a forest where it could get hurt, (1) if it weren't trained from a foal, it wouldn't go there. (1) I think that when a horse feels that it is dangerous somewhere, it doesn't go there. But you could still go there on a motorbike.
33 **Aneta:** I think there's this real difference because one is a living thing and the other is a machine.

The extract clearly shows that the chosen method of asking questions led students to implement an open discussion. The students not only asked questions but also reacted to what their peers were saying; they listened to each other and inter-animated their voices. For example, Jana pointed out in line 8 that the previous answers were not really connected to Aneta's question in line 1. Viky constructed her answer in line 10 by building on Klara's statement from line 7. At the same time, the extract also includes examples of student thoughts with reasoning (in lines 10, 27, 31, and 32). On the other hand, it is rather problematic that this particular activity did not add to meeting the aim of the lesson, which was to interpret a short story with ethical implications. The picture chosen by Daniela was not directly related to the short story; also, the entire discussion centered on the feelings of the boy riding the horse. Daniela

5.2 The Series of Lessons that Daniela Taught During the TPD Program

did not succeed in connecting the discussion in Extract 5.13 to the interpretation of the short story. Simply said, the problem with purposefulness emerged again here.

Daniela stated in the subsequent interview that this had been her first time using such a method and therefore its implementation was taxing for her as she was not used to it. She expressed doubts about whether the lesson had been interesting for the students, whether the activity had taken too long and been monotonous. It might be that Daniela's frustration from the previous lesson—in which the students had found the genre transformations too difficult and not attractive—was expressed at this moment in the interview. She had therefore chosen an activity she assumed would be liked by her students as it involved working with a picture, scissors, and glue. The researcher pointed out that this particular aim was met since the students were engaged the entire time and worked eagerly. In contrast, she pointed out that the principle of purposefulness was violated since the chosen activity was not directly linked to the story that was later read and interpreted and was not in any way linked to any educational aim of the lesson.

Extract 5.14: Interview after Lesson 6

1 **Researcher**: What types of questions did the students ask? How content are you with the (.) questions that your students asked?
2 **Teacher**: Yeah, I think it was kinda OK (.) First they had to find out who the guy is. And then they asked questions related to the text, and I wanted them to ask those questions, like (.) if he's happy or sad, if he's in unity with the horse, and I wanted them to ask those questions, and otherwise I would've led them to ask those questions, because I needed them to understand why the boys stole the horse and what it meant for them.
3 **Researcher**: Yeah, that was a nice debate you had. But I can't shake the feeling that from the perspective of the entire lesson this was <u>like wasted time</u>, and maybe your mentioning of monotonousness a moment ago stems from the fact that they couldn't do anything other than guess what was in the picture.
4 **Teacher**: Hmmmm (.) that might be right.

In the quoted extract, the researcher questioned whether the activity was effective in relation to the lesson's aim, as the teacher had assumed. First, most of the activity (such as the work with scissors and glue and brainstorming questions) took place in silence even though the aim was to induce open discussion. Second, although open discussion was induced once the students started speaking, it was not relevant to the task of interpreting the text. It was not possible to interpret the behavior of the characters in the short story based on examining a picture not directly connected to the text. Focusing on the chosen indicator weakened Daniela's awareness of her own educational aims.

Daniela recognized lack of the purposefulness during the interview (line 4). Her recognition became the basis for a change in the following lesson, in which Daniela focused the most on implementing the principle of purposefulness.

Lesson 7: Students' questions and the teacher's answers

In the next recorded lesson, Daniela again decided to implement an activity in which the students would ask questions. This time, however, the method of execution differed. The topic of the lesson was fantasy. Daniela first briefly presented the main features of the genre and then asked the students to create questions on topics about which the students wanted to know more. Daniela had been inspired by one of the model methods discussed in the third workshop in which the teacher consciously provides students with only a limited set of information, then the students create questions to explore the gaps, and finally the students collaboratively seek answers. Daniela's method of execution is captured in Extract 5.15.

Extract 5.15: Lesson 7

The teacher provided her students with an incomplete set of information and then asked them to create their own questions that would make the information complete.

1 **Teacher:** So, the fantasy genre describes a story that takes place (.) in a different reality than the one where we are right now. (2) Some characters can actually be supernatural. (.) And fantasy was inspired by a whole lot of other genres and favors certain historical periods. (1) And now you'll be writing questions. (.) Each you will <u>try to come up</u> with two questions about what else you'd like to know.

2 —

3 **Teacher:** So, who wants to ask me a question? ((*Klara is raising her hand*)) Yes, Klara?

4 **Klara:** Which genres inspired fantasy?

5 **Teacher:** ((*scanning the other students*)) Any ideas? Any genres that inspired fantasy? (.) Well, it certainly got inspired by fairy tales. (.) That's for sure, because fairy-tale characters also feature in fantasy. Like, for example? ((*giving the students an inquiring look*))

6 **Petr:** Dragons.

7 **Teacher:** Yes, dragons, for example ((*nodding her head*)).

8 **Tereza:** Witches.

9 **Teacher:** Yes, witches can also be found in fantasy. And wizards, for sure. So this is how fantasy was inspired by fairy tales. (1) And then (1) then it was also inspired by fables because there are supernatural characters in fables, as well, which is related to (1) some place, some characters, something is said about something. So there is inspiration in that. And it was also (1) inspired by medieval knight romances. Because in the Middle Ages people wrote stories about how brave knights are, what they can do, and what battles they can win. So this can be found in fantasy, too. Because in fantasy there are, (.) for example, (.) some brave heroes who managed to do something great. So, fairy tales for sure ((*counting with her fingers*)), fables for sure, and medieval romance. So, another question? ((*scanning the students when Kristyna raises her hand*))

10 **Teacher:** ((*looking at Kristyna*)) Yes?

11 **Kristyna:** Which historical periods?

12 **Teacher:** Which ones? Would you know? [Which–]

13 **Tereza:** [The Middle Ages.]

14 **Teacher:** Mostly the Middle Ages, excellent. Would you happen to know of an example of fantasy that takes place in the Middle Ages?

15 **Tereza:** *Crystals of Power*, for example.

16 **Teacher:** *Crystals of Power*. And?

17 **Vitek:** *Ranger's Apprentice*.

18 **Teacher:** Yes, *Ranger's Apprentice*, because there are castles and kingdoms.

5.2 The Series of Lessons that Daniela Taught During the TPD Program

In comparison with Lesson 6, Lesson 7 moved away from dialogic teaching. The questions asked by students (lines 3 and 10) rather mechanically derived from what the teacher left unsaid ("And fantasy was inspired by a whole lot of other genres and favors certain historical periods"). While the teacher answered at length (line 8), the students were provided with few opportunities for their own utterances; Daniela only enabled them to complete her own factual answers to questions of low cognitive demand (lines 5, 7, 14, and 16). Questions of high cognitive demand that students could answer appeared only in lines 10 and 11. The teacher allowed one student to answer the question (line 12) and then other students to give examples (lines 14 and 16), but she alone explained why fantasy is often portrayed in the context of the Middle Ages (lines 17). In comparison with the previous recorded lesson, the students also did not react to the utterances of their peers and there was no voice inter-animation. The lesson resembled Lessons 1–2 and 4 in which the students eagerly participated and followed the teacher's instructions, but in which their voices were suppressed.

In the subsequent interview, the researcher pointed out that Daniela was dominant in the classroom discourse and that the students received little space for their own utterances (except for creating questions for the teacher). The researcher also stated that open discussion was not implemented, and the interaction was dyadic and took the form of students communicating with the teacher instead of students communicating with other students.

Extract 5.16: Interview after Lesson 7

1 **Researcher:** They ask questions but the person who answers them is mostly you.

2 **Teacher:** But it wasn't really my aim for them to answer in this part of the lesson.

3 **Researcher:** Hmmm.

4 **Teacher:** Cause this was the first time (.) we talked about fantasy, so I didn't count on them knowing an awful lot about it, or that they would know some novels, but I just wanted them to get the information from me. I wanted them to ask me about whatever they were interested in. So–

5 **Researcher:** So you think that it was basically OK? ((*asking inquiringly*))

6 **Teacher:** So, yeah. (1) Sure, I guess I could have asked (1), there were lots of opportunities as I now see it. They probably could've produced it on their own. They certainly could've managed to deduce what fantasy takes from individual genres, but I didn't really have the ambition for them to get everything on their own. I just wanted this to be a version of frontal teaching (.) but I wanted them to be more active because they would be asking those questions. So, I wanted them to learn something. So they could work better in the next part of the lesson and could find the features of fantasy in the chosen extract and in the next sessions.

7 …

8 **Researcher:** It can be seen that they want to talk in some of these moments, but you're sorting of jumping in and interrupting them, hmm. So, I don't really know. This happened several times when Vitek wanted to say something (.) but with others, too. Because they (2) really know about this thing. Vitek constantly returns to *Ranger's Apprentice*. He's always talking about that series.

9 **Teacher:** Well, he's gonna present about that book, so he'll get his turn. ((*laughter*))

According to Daniela, she did not emphasize the features of dialogic education because she had mastered them already (asking open questions of high cognitive demand, uptake, open discussion). Instead, she prioritized the goal for her students, "So, I wanted them to learn something." Daniela focused on the principle of purposefulness to present students with information that is part of the school curriculum. Again, this emphasis stems from Daniela's previous interview with the researcher and what she saw as the most problematic. Therefore, purposefulness in the lesson was more than achieved, but not the indicators of dialogic teaching. From that perspective, Daniela's seventh recorded lesson was substandard, as all of the indicators decreased sharply (as can be seen in Fig. 5.1). This situation is inversely proportional to the situation in Lesson 6 in which there were high values for all indicators, but in which the principle of purposefulness was violated.

The researcher was rather critical during the reflective interview (as can be seen, for example, in line 7) when she pointed out how little space the students were given to practice talk with reasoning. The teacher reacted by defending herself by referencing her educational goals (lines 2 and 4). Despite this, the interview influenced her to structure her next lesson in such a way that the students would communicate the most on the topic of their favorite fantasy books.

Lesson 8: Student talk without reasoning

Fantasy remained the central topic of the next lesson, as well. On the other hand, the form of talk completely changed. The students gave mini-presentations on their favorite fantasy novel or television show that they had prepared at home. After presenting, the students received follow-up questions from their peers and the teacher that they answered (as shown in Extract 5.17, in which Risa responds to questions from his peers). Even though the lesson included a high degree of student talk, the indicators of dialogic teaching still remained low. This is especially apparent with the indicator of student thoughts with reasoning, which was the lowest in Lesson 8 out of all recordings.

Extract 5.17: Lesson 8

Risa gave a mini-speech on Christopher Paolini's Eragon *in which the main protagonist finds a dragon's egg from which a dragon hatches. Other students asked Risa questions about the plot and the length of the novel.*

1 **Kristina:** How did he get the egg?
2 **Risa:** Well, it was guarded by an elf, Arya, who was helping the Varden, and she stole the egg from the king. She was supposed to guard it and (.) because the king's people got her (.) they surrounded her with a ring of fire and (.) she couldn't escape so she used a spell to send the egg away and (.) she didn't know where it ended up, and it ended up with Eragon. And then the egg hatched. ((*nodding at Klara who is raising her hand*)) Yeah?
3 **Klara:** You said that the king kept three eggs. But what happened to the other two?
4 **Risa:** They didn't hatch because a dragon only hatches when it's close to a rider. (1) So it basically chooses him.
5 **Katka:** I'm interested in how many pages the book has.

5.2 The Series of Lessons that Daniela Taught During the TPD Program

6   **Risa:** (*looking at the number of the pages in the book*)) Well, (1) 487 in total, but that includes the acknowledgments.

Extract 5.17 shows that open discussion did not take place even though the students were interacting with one another. In this extract, interaction always took the dyadic form of one student talking with another. Yet, they never transcend this boundary. In line 1, Kristina asked a question that was answered by Risa (line 2), which ended their interaction. Then, Klara asked another question in line 3 and Risa answered in line 4, which was repeated in lines 5 and 6. Each interaction concluded with Risa's answer—the other students do not enter, and they do not ask follow-up questions or form other questions based on what was already said by their peers.

While Risa responded at length, his responses did not include reasoning, they merely described the plot of the novel (lines 2 and 4) or provided his peers with factual information about the novel (line 6). Therefore, even though this lesson was student-centered to a significant extent, it failed by not making the students develop more challenging cognitive processes to the same extent as it managed to enable them to inter-animate their voices.

During the interview, the researcher was less critical than in the previous interview because the teacher admitted before the start of recording that she was nervous. It was clear that the previous interview brought about feelings of failure in Daniela. The researcher attempted to soften this impression by frequently encouraging Daniela, appreciating the positive features of the lesson (such as the good quality of the mini-presentations and the good delivery by the presenting students). Daniela responded by saying that she asks her students to present often and in various formats, which is why they were comfortable with the task. This statement was used by the researcher as a bridge to her only critical commentary regarding the lesson: the absence of open discussion. This shifted the reflective interview to the question of how to achieve what had been eluding Daniela so far: the type of discussion in which students react to one another and inter-animate their voices.

The rest of their discussion focused on the creation of a methodological plan for the next session. Daniela decided to use Tolkien's *The Lord of the Rings* and focus on the characters Frodo and Aragorn. She decided that the students would vote on which of the characters played a more vital role in the story. The aim was defined on two levels: the content level (so as to make students realize that both characters were important to the story) and the formal level (so that the students could voice various opinions and the indicators of dialogic education would be met).

Extract 5.18: Interview after Lesson 7

1   **Teacher:** I could ask them to create a fictional fantasy hero. So with two groups (.) each would have one hero. And I'd start with a brief intro about who can be a hero, that it can be somebody like Aragorn or also somebody like (.)
2   **Researcher:** Frodo.
3   **Teacher:** Frodo. Yep, exactly, hmm. So they'd know that they have choices and then they can make the hero on their own, whatever they want it to be, and they should give the hero a character trait, maybe something less obvious, and they can put it into an

experience the hero goes through. And now I'm stuck and don't know what the next step is. (1) If the first group should ask the second, or if one group should present their hero and the other should ask follow-up questions, you know? My first idea was that they'd create a hero of their own and the other group would ask them questions to find out what character features the hero has.

4   **Researcher:** Hmmm. (.) And the whole thing could be flipped. But that is just an idea, OK. Maybe they could find out that the heroes could be different?
5   **Teacher:** Different, hmm.
6   **Researcher:** But how can you guarantee that each of the groups will create a different hero?
7   **Teacher:** Perhaps I could have them read an extract. And maybe the names would be omitted, you know. (.) Each group would have one text which'd indirectly describe the character trait of the hero and I could black out the names so that they couldn't guess which novel the hero was taken from, and based on that they could complete the character portrait of that hero.
8   **Teacher:** And I'm thinking that we could turn this into a game. You could tell them that this is a game (.) and that the group that better defends their hero, which would be better, and they could …
9   **Researcher:** And the message would be that they're both, in fact–
10 **Teacher:** [Both are important.]
11 **Researcher:** [Both are important] or useful in that story.

Extract 5.18 portrays a sequence in a collaborative debate in which the teacher weighs aloud the various routes her lesson could take, and the researcher adds her own suggestions. Both participants react to each other and develop the other's ideas. A recurring pattern appears: a suggestion is stated and immediately questioned (e.g., "But how can you guarantee that each of the groups will create a different hero?"). This enables the two communication participants to make the plan more and more precise. It is also apparent that this interview differed from the preceding ones: both communicating participants focused more on the coming lesson than the previous one.

Lesson 9: Open discussion with rich argumentation with a resistant group of girls

The brainstormed plan was used in Lesson 9 with a core activity that had students establish which hero is more heroic. Students first received two extracts: one described Aragorn, and the other described Frodo. They were presented with the task of completing the character descriptions. The students were then divided into two groups according to their preferences and defended their choice of a more heroic hero in discussion. The majority of the dialogic teaching indicators clearly increased during this activity; this was especially the case for student thoughts with reasoning and the length of open discussion. Still, the number of open questions of high cognitive demand decreased, which could be explained by the fact that the open discussion in which the participants reacted to one another consumed all of the space available for asking questions.

5.2 The Series of Lessons that Daniela Taught During the TPD Program

Extract 5.18: Lesson 9

1. **Teacher:** So, Vitek, tell me why you think <u>Aragorn is a hero</u>?
2. **Vitek:** I think he was afraid at first, but then he overcame his fear and led the army into victorious battle and so decided to take the burden on himself and in that way he helped everybody succeed.
3. **Teacher:** What do you think? ((*looks at the other group*)) Why do you think Frodo is better?
4. **Viky:** Frodo is stronger because he resisted the ring.
5. **Tereza:** His will is stronger.
6. **Vitek:** COME ON we can't really know that he had (.) <u>you can't really know</u> that his will was stronger than Aragorn's, because Aragorn never carried the ring, so (.) he never experienced it ((*gesturing toward the other group*))
7. **Klara:** Aragorn saved a few people by curing them, but Frodo saved the whole country by destroying the ring.
8. **Vitek:** BUT ARAGORN SAVED THE WHOLE COUNTRY. By (.) leading the army into the battle and becoming the King of Gondor.
9. **Risa:** But, if the ring had gotten to the bad guy, (.) what was his name? The bad guy, so then (.)
10. **Tereza:** That guy Sauron?
11. **Risa:** Sauron. So then (.) <u>he'd have easily wiped everyone out</u>. So Frodo's task was much more important.

Extract 5.18 portrays a discussion with very clear opinions on both sides expressed in reaction to one another. The student responses are complex and include reasoning (lines 2, 4, 6, 7, 8, and 9–11). The eager participation of the students cannot be overlooked—they truly attempted to defend their positions (as can be seen in Vitek's gesticulation and raised voice in lines 6 and 8). Still, the debate remained matter-of-fact and the students sought new ways to bolster their cases. Extract 5.18 describes a classroom talk that was of high quality not only because of the high indicator levels, but also because it was purposeful since the students were thinking about individual characters and evaluating their role in the novel as a whole.

In the subsequent reflective interview, the researcher emphasized the quality of the students' responses along with the inclusion of open discussion. Daniela responded by saying that in her previous lesson she had tried hard to make her students ask questions because she had assumed that student questions would by default induce open discussion. However, this assumption—which had been proven false by Lessons 7 and 8—was abandoned in Lesson 9.

Extract 5.19: Interview after Lesson 9

1. **Researcher:** One of the things that really went well was they <u>really spoke very nicely</u> and had lots of arguments and they, like, were really <u>in a true discussion</u>, lots of them very engaged, and they reacted to one another. And that didn't really happen before.
2. **Teacher:** Well (.) before I really just tried to <u>make them ask questions</u>. And I'm not into that anymore.
3. **Researcher:** I see.

Both the researcher and the teacher also discussed the two groups' level of engagement. The students first received pictures of both heroes and extracts in which they each featured. Based on these extracts, the groups were to complete character portraits of both heroes and then chose the one they perceived as more heroic and divide themselves into two groups based on their preference for Aragorn or Frodo. The teacher had assumed her students would be familiar with both characters even before reading the extracts by being familiar with either the novel or its movie adaptation. This assumption was not fully confirmed and resulted in some information asymmetry: students with prior knowledge were able to argue better than students with knowledge gained only from the extracts. Daniela also noticed some distance and unwillingness to participate among a group of girls who had not been familiar with either the book or the movie adaptation and visibly showed distance from the fantasy genre.

Extract 5.20: Interview after Lesson 9

1 **Teacher:** And a group emerged in the corner, and they just very visibly showed me that they're just not into fantasy. Because I'd hoped they'd already know the necessary information from the books and movies. From *The Lord of the Rings* and *The Hobbit*. And that the extracts would just refresh that in their memory. But they just kept telling me they didn't know these things and it's just not clear from the extracts. And when they were supposed to write those character portraits of the heroes, the girls just completely bailed and wrote that Aragorn was a show-off and Frodo was a fag.

Even though the values for the indicators were outstanding in this lesson, which was also very purposeful, the principle of collectivity turned out to be problematic. While some students participated eagerly, some other students chose not to. Hence, the teacher decided to create a simple plan for her next lesson based solely on a text with which all of the students would get familiarized during the lesson.

Lesson 10: Excellent teaching

In Lesson 10, we observed a substantial increase in the indicators (see Fig. 5.1) and a significant simplification of teaching methods—the students read aloud an extract from Mary Shelley's *Frankenstein*. The reading was divided into parts, it was interspersed with a plot summary, and the students were asked to answer questions. The students expressed differing opinions, which led to open discussion. The fact that the students were seated in a circle made the participation of all students easier. After the students finished reading the text, Daniela asked them how a scientist should behave if they know they have created a dangerous monster. The following extract captures how the students dealt with the question.

Extract 5.21: Lesson 10

1 **Johanka:** I think he could put him in jail and experiment on him, use him for medical testing and similar things.
2 **Teacher:** Wow ((*laughs hesitantly*)) What do you think about that?
3 **Kristyna:** It's better than killing him.

5.2 The Series of Lessons that Daniela Taught During the TPD Program

4 **Teacher:** Better than killing him? ((*points at Risa, Jindra is raising his hand*))
5 **Risa:** It would be better than using rats.
6 **Viky:** He's dead anyways, so (.)
7 **Teacher:** And why is it better than testing on rats?
8 **Viky**: Because rats are still alive.
9 **Teacher:** Like, rats are still alive but Frankenstein's monster is not?
10 **Klara:** No, he was dead.
11 **Teacher:** What was he?
12 **Klara:** Kinda artificial.
13 **Hanka:** He was artificially created.
14 **Teacher:** Artificially created (2)
15 **Viky:** And dead, too.
16 **Teacher:** So since he was artificially created, we don't think of him as a human being that would feel emotions or have a right to life.
17 **Hanka:** Well, a right to life, one can't really say (.) well, I don't know, but if somebody takes one leg from Franta, another from Vitek, and he sews them up like this ((*laughing*)), maybe the result has feelings, but I don't think it has a right to life, when it was artificially created.
18 **Teacher:** That's an interesting opinion. Do you agree with Hanka on this? That artificial creations ((*Jindra is raising his hand*)) have no right to life like people do?
19 **Viky:** Well, in theory, he is created from (.) I mean Frankenstein didn't kill people so that he could make this monster (.) so in theory he's created from those dead bodies, so basically he is also dead.
20 **Vitek:** But he is alive.
21 **Teacher:** Is he alive?
22 **Vitek:** He kinda seems alive to me.
23 **Viky:** He is alive, but he is dead matter, too.
24 **Vitek:** But life was breathed into that dead matter.
25 **Teacher:** ((*students are murmuring*)) Well, so the scientist chose not to kill him, the monster. At that moment, he was horrified, but he didn't kill it. But he's still responsible for what he created ((*Aneta is raising her hand*)), he doesn't like it, in fact he is disgusted by it, but he didn't really consider killing the creature, because he considered it to be alive. So? ((*pointing at Aneta*))
26 **Aneta:** So about that killing, I think that it's like when a mother gives birth to a baby ((*the teacher is nodding her head approvingly*)), so there's an emotional bond and when I give life to something I can't just kill it.
27 **Teacher:** Thank you, Aneta. I didn't really want to start that myself, but I was waiting for how we would get to it, so (.) when parents give life to a baby, (1) the baby is alive because of the parents. And imagine if the parents didn't like the baby, so would they do medical testing on it? ((*students are murmuring*)) Or would they kill it? You know what? <u>We won't</u> ((*Aneta is raising her hand*)), <u>we don't really need to go so deep to get to Frankenstein. It's for you to think about whether these two scenarios are in some way similar.</u> ((*pointing at Aneta with her palm*))
28 **Aneta:** It's like when a child gets born with a disability, so its parents won't donate it for testing or kill it.

In this extract, we can observe a developed discussion with clearly profiled and different voices. The students discuss whether an artificially created being can be considered alive and whether it is justified to treat it in any way imaginable. The participants were eagerly engaged in the discussion along with the teacher, who clearly made her opinion known (lines 16, 25, and 27). Yet, her participation in the discussion was still very egalitarian—she did not claim all the power into her own hands as evidenced by the fact that the students did not have a problem with contradicting her and expressing differing opinions. During the lesson, the students formulated an outstanding number of thoughts with reasoning (as can be seen in Fig. 5.1 and lines 17, 19, 26, and 28 in the extract). At the same time, classroom talk was at all times concentrated on the discussed text, its possible interpretations, and their real-life applications (in spite of the novel having certain fantasy elements). From the perspective of dialogic education, the tenth lesson was exemplary, which is also seen in the fact that the majority of students participated in it.

5.3 How to Understand the Nonlinear Development of Change

In this section, we offer some interpretations for why the nature of transformation, was as we have described through Daniela's case, nonlinear and switching between success and lack of success.

We entered the project estimating that a possible change would be gradual and divided into steps. It is known that implementing change into teaching takes time (Adey 2006; Butler et al. 2004). For TPD programs, this concerns the program length as well as the program phases, their interconnection, and the accumulation of achieved progress. We implemented phases in our project by introducing the individual indicators of dialogic teaching. For example, the teachers were to include a higher number of questions of high cognitive demand after their participation in the second workshop, and triadic interaction (i.e., discussion among students) after the third workshop. These phases made use of the teachers' ability to ask open questions of high cognitive demand since proper discussion cannot happen without a well-asked question first. We facilitated the process taking part in phases by reflecting on each recorded lesson after it was taught, appreciating progress, and planning how it could be furthered in the subsequent lesson.

However, the data from Daniela's lessons show that the transformation of teaching practices was not linear, nor did it occur in step-by-step increases in the observed parameters. Instead, progress alternated with regression. The question arises as to what drives the process of change in a sequence of consecutive lessons. We can also ask why at some moments progress does not take place but instead downturns occur.

5.3.1 *Critical Reflection as the Motor for Change*

Our data show that the nature of classroom talk was different in consecutive lessons. They also reveal that there was a clear connection between what was said in the reflective interviews and what happened in the following lesson. After each reflective interview, the teacher paid attention to one of the several stimuli that were discussed in the interviews. However, this correspondence between the content of the reflective interview and the subsequent change in teaching practices was always partial. Several issues always emerged from the data analysis and its reflection during the reflective interview, and the teacher made a choice about the direction of change in the subsequent lesson. This choice was not necessarily predictable. For example, the fact that the implementation of open discussion was absent was discussed in the reflective interview after Lesson 7. In Lesson 8, however, this parameter did not change because the teacher focused on dealing with another problem, namely how to increase student talk time. It can be seen, then, that the correspondence is with one of several possible issues and the choice of issue is up to the teacher. Our observation that teachers choose what aspect of their teaching to change is also supported by Gomez Zaccarelli et al. (2018), who claimed that teachers can consciously prioritize one aspect that they will change over others.

Even though it is not possible to completely predict which stimulus reflected in the interview will be heeded by the teacher, a pattern nonetheless emerged: Daniela primarily responded to critical ones. This also explains the changes between consecutive lessons because Daniela attempted to improve what had been assessed as imperfect by herself or by the researcher. In contrast, Daniela did not focus on the features of her teaching practices that had been recognized as examples of good teaching. At times, Daniela's loss of interest in these features was such that the values for the praised feature even decreased. This was recorded when Daniela was satisfied after Lesson 3 with how she handled open questions of high cognitive demand and discontent for not meeting the principle of purposefulness. In the subsequent lesson, Daniela's handling of the purposeful principle was exemplary, and the values for the indicator of open questions of high cognitive demand decreased significantly. Similarly, Lesson 6 was appreciated for including student thoughts with reasoning to a great extent and criticized for not meeting the principle of purposefulness. In Lesson 7, she upheld the principle perfectly, but the number of student thoughts with reasoning decreased markedly.

5.3.2 *The Phenomenon of Unintended Consequences*

Our data further show that a change implemented by the teacher can have unintended consequences. For example, in Lesson 4 Daniela did not aim to decrease the number of open questions of higher cognitive demand. This effect was an unintended consequence of Daniela's attempt to increase the value of the principle of purposefulness.

Based on the data we collected in the lessons of Daniela and other teachers, the effects of changes and their unintended consequences accumulated over many consecutive lessons. This is well illustrated in Daniela's Lessons 6 through 8. When the analysis showed that purposefulness was not met in Lesson 6, Daniela increased the value for purposefulness but at the same time minimized the space in which students could communicate with one another—in this lesson, students could only ask questions that she could answer. After this was discussed in the next reflective interview, Daniela massively increased the space for student communication, but students only monotonously gave their presentations and no real dialogue with inter-animation of the participants' voices occurred. Only in Lesson 9 did Daniela manage to achieve a lesson that was purposeful and in which the students reacted to one another.

It can be understood that teachers need to solve a series of gradually emerging problems before they can achieve the ideal of dialogic teaching. This also explains the well-known statement according to which any change in teaching practices takes a long time and so effective TPD programs also need to be of a sufficient length (see, e.g., Adey 2006; Butler et al. 2004; Desimone 2009). The necessary time period cannot be predicted as one cannot predict the scope and nature of problems that will appear during the implementation of changes.

We consider the identification of the phenomenon of unintended consequences to be very significant because it enables us to understand why changes in dialogic education do not have a straightforwardly linear trajectory. The effects of unintended consequences of well-meant alternative practices can accumulate to such grandiose proportions that they stop progress or even revert it.

5.3.3 The Role of Gestalt in the Process of Change

Why and how do teachers regress during their transformations? We will use the rapid decrease in the values of all indicators after Lesson 6 as our starting point in interpreting this phenomenon. What happened between Lesson 6 and Lesson 7? In Lesson 6, Daniela attempted to implement some recommended dialogic techniques and emphasized her students asking questions and responding to one another. After discussing this in the subsequent reflective interview, Daniela abandoned the experiments of the previous lesson and return to the safe ground of traditional and authoritative teaching—in Lesson 7, she lectured. Daniela could lecture well even before she entered the program and so, in other words, she returned to her gestalt (Korthagen et al. 2001).

Korthagen et al. (2001) used the term *gestalt* to describe the interplay of cognitive and emotional factors that make teachers act in certain specifically stable ways. The term describes behavior that goes unacknowledged by teachers, and it is very probable that such behavior dominates ordinary teaching practices (Korthagen and Kessels 1999; Korthagen et al. 2001). Gestalt describes habitual behavior, and each teacher has a number of gestalts that characterize their style of teaching. If teachers want to transform their teaching, they need to overcome their gestalts.

5.3 How to Understand the Nonlinear Development of Change

We familiarized the teachers participating in our program with the concept of dialogic teaching, and they decided to change their teaching styles accordingly. Since their gestalts differed in the distance from the ideal of dialogic teaching, the degree of change in their existing teaching styles also differed. They found some of the requirements easy to meet because doing so only required strengthening patterns that were already present in their teaching practices. For example, most of the teachers already asked their students open questions of high cognitive demand. However, other requirements demanded more serious changes in teaching practices—implementing open discussion turned out to be the most challenging requirement as it had not featured in their prior teaching at all.

If teachers are to acquire new skills and techniques, they need to overcome their gestalts and create new patterns of behavior. The original gestalts do not disappear; they remain a part of the teacher's repertoire and can even dominate their practices at the expense of the new skills and techniques under specific conditions. This understanding enables us to explain the numerous increases and decreases in the indicators. When teachers managed to implement new dialogic techniques, the values rose. When teachers backslid to their gestalts, the values dropped. This pattern took place several times in Daniela's lessons. The changes between Lesson 3 and Lesson 4 are an example. The indicators increased significantly in Lesson 3, in particular the indicator for open questions of high cognitive demand. After reflecting on the lack of purposefulness in the lesson, however, Daniela returned to her gestalt in Lesson 4. This lesson was similar to the lessons recorded prior to the start of our program—the students were active and eager to communicate, yet they received few opportunities to create thoughts with reasoning because Daniela asked them only simple questions that did not challenge them. Both Daniela and the students felt at ease under such conditions, but the progress achieved in the previous lesson was to a great extent lost.

Daniela's return to her gestalt happened again in Lesson 8. In the previous interview, the limited space for student talk was reflected critically. Daniela had designed Lesson 7 such that her students would ask questions and she would provide them with elaborate answers. In the next lesson, Lesson 8, Daniela significantly increased the opportunities for students to talk but without taking into consideration any of the newly acquired techniques. Instead, she returned to what she and her students had mastered well even before the start of the TPD program: a lesson in which the students give mini-presentations. Her decision resulted in a lesson that was student-centered. However, there was no inter-animation of voices and the students did not try out more challenging thinking processes. Once again, Daniela and her students felt at ease under such conditions and enjoyed the lesson. These examples illustrate our finding that phases of progress and regression alternated during the course of our development program, which was caused by the fact that the teachers switched between using new techniques and returning to their old gestalts.

This raises the question of what exactly causes the backslide to gestalt. Our data convincingly show that frustration and feelings of failure triggered regression. For instance, Daniela mentioned before the recording of Lesson 8 that she was nervous and uncertain about the quality of her teaching in the upcoming lesson. Thus, the mechanism of backslide to gestalt can be described as follows: because of frustration, teachers start to question the new skills and techniques that they are acquiring and trying to master. Simultaneously, the teachers are not capable of correctly analyzing the causes of their current problems nor finding the proper solutions. They therefore return to their gestalts as if to ingrained behavioral shortcuts. Further, they feel more comfortable with their return to the gestalt as it includes familiar techniques and ways of teaching and eliminates the feelings of frustration caused by attempts at implementing new techniques. At the same time, the process of change that had previously begun is interrupted.

Our findings show how complicated it is to change teaching practices. We stated that critical reflection drove the process of change and that there would be no change without the teacher taking a critical stance toward her own practices. At the same time, looking critically at their own teaching occasionally made teachers feel frustrated and incompetent, which triggered a return to their gestalts. Therefore, the question arises of how to provide teachers with critical impulses and prevent them from returning to their gestalts.

5.3.4 Reflection as a Way to Overcome Gestalt

There is a consensus in the scientific community that reflection is an essential component of teacher education (Beauchamp 2015; Hatton and Smith 1995; Korthagen et al. 2001; Lane et al. 2014). Reflection is understood as a bridge between teachers' knowledge and their behavior. Berson et al. (2015) claimed that education aiming at changing the teaching practices of teachers urgently needs to include space for reflection since it is essential to observe how new patterns of behavior emerge during the process of change and understand their logic and character. We used Korthagen's model (Korthagen and Kessels 1999; Korthagen et al. 2001) while designing our TPD program. This model is based on the statement that teachers are aware of some components of their actions that would otherwise go unnoticed. This feature is particularly useful in implementing dialogic teaching because typically communication largely takes place outside the conscious examination of its participants (Gröschner et al. 2020). Within this context, we can therefore explain why our participants backslid to their gestalts but did not stay with them. Since the teachers reflected on their behavior in reflective interviews, they could identify unproductive gestalts and seek alternative patterns of behavior.

Extract 5.8 serves as a good example of this observation. In the extract, Daniela realized—aided by the researcher—that Lesson 4 was not cognitively challenging enough. Daniela said that the whole lesson was "friendly" to the students and "chill" for herself. This zone of comfort often characterizes gestalt. During the interview, however, the teacher stated that the cognitive challenge was too low and that this was in conflict with the newly implemented techniques. At the same time, Daniela started developing new alternative techniques for her next lesson and proposed raising the level of challenge by interconnecting the students' knowledge of literature and history and working with texts the students themselves created.

5.3.5 Teaching Methods as Instruments for Implementing Change

There are programs based on how teachers appropriate certain teaching methods or instructions for teaching activities (Chinn et al. 2001; Hennessy et al. 2011; Gomez Zaccarelli et al. 2018). It is presumed that if teachers follow certain procedures, changes in indicators and other attributes of dialogic education will manifest. In our TPD program, we used the indicators of dialogic teaching as a starting point and intended to discover collaboratively, in discussion with the teachers, proper teaching methods for meeting the indicators. Therefore, each workshop and reflective interview included a discussion of possible teaching methods. The researchers presented viable methodological approaches to teachers who discussed them and suggested alternative approaches. The decision as to which method would be chosen and used was always left to the teachers.

Data recorded during the interviews show that the teachers were thinking about teaching methods intensely. While the researchers emphasized the indicators and principles of dialogic teaching during the interviews, the teachers more often spoke of methods. This is also exemplified by Extract 5.8, discussed above. While the researcher focused more on questions (lines 7 and 9)—and thus highlighted the importance of the indicators of dialogic teaching—Daniela focused more on teaching methods and their applications. For example, she mused about how best to divide the students into groups, the format of their homework, and the nature of the materials with which to equip them (line 8).

This emphasis on methods is understandable if we take into consideration the way in which the TPD program was organized. The teachers were first presented with the indicators and principles of dialogic teaching. These were presented as desirable components of teaching that were expected to appear in their teaching practices. Therefore, the teachers found themselves in a situation in which they needed to find a viable method to ensure implementation of the indicators and principles in their lessons. And while the indicators and principles were given, space for the teachers' autonomy (and responsibility) opened with the choice of methods. The selection, design, and execution of a particular teaching method became an instrument for teachers for implementing dialogic indicators and principles in the classroom. It is therefore understandable that the teachers gave the methods intense thought and wanted to discuss them during the interviews.

The teachers followed three paths when planning methods for implementing dialogic teaching. In the first, they used a method that they had known from their past experience. In the second, they used a method that was presented to them at one of the workshops. In the third, they creatively fashioned a brand new method. All of these approaches were observed in Daniela's lessons. First, Daniela used a familiar method in Lesson 3. She had been to a teacher development workshop on drama education in which she had acquired the technique of impersonating a literary character. Second, she used a method presented at one of our workshops in Lesson 7, in which she implemented the technique of an incomplete lecture during which students are provided with only a partial set of information and are asked to create questions to fill in the gaps. Third, there were examples of Daniela's own methods, as exemplified by her activity in which the students were to glue a picture into their notebooks and then brainstorm questions relevant to the picture, as seen in Lesson 9.

Even though Daniela, and the other teachers as well, chose her methods deliberately, our case study reveals that the chosen methods did not serve her well at all times. Methods need to be understood as tools; the effects that a given method brings about are not caused by the method itself but rather by the teacher's use of the given tool. For example, the method of an incomplete lecture can help to bring about discussion between students and teachers. However, this did not happen in Lesson 7 because Daniela herself answered the questions from her students and did not engage her students in knowledge creation.

Our data show that the teachers were only rarely successful during their first attempts at using a given dialogic teaching method. They met their lack of success with one of two responses. In the first case, they abandoned the method and chose another, which in some cases resulted in a series of experiments with multiple methods, as was the case with Daniela. In the second case, the teachers chose to stay with the method but improved its use or modified it (as can be seen in the case of another teacher from this sample, Hana; see Sedova 2017). In either case, we observed that all of the teachers chose and calibrated methods so that they would serve them well. In the final stage, teachers no longer imitate the form that a given tool has. Instead, they understand the underpinning logic of the tool and can therefore adapt the tool, intensifying the effects of its use.

We can see this evolution in Daniela's final lesson, during which she used the same method as in her first lesson in which her students read a text and were led by Daniela's questions to interpret the text. Unlike in Lesson 1, however, the indicators of dialogic teaching were met in Lesson 10 when Daniela asked open questions of high cognitive demand, gave her students space and time to create elaborate answers, used uptake to motivate student reasoning, and managed to implement open discussion among the students. The result was student talk that was collective, purposeful, and of high quality.

5.4 Summary

This chapter used Daniela's case to illustrate the nature of change toward dialogic teaching, a change that was neither gradual nor constant. Instead, this change was nonlinear and phases of progress alternated with phases of stagnation and, in some cases, even phases of regression.

In our efforts to explain such changes, we observed that critical reflection played a vital role in teacher stimulation. The teaching components that were labeled as not being examples of good teaching became the stimuli for change in subsequent lessons.

Further, we found out that a change in one component of teaching practices often triggered a chain reaction that influenced other components. This led to unintended consequences—unplanned changes that could even result in regression in one or more of the elements of dialogic teaching.

We identified an important source of change resistance in teacher gestalt: routine behavior patterns that make teachers feel comfortable and safe. We showed that during the TPD program, the teacher sometimes experienced frustration that drove her to her gestalt. This resulted in blocking of planned changes and the (often unacknowledged) freezing of teaching practices in their prior state, before the process of change was initiated. We showed that through reflective interviews, it was possible to make the teacher aware of her gestalts as well as to be sensitive to unintended consequences during the transformation.

Finally, we described the teacher's experimentation with teaching methods as the main instrument by which she drove the implementation of dialogic teaching indicators and principles into her practice.

References

Adey, P. (2006). A model for professional development of teachers thinking. *Thinking Skills and Creativity, 1*(1), 49–56. https://doi.org/10.1016/j.tsc.2005.07.002
Beauchamp, C. (2015). Reflection in teacher education: Issues emerging from a review of current literature. *Reflective Practice, 16*(1), 123–141. https://doi.org/10.1080/14623943.2014.982525
Berson, E., Borko, H., Million, S., et al. (2015). Practice what you teach: A video-based practicum model of professional development for elementary science teachers. *Orbis Scholae, 9*(2), 35–53. https://doi.org/10.14712/23363177.2015.79
Butler, D. L., Novak Lauscher, H., Jarvis-Selinger, S., et al. (2004). Collaboration and self-regulation in teachers' professional development. *Teaching and Teacher Education, 20*(5), 435–455. https://doi.org/10.1016/j.tate.2004.04.003
Chinn, C. A., Anderson, R. C., & Waggoner, M. A. (2001). Patterns of discourse in two kinds of literature discussion. *Reading Research Quarterly, 36*(4), 378–411. https://doi.org/10.1598/RRQ.36.4.3
Desimone, L. M. (2009). Improving impact studies of teachers' professional development: Towards better conceptualisation and measures. *Education and Research, 38*(3), 181–199. https://doi.org/10.3102/0013189X08331140
Gomez Zaccarelli, F., Schindler, A.-K., Borko, H., et al. (2018). Learning from professional development: A case study of the challenges of enacting productive science discourse in the classroom. *Professional Development in Education, 44*(5), 721–737. https://doi.org/10.1080/19415257.2017.1423368
Gröschner, A., Jähne, M. F., & Klass, S. (2020). Attitudes towards dialogic teaching and the choice to teach: The role of preservice teachers' perception on their own school experience. In N. Mercer, R, Wegerif, & L. Major (Eds.), *The Routledge international handbook of research on dialogic education*. Abingdon: Routledge.
Hatton, N., & Smith, D. (1995). Reflection in teacher education: Towards definition and implementation. *Teaching and Teacher Education, 11*(1), 33–49. https://doi.org/10.1016/0742-051X(94)00012-U
Hennessy, S., Warwick, P., & Mercer, N. (2011). A dialogic inquiry approach to working with teachers in developing classroom dialogue. *Teachers College Records, 113*(9), 1906–1959.

Korthagen, F. A. J., & Kessels, J. P. A. M. (1999). Linking theory and practice: Changing the pedagogy of teacher education. *Education and Research, 28*(4), 4–17. https://doi.org/10.3102/0013189X028004004

Korthagen, F. A. J., Kessels, J. P. A. M., Koster, B., et al. (2001). *Linking practice and theory: The pedagogy of realistic teacher education.* Mahwah: Erlbaum.

Lane, R., McMaster, H. J., Adnum, J., et al. (2014). Quality reflective practice in teacher education: A journey towards shared understanding. *Reflective Practice, 15*(4), 481–494. https://doi.org/10.1080/14623943.2014.900022

Sedova, K. (2017). Transforming teacher behaviour to increase student participation in classroom discourse. *Teacher Development, 21*(2), 225–242. https://doi.org/10.1080/13664530.2016.1224775

Chapter 6
The Case of Marek: Tension and Conflict in a Dialogic Teaching System

Abstract In this chapter, we will focus on the teacher Marek. In describing his case, we want to demonstrate that dialogic teaching is a complex and interlinked system consisting of elements (indicators, principles, and methods) that influence one another in either a synergistic or a discordant way. Tensions or even conflicts such as those documented here can arise between these elements.

The organization of this chapter is similar to that of Chap. 5. At the beginning, we present some contextual information about the teacher Marek. Next, we describe individual lessons he taught during the TPD program to show how his teaching practices changed. The data from the lessons are complemented by data from the reflective interviews to present how Marek was thinking about the transformation process. Finally, we offer some interpretations for why tensions and conflicts may arise in a system of dialogic teaching. Further, we focus on the most harmful instances in which the principles of purposefulness and collectivity were broken. We explain the sources of this and show how Marek and other teachers in our sample overcame the tension and saved the principles essential for dialogic teaching.

6.1 About Marek

Marek participated in the TPD program during the 2014/2015 school year. At the start of the program, Marek had been a secondary school teacher for 12 years, ever since he had graduated with a degree in teaching English and Czech language and literature. Apart from the courses that he was certified to teach, Marek was also teaching media education and information and communication technologies. Marek thought of himself as of a skilled teacher and a very gifted manager. He was a self-confident teacher with high self-esteem.

We accompanied Marek to the classes of Czech language and literature that he taught to seventh-grade students four times a week for 45 min. Of the four classes, one was devoted to literature. Marek was teaching this class for the second year. It comprised 19 students at the start of the year (18 at the end because one male student relocated to another town because of his parents' work). Boys made up two-thirds of the class; there were seven girls. One of the boys, Karel, was a new addition to the class since he had failed to complete the previous year and had to repeat the seventh grade with students who were one year younger than him. The school at which Marek was teaching is situated in a conservation area in the city's historic center. The students' socioeconomic background was either middle or working class.

6.2 Series of Lessons Marek Taught During TPD Program

Observations of Marek's classes confirmed the findings from the case of Daniela (see Chap. 5) that the implementation of dialogic teaching into practice is in no way linear. In Marek's case, the development also included phases of both progress and regression. The development overview is shown in Fig. 6.1. Lessons 1 and 2, recorded before the start of the program, represent a phase of their own—they show Marek's teaching before he was motivated to implement any changes whatsoever. Since interactions between the teacher and the students appeared in such classes only sporadically, most of the measured values approximated zero. A turning point in Marek's teaching was the third recorded lesson, which took place after our first and second workshops. Having acquainted himself with the nature of the project, Marek changed his conception of teaching. This had an immediate positive influence on all the measured indicators. The values of individual indicators oscillated, ending high in student thoughts with reasoning and open discussion, but apparently lower in open questions with high cognitive demand and uptakes. This development is interpreted below.

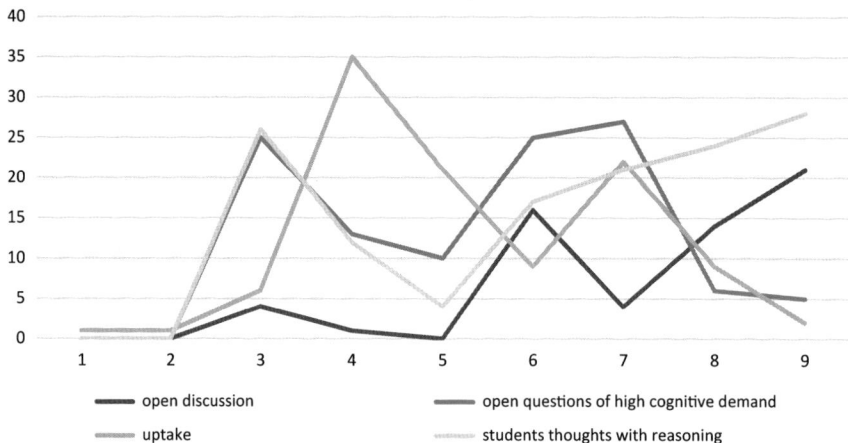

Fig. 6.1 Development of indicators over consecutive lessons

6.2 Series of Lessons Marek Taught During TPD Program

Lessons 1 and 2: Before entering the TPD program

Marek entered the program as a teacher with a clear image of what high-quality teaching of literature should look like. His main declared aim was to motivate his students to think about the readings. Marek was confident that his teaching met this aim and that his students were able to use their critical thinking skills. Marek emphasized thinking as a key skill. He favored independent student work since he believed that this mode of work enables students to practice independent thinking despite the substantial number of students in the class. Typically, his students worked independently on tasks that Marek provided via worksheets. These worksheets were created by Marek and guided students to read authentic texts (fiction and non-fiction) for understanding and to respond to them with their own writing. Such tasks were then evaluated by Marek outside of class time. The results were often exhibited in the classroom or summarized by Marek in the following class. Student verbal participation in classroom talk was considered only a pleasant way of passing occasional intervals of time. In other words, student participation was not a means for Marek to support his chosen aim of student thinking. The students thus contributed with only very short periods of talk and did so in two ways: they were engaged in motivational activities that preceded their independent work and they demonstrated their understanding of the instructions necessary for completing their independent work (e.g., by being involved in class talk of an organizational character).

This description characterized the lessons recorded before the start of the program. Both of these lessons examined an extract from "The Water of Life," a short story written by Otakar Batlička, a Czech author of young adult literature. During Lessons 1 and 2, Marek's students participated in classroom talk in only one of the two described ways, as seen in Extract 6.1.

Marek used a motivational activity in which he asked his students to predict the content of the story based on its title. He asked them to brainstorm a few ideas in writing that they were then to tell their neighbors. His students then presented their ideas in front of the whole class, as documented in Extract 6.1.

Extract 6.1: Lesson 1

1   **Teacher:** Take a pen into your hand, a piece of paper, and try to jot down (.) on the paper (.) three, four (1) plot ideas based on the short story title "The Water of Life."
2   **Ss:** ((*murmuring and preparing the necessary things*))
3   **Teacher:** Write it on any piece of paper, rip a sheet from your notebook. (2) What could the story be about…
4   **Ss:** ((*writing their ideas*))
5   **Teacher:** ((*Walking around the classroom and observing what the students are writing. Stops behind some students and tells them their writing is illegible. Delivers short comments on what his students have written.*))
6   **Teacher:** (*two minutes in*) So, most of you have written at least two lines. So, please, (*starts dividing the students into pairs*) Olda, Nikos, (.) Ota, Vojta, (.) Jenda, Vasek, (.) Ondra, Kuba, (.) Eda, Jirka, David will join them, (.) Kamca, Jana, (.) Pavla, Dana, (.) Lucka and Dita. Try to talk about the ideas you had.

106   6   The Case of Marek: Tension and Conflict in a Dialogic …

7 ((*Ss sit in their designated pairs and discuss the task. T writes the word "expectation" on the board and then starts monitoring the groups.*))
8 **Jenda:** So we're, like, to choose (1) the best idea?
9 **Teacher:** (*nodding*) Yep, exactly. You choose in your pairs the one that you think might be the right one (2) out of all the options (1) and then we'll put all of your choices on the board. (1) So, talk this through and I'll write it on the board. (3) All set? (1) Magic, Nikos, let's start.
10 **Nikos:** It could be a documentary about a river that's full of life, like either there is plenty of fish in it or it has some healing properties.
11 **Teacher:** (*writing on the board*) So, gentlemen? (*points at Ondra and Vojta*)
12 **Vojta:** It is about the water of life; whoever drinks it gets cured.
13 **Teacher:** All right. Dana and Pavla? (*points at these girls*) What do you have?
14 **Dana:** It's about some river…
15 **Teacher:** I don't follow.
16 **Dana:** And it's a river worshiped by a tribe, yeah, some tribe.
17 **Teacher:** Hmm, so you mean like some sort of a holy river?
18 **Dana:** Yes.
19 **Teacher:** I see. (*writes on the board*) Alright. Jana and Kamca? (*points at these girls*)
20 **Jana:** We have the same as Vojta.
21 **Teacher:** Hmm, that thing, OK. (*writes a check mark next to Vojta's suggestion*) Lucka (.) and Dita?
22 **Lucka:** The same.

The extract starts with a short period of independent work by students who are then to discuss their ideas in pairs. The teacher then asks one student in each pair to share their ideas. While he chooses which boy will speak, he allows the girls to choose which of them will speak. Although the teacher writes the students' ideas on the board, he provides no feedback, nor does he make them elaborate on their statements. At the same time, he does not force his students to provide him an answer. He also accepts student answers that had previously been suggested by other students. Moreover, the brainstormed ideas on the board are not in any way used later in that given class. In this particular case, Marek asked a question that can be considered an open question of high cognitive demand. After all, the students could have created their own stories inspired by the title provided. Nevertheless, many of the responses were examples of cognitive non-correspondence: the students made their task easier by reusing the answers of their peers. In addition, there was no uptake through which the teacher made the students return to their answers. Clearly, the aim of the activity was not to make students create elaborate answers with reasoning. Instead, it appears that Marek wanted to motivate his students to read the short story. The student responses had no other purpose in the given class: their expectations were never confronted with the reality of the short story. The quality of the student responses was not important to Marek and, accordingly, he never tried to deepen the replies. In sum, this activity did not match Alexander's (2020) principles of cumulativity and purposefulness.

6.2 Series of Lessons Marek Taught During TPD Program

As for the use of time in the activity, most of it was used by students in writing down possible reasons for the short story's titles. The students who shared their ideas for plots needed only seconds to do so; Marek's activity did not provide them with the chance to discuss or deepen their ideas. Eventually, half of the students participated in presenting their ideas to their peers orally (with one representative for each pair). Still, some reported that their idea had already been stated (lines 20 and 22). The aim of this activity in which students participated in classroom discourse was to motivate the students; it represents the first type of classroom discourse in Marek's classes.

The second type of classroom discourse was of an organizational character: Marek gave the students instructions about particular activities and informed them about their goals. Extract 6.2 shows how Marek ascertained whether his students understood the instructions described in the worksheets.

Extract 6.2: Lesson 1

1. **Teacher:** And now, on to task two. Please, let's read the instructions (*pointing at Kamila*).
2. **Kamila:** (*reading from the worksheet*) An interview with an adventurer. How do you imagine an important adventurer? Choose a main character from the story and describe how the character looks and acts. You will then take the role of a journalist and create an interview with at least 10 questions. The questions need to be open; yes–no answers will not be accepted. The answers will need to be written down on a separate piece of paper.
3. **Teacher:** Do you understand what I want you to do?
4. **Ss:** Yes. No.
5. **Teacher:** So when I collect the worksheet, what will you hand in? (1) What will I be holding in my hands?
6. **Nikos:** A report, a piece of paper.
7. **Teacher:** I'll have a piece of paper, but what will it say?
8. **Nikos:** It'll describe a bad guy.
9. **Vasek:** An interview?
10. **Teacher:** An interview. With who? With a character, right? As I was saying, I'd like to have the character's features somewhere at the top of that of piece of paper so I know how you imagine the person. Let's turn the page (*turning the page*).

This activity had the potential to be meta-cognitive; for example, the students could have discussed the ways in which the task could be completed, the order of their actions, and so on. However, the entire activity was managed only by the teacher and as such fell under organizational communication. The teacher asked closed questions of lower cognitive demand and the students summarized what they were told. The teacher's feedback only verified whether the information provided by his students was correct.

The aim of the activity seems to have been to clarify the instructions, but this did not happen. Student answers showed a misunderstanding that was not dispelled by the teacher (line 8). The students kept asking questions about the instructions even during the time dedicated to their independent work. It is clear that they still had some doubts about the instructions. When interpreting their participation, we could speculate about what the real purpose of the student verbal participation was. It remains unclear whether the goal was to deepen their understanding of the instructions or just signal that they were expected to work independently from that point on. In the latter understanding, student participation becomes a ritual for transition to the next activity.

To summarize the nature of classroom discourse in the lessons prior to the program, Marek did not use student talk as a means to an end that he himself considered key: developing student thinking. He reserved that role for independent student work. His students were allowed to talk in only two types of whole-class activities: motivating students to work on another task or clarifying the instructions for their independent work. Thus, student talk in Marek's pre-program classes served different purposes than those typically described in the literature on dialogic teaching. All of the measured indicators also revealed the secondary role that whole-class interactions had in Marek's teaching: student thoughts with reasoning, teacher uptake, and triadic interaction were not represented in either of the two lessons (see Fig. 6.1). Open questions of high cognitive demand appeared only rarely: once in each lesson. Dialogic teaching as a tool to deepen student thinking was rather removed from Marek's typical style of teaching.

Lesson 3: Interaction as a part of teaching and a steep rise in indicators

Marek's third recorded lesson took place after he participated in the first and second workshops of our development program in which he was acquainted with the concept of dialogic teaching and its indicators. Due attention was paid to open questions of high cognitive demand and uptake. The aim of the third recorded lesson was to increase these two indicators. Marek himself expressed certainty that such an aim would be achieved easily because he had emphasized the role of open questions in teaching even before taking part in the workshops. Even though their presence in Marek's teaching was rare (see above), he was adamant that they were very compatible with his teaching practices.

As the topic of his third lesson, Marek chose the story of David and Goliath. To maximize opportunities for student talk, Marek swapped independent work for activities in which students respond orally. They were provided with two texts: the first gave them instructions on how to proceed in investigating crimes. The second contained the story of David and Goliath. The student task was to decide whether the story was an example of a murder or self-defense and justify their choice with evidence. Instructions for collecting evidence were provided in the first text on how to investigate crimes. Overall, the instructions were complex. To complete the task, the students had to read two advanced texts and apply their understanding of the first (how to categorize a crime) to the Biblical story. The students faced these challenges independently. After approximately 20 min, they were to present and justify their decisions. Extract 6.3 captures a part of this activity:

Extract 6.3: Lesson 3

1 **Teacher:** I believe that at this point you can somehow explain whether this was a murder ((*pointing at the board* – 3)) or manslaughter or some other situation. So. (.) Think this

6.2 Series of Lessons Marek Taught During TPD Program

through for a moment and then you'll explain and justify. (2) And I hope you won't be just making something up.

2 **Nikos:** I know. ((*3 – students gradually starting to raise their hands*))
3 **Teacher:** So two, three, four, five people are volunteering. Jana, Dana, and the rest, listen carefully because your task (2) is to either agree, and explain why you agree, or disagree. And explain why you disagree. So, let's go in the order in which you raised your hands. ((*looking at the far side of the classroom and points at Oldrich*)). Oldrich.
4 **Oldrich:** ((*raising his hand*)) Well, it could be both. Murder and manslaughter. Murder because Goliath asked David to beat him. And ((*gestures*)) they had a bet. If he beat him, the Philistines would serve the Israelites, and if not then the other way around. But it also could have been a battle, because they attacked, I mean the Philistines, the Israelite army. So I side more with the murder option ((*uses hands to mime balancing things*)).
5 **Teacher:** So, I'd be really interested to know why you think so because we've described murder in very specific terms. ((*points at the board where the attributes of murder are listed*))
6 **Oldrich:** (1) Well, deliberation.
7 **Teacher:** That murder is deliberate and planned and the murderer is conscious of what they're doing ((*paraphrasing the attributes on the board*)).
8 **Oldrich:** Yes, he thought about how he was going to kill him.
9 **Teacher:** I see.
10 (…)
11 **Teacher:** Jenda, do you agree with what Oldrich said? ((*Jenda has his head down on the table right in front of the teacher and appears not to be paying any attention*))
12 **Jenda:** No.
13 **Teacher:** Why don't you agree? Try to explain your opinion. Ladies ((*turns and gives the girls who had started talking a look of warning*)), you'll be able to talk in a second ((*turns back to Jenda*)).
14 **Jenda:** Because ((*pause*)), I can't explain it.
15 **Teacher:** So, think about it. I'll get back to you soon. Nikos?

Marek managed to enliven his interaction with his students by asking open questions of high cognitive demands. The students could choose how they would close the matter but at the same time they needed to understand the story, apply the definitions of murder and manslaughter, and base their verdict on one of the steps described in the text on how to categorize crimes (high cognitive demand). The requirements put on the students were specified by Marek (lines 1 and 3), who instructed them not to just make something up but rather to justify their choice with evidence. He further stressed this in his uptake (line 7). Students were partially prepared for such a challenge from their previous independent work and attempted to provide reasoning for their opinions. The most elaborate response was uttered by Oldrich and consisted of 65 words (line 4). Oldrich's response can be contrasted with a typical response from Czech lower-secondary students, which is on the order of one or two words. Instead of choosing a one-sided answer, Oldrich pointed out that both options could be valid and provided evidence for both variants. Marek responded with uptake (line 5) and appealed to Oldrich to enrich his response by including some of the attributes listed on the board. Oldrich reacted by mentioning prior deliberation and planning (lines 6 and 8). If we observed the extract in its entire context, we would see Marek asking three more students to provide their points of view. Their answers did not reach the quality of Oldrich's response, but they could definitely be considered examples of student thoughts with reasoning. It can also be noted that some students found the task too challenging or simply not inspiring enough, as was the case for Jenda (lines 12 and 14).

In summary, the third lesson was characterized by a steep rise in the indicators. The degree of open questions of high cognitive demand and student thoughts with reasoning were the first peaks recorded during the program (see Fig. 6.1). Individual student responses were connected and helped with achieving the planned instructional aim. Thus, this activity meets the criteria associated with the principles of cumulativity and purposefulness.

During the subsequent reflective interview, the researcher commented favorably on the nature of the questions asked by Marek.

Extract 6.4: Interview after Lesson 3

1 **Researcher:** After reviewing the recording, I have to say you asked questions really well.
2 **Teacher:** Thank you.
3 **Researcher:** You see? Here (1) and here ((*they inspect a line in the transcript*)). When you described murder and manslaughter, you led them (.) and they automatically started comparing and the whole thing shifted into comparison and closer to higher cognitive processes. (.) So about the questions, we don't really have much to work on.
4 **Teacher:** Sure.

This extract documents how the researcher praised Marek. At the beginning of this case study, we described Marek as a teacher with high self-esteem who was confident in his ability to teach. Marek's high self-esteem may appear to be justified: the indicators went up the moment he wanted them to increase. Nonetheless, the nature of classroom talk in the third lesson may be seen as problematic if we take into consideration how well Marek did in meeting the principles of dialogic teaching, especially on the principle of collectivity. The extract clearly shows a trend of unequal participation by various student groups. This is documented by line 3 in Extract 6.3 in which Marek is talking to a group of female students. As line 3 shows, the girls were supposed to try to listen. It can be noted that Marek was doubtful about their ability to do so and that he assigned them a task of a passive nature. The lack of success with such an instruction is apparent as Marek had to repeat his appeal again even before the end of the extract (line 13). Even in that case, Marek's warning is an example of rhetoric: even though he let the girls know twice that they were to fact-check their male peers, Marek did not give them the space to do so. Thus, while five students (Oldrich, Nikos, Vojta, Ota, and Vasek) volunteered to participate and were enabled to do so, the other students were not productively engaged in classroom talk. This is exemplified by Jenda (lines 12 and 14), who was not able to justify his opinion, and by the girls who participated only as listeners.

6.2 Series of Lessons Marek Taught During TPD Program

Only seven students spoke in an activity that Marek had planned to be for the whole class; that is less than half of the students present. Five of these students actively volunteered from the start (and spoke at length once given permission). Jenda is the sixth student and Lucka the seventh (as she contributed with a one-word answer to a question of low cognitive demand). We believe that Marek called upon Jenda and Lucka to participate in classroom discourse in an effort to discipline them. Jenda was resting his head on the table right in front of Marek. Lucka was called on in a moment during which she was talking to her neighbor.

It can be concluded that Marek prepared his lesson to maximally meet the indicators of dialogic teaching. He was not as successful with the principles. This was especially the case for the principle of collectivity—while some students spoke at length and participated several times, others did not get engaged at all or contributed with only a word or two. This differentiation in student participation was further empowered by their seating arrangement. Jenda and the students who were actively communicating with the teacher sat right in front of Marek—they created a barrier of sorts between Marek and the remaining (less communicative) students. When the communicative students were speaking or volunteering to do so by raising their hands, it might have been more difficult for Marek to see the other students at the back. The students at the back were much less eager to communicate (see Fig. 6.2 for the class seating arrangement).

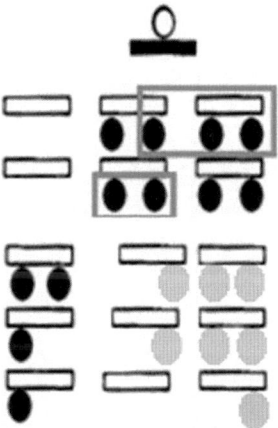

Fig. 6.2 Seating arrangement for students in Marek's class

Legend:

Blue: The communicatively actively students Vasek, Vojta, Oldrich, Nikos, Ota;
Gray: the girls;
Green: Karel, who was repeating the grade.

Note: The distance between the second and third rows is intentional and reflects the arrangement of tables in the classroom.

During the subsequent reflective interview, the researcher opened the topic of differing student participation. Marek primarily connected the topic to the girls in the classroom.

Extract 6.5: Interview after Lesson 3

1. **Researcher:** Five of them volunteered. Those were: Nikos, Oldrich, Vasek, Vojta (.) and Ota. Ota volunteered.
2. **Teacher:** Hmm. They're really lazy, those ladies.

It follows from the interview that the teacher was aware of the different degree of student participation. Marek was not surprised when the researcher mentioned that five students volunteered, and he had a ready explanation to offer. He proposed that character features were the underlying cause and that the girls were not willing to work in his class, which he explained as their perceived laziness. Later during the same interview, Marek used a different explanation, based on the students' different skills: "I think that the students basically have two different approaches to learning in this class. Half of them think I'm asking about crystal-clear things, because they get it, and the other half just don't know what's going on at all." In his second explanation, the students were not lazy; instead, their cognitive skills were deemed not proficient enough to follow Marek. Nonetheless and no matter which rationale Marek used, he divided the students in his class into two groups. The first included five members whose cognitive powers enabled them to easily process even the complex instructions for the David and Goliath lesson. The second group included students who were less cognitively equipped and thus were not able to participate. All of the girls in the class and the remaining boys were part of the second, larger, camp of students who according to Marek "think slowly." Marek clearly believed in a typology of students and intuited that they participated to different degrees. However, this difference became visible only when student talking time increased.

Marek's aim for the next recorded lesson was to maintain the values for the indicators and engage more students from both groups in talk. He mentioned during the interview that he would have to devise a way to engage more students.

Extract 6.6: Interview after Lesson 3

1. **Teacher:** Yeah, I'll think about how to involve even those who (.) think slowly. (.) Actually, they don't think, because they believe it's useless.
2. **Researcher:** Well, it seems to me that they're not thinking because they know that even if they were thinking, they would still be slower (.) and wouldn't get a chance to speak.
3. **Teacher:** No, we'll go about it differently. I'll create those two groups. In essence, I'll create two types of tasks. All the weaker students, (.) they'll start, (1) yeah. Each of those groups will work with a different set of materials. So, the weak ones will have specific instructions, simple stuff they can establish and check (1) and the other guys, they'll do the advanced thing, the higher level thinking. That's possible, in theory.

Contempt was apparent in Marek's description of the students who participated less (line 1). In her reaction, the researcher tried to propose that the students' lesser engagement could be connected to the fact that they receive few opportunities to speak. Marek did not respond to the suggestions and instead proposed scaling the difficulty of the activities in the next lesson so that all of the students could participate: the weaker students at the start and the gifted students later. This proposal had not been tested by Marek, and he described it as a theoretical possibility. The extract from Lesson 4 shows how Marek managed to execute his plan.

Lesson 4: Fall of indicators as a result of attempts at higher student participation

Marek chose chivalry as the topic for his next class, during which he planned to make more students participate. He did not let his students know the topic beforehand as he wanted them to deduce it for themselves. Marek intended this deductive process to be a warmup activity for the less talkative students. Marek had mentioned this type of activity in his previous reflective interview. Extract 6.7 shows how Marek carried out the activity.

Extract 6.7: Lesson 4

1 **Teacher:** So try to think of the names of all the fairy tales that you've ever read and name one particular group of people that has some duties and at the same time some rights.
2 **Oldrich, Nikos:** ((*raising their hands*))
3 **Teacher:** Let's wait for more people. (1)
4 **Nikos:** ((*murmuring*)) Dwarfs.
5 **Oldrich:** ((*loudly repeats what Nikos said*)) Dwarfs.
6 **Teacher:** Dwarfs. ((*laughing*)) They didn't have many rights, dwarfs. They had the right to work.
7 **Dita:** ((*raising her hand*))
8 **Teacher:** Yes, Dita?
9 **Dita:** Kings?
10 **Teacher:** Kings ((*nods approvingly*)), thank you. (1) And there was one group below them on the social ladder.
11 **Nikos, Oldrich, Dita:** ((*raising their hands*))
12 **Nikos:** Well, (1) I don't know, but what about monks? Do they fit?
13 **Teacher:** Those were basically priests, monks. Hmmm, who's next?
14 **Ondra:** ((*raising his hand*)) Me!
15 **Teacher:** ((*points at him*))
16 **Ondra:** A prince or a princess.
17 **Teacher:** Those were members of royal families. But thanks for participating today. That's cool.
18 (…)
19 **Oldrich, Nikos, Jana, Kamila, Vojta:** ((*raising their hands*))
20 **Teacher:** Kamila.
21 **Kamila:** Well, food tasters.
22 **Teacher:** And what rights did they have?
23 **Kamila:** Well, if somebody brought food, they tasted it to find out if it's poisoned or not.

24 **Teacher:** Was that their right or duty?
25 **Oldrich:** Duty.
26 **Kamila:** Duty.
27 **Teacher:** Well, that means, my question was about rights. About a group of people with special rights.
28 **Oldrich:** ((*raising his hand*)) I know!
29 **Teacher:** Wait, Oldrich, let's give a chance to Vojta. ((*points at Vojta, who is raising his hand*))
30 **Vojta:** What about servants? A servant…
31 **Oldrich:** Priests.
32 **Teacher:** Priests.
33 **Vasek:** Soldiers?
34 **Teacher:** Some soldiers. Jana? ((*points at Jana*))
35 **Jana:** Jews?

Marek initiated this interaction with a question asking students to identify a medieval group of people with special duties and rights. Even though the question appears to be open ended, it was not. Since Marek wanted to hear one particular answer from his students, it was a closed question. The extract captures a pseudo-inquiry (see Sect. 1.3.3) in which the teacher expects only one correct answer that the students try to guess.

The reality of the lesson was rather distant from Marek's initial plan. He presumed the students would figure out the correct answer quickly. However, he had to wait 15 min to hear it as the students listed various groups of people other than knights. This procedure was a violation of the principle of purposefulness as Marek dedicated a third of the class time to a guess-what-the-teacher-is-thinking activity. Marek also expected that only the students whom he considered slow would participate in this activity. He thought the more cognitively gifted students would get engaged later in the class by solving the more cognitively demanding tasks. This expectation was also not confirmed. All of the students participated in the very first activity, no matter which label they had been given by Marek. In addition, there was no follow-up activity of high cognitive demand for the supposedly smarter students. Even the subsequent activities followed the lead of the first one: the students again guessed what the teacher was thinking or tried to recollect what they already knew.

As for the measured values, there was a decrease in open questions of high cognitive demand and, in turn, student thoughts with reasoning was less frequent as well. The only indicator that increased was teacher uptake, which Marek amply used in situations in which students mistook duties for rights and rights for duties (as can be seen in Kamila's responses in lines 21 and 23).

The regression in indicators influenced Marek's attempts to meet the principle of purposefulness. This can be seen in several key moments. The first is related to a change in calling on students. After Marek asked his question, the students he had labeled as communicative (Oldrich and Nikos) immediately raised their hands. But Marek did not call on them. Instead, Marek let them know that that the question

6.2 Series of Lessons Marek Taught During TPD Program

would be answered once more students volunteered. Nikos and Oldrich used humor to overrule Marek's decision (dwarfs, lines 4 and 5). Marek accepted the joke, laughed, and then—still in jest—explained why this response was incorrect (line 6). When a girl, Dita, volunteered, Marek immediately granted her the floor (lines 7 and 8). This moment shows a significant change in Marek's teaching practices: the students were not called on in the order in which they raised their hands. Dita did not offer a productive response since kings as a social group had already been discussed previously. Nonetheless, Marek's response is positive in that he thanked Dita for her participation. He also built on Dita's response in the subsequent clue that he gave to the students (by suggesting that knights were a group one step below kings on the social ladder of medieval society). Nikos and Oldrich continued to raise their hands and even Dita tried again to correctly answer the question, undeterred by the failure of her previous answer (line 10). Ondra, who according to Marek is one of those who "think slowly," guessed that the group in question might include princes and princesses (line 16), which was not correct. Marek's replies to incorrect answers are telling and show which students participate routinely and which sparingly. In this lesson, Marek differentiated his response accordingly: he thanked Dita and Ondra for their participation and did not entirely reject their response. He did not thank Oldrich or Nikos for their participation and openly demonstrated why their responses were incorrect. Since both Oldrich and Nikos speak frequently, Marek might not have been worried that his feedback would undermine their further participation.

His behavior led to an increase in the number of students who volunteered to speak; even other girls did so. Marek called on Kamila (line 20), who mentioned food tasters. Marek neither validated nor rejected her answer. Instead, he asked her about the rights of food tasters and thus led her to realize that her answer was incorrect. He helped her revise her own answer. Oldrich continued to raise his hand and verbally remind Marek that he was in the class (line 28). Yet even in this case, Marek favored his new strategy and gave a chance to Ondra, who proposed yet another unsuccessful answer. The activity continued in this manner for the next several minutes.

Eight of the total 16 present students spoke in the lesson (the numbers were different in Marek's previous lesson, in which 7 out of 18 students spoke). Student participation mildly increased in this lesson, even though the change was by no means radical. It must be noted that the instruction that Marek chose enabled students from both groups to participate. It is no surprise that all of the communicatively active students who were present participated. Four students whose ability to participate had previously been questioned by Marek spoke as well.

Marek changed his teaching practices in Lesson 4. He did not call on students in the order in which they raised their hands. This gave the other students space for talking. He deliberately provided the students with feedback that did not deter them from further participation. The feedback that Marek gave to the two different groups was markedly different. Over time, such strongly differentiated feedback could result in the students realizing how differently Marek perceives each of their groups, if they did not already know. Still, Marek's approach in Lesson 4 encouraged previously less talkative students to actively participate. In this lesson, Marek's teaching was closer to meeting the principle of collectivity. At the same time, the activities he chose to reach this end were largely purposeless.

In sum, Marek's attempts to engage more students went in the right direction. Nonetheless, the attempts were accompanied by a decrease in the measured indicators (see Fig. 6.1). Interestingly enough, Marek was not aware of the decline in indicators. From his perspective, the chosen activity developed analytical thinking.

Extract 6.8: Interview after Lesson 4

1 **Researcher:** Those questions you asked them, they were questions of low cognitive demand (.) and closed ended because there was just one right answer. (.) You want them to say just one right thing and that's knights. That's why the question is closed ended. (.) And the thing with closed questions of low cognitive demand is that you can't scaffold them. Because the students either know the answer or they don't.

2 **Teacher:** That means that it isn't possible (1) to point them to the correct answer?

3 **Researcher:** It's possible. But only by giving them clues so that you narrow down the options for their guesses. You give them clues so that they can guess correctly. But you can't scaffold the process for them like you could when they're trying to identify a subject in a sentence. You can't show them the process.

4 **Teacher:** But isn't it true that by giving them the clues I give them information that eventually creates a funnel of sorts and that funnel leads them to the correct answer? Because I say that those kids know a lot of things and by my giving them clues, they can recollect the right answer. Because I told them at the beginning that there is a group of people, that there are fairy tales, and then we would talk about a handful of things (.) and we would get to those knights.

5 **Researcher:** But this didn't really help them find the right answer.

6 **Teacher:** No, it didn't.

7 **Researcher:** Because, yeah, (.) you can't really scaffold this question. You can narrow down the number of options, but that isn't scaffolding. And that makes them think about what you're thinking and they're trying to guess it. But this does not train their analytical thinking. You reduce the number of options and lead them to something. But (.) you have different connotations than they do (.) – you know some fairy tales about knights, but they know different ones. So when you say they know the group from fairy tales, for you it's clearly knights, but for them it could be ogres ... But when you scaffold something, all the participants can get to the correct answer by following the same path.

8 **Teacher:** Yes, I see.

Only during his interview with the researcher did Marek identify the nature of the questions that he had asked. Even though he first tried to claim that his instructions developed the students' analytical thinking, he eventually accepted that when they were asked questions of low cognitive demand the students could only guess at the right answer.

Lessons 3 and 4 showed that Marek is capable of either preparing cognitively demanding instructions or engaging students from both groups. Yet combining a cognitively challenging set of instructions with engagement of as many students as possible turned out to be, at that moment, an unsolvable challenge. Due to his high self-esteem, Marek did not accept the situation easily. He attributed his failure to the differing abilities of his students and to the parameters of dialogic teaching. This can be seen in his questioning the possibility of creating a set of instructions that all students find cognitively challenging: "If you want to implement dialogic teaching, you need to ask a clever kid a difficult question. And a kid who needs more help an easy question." He persisted in thinking that questions need to be differentiated in relation to who should answer them. In this regard, he saw the female students as the most problematic: "That's all that the girls have in them." Marek believed that they could not handle more challenging instructions and that their supposedly better classmates would make fun of them because of their answers. "They'd just tear them to pieces. I'm sure of it. They'd ridicule them or something. Their social relationships are not very strong. (…) Yeah, they'd be so ashamed and those clever guys would control things as they see fit, but, hey, we'll see, I'm open to surprises." Apart from the principle of collectivity, Marek mentioned the possibility that the principle of supportivity would also not be met. We believe that at that phase Marek needed to rationalize his failure by relating it to the shortcomings of his students and thus justify his way of teaching. He therefore sought external reasons to explain why it had not been possible to synchronize open questions of high cognitive demand with the principle of collectivity.

It can also be noted that Marek distanced himself from the development program and its aims. He wanted to go against the method for instructing students given by the nature of the program (whole-class communication) and return to his previous way of teaching: "That's the way it's going to be. I have a lesson ready just for that. It will be on the thinking of medieval men. And it will be (.) again learning in groups. So, you can record it willy-nilly, I don't care." Marek's return to gestalt is similar to Daniela's retreat in her Lessons 4 and 8 (Chap. 5). It is telling that Marek invited the researcher by saying that she could record the lesson because he did not care. That is a break from his previous conception of teaching in which he presented his classes as exemplary. We believe that Marek reacted this way because his self-esteem had already been put into question twice. It turned out that Marek's early assessment—in which dialogic teaching was identical to his way of teaching—was not accurate. Dialogic teaching was more difficult than Marek had expected.

Lesson 5: The growing discrepancy between the indicators and the principle of collectivity

In the fifth recorded class, Marek continued with his examination of medieval topics. He chose the genre of travel literature and one of the key authors from that time, Marco Polo. The first half of the lesson was planned as an introduction to the topic and Marek spent it talking with his students about traveling in the Middle Ages. As he had planned, Marek returned to working in groups in the second part of the lesson. He intended to use group work to engage more students in communication by having them solve a cognitively challenging task. Marek believed that groups that included students at equal levels would enable all of the students to participate at the level they needed without facing shame.

In the introductory activity, which lasted half of the lesson, students discussed traveling in the Middle Ages. Marek asked questions of low cognitive demand and received responses of corresponding quality with no reasoning, as the following extract shows.

Extract 6.9: Lesson 5

1 **Teacher:** Can you imagine how these medieval people traveled? How would it probably have looked? How many times per year they would travel and how far?
2 **Kuba, Nikos:** ((*raising their hands*))
3 **Teacher:** Yes, Jenda?
4 **Jenda:** So, in the Middle Ages the people with power would travel in chariots when they wanted to get something done. But these days we use trams and cars.
5 **Teacher:** And what about, (2) say, normal people? How did they travel?
6 **Jenda:** ((*appears to be deep in thought*))
7 **Dana, Kamila, Nikos:** ((*raising their hands*))
8 **Teacher:** If you know something about it. If you say you don't know, then…
9 **Jenda:** ((*uncertainly*)) They traveled in chariots or just walked?
10 **Teacher:** Well, and how often? (1)
11 **Jenda:** Well, (1) when they needed to buy something and the shop was far away. When they were living in a village and the shop was in the town…
12 **Teacher:** ((*starts moving his leg*)) How did they do it?
13 **Kuba:** They walked.
14 **Teacher:** (*nods*) They walked. ((*looks at Jenda who shrugs his shoulders*)) They just set off. Vasek? ((*points at Vasek*))
15 **Vasek:** They went to the markets. (.) And, (.) yes, to the markets.
16 **Teacher:** So they traveled when they needed it?
17 **Vasek:** Yep.
18 **Teacher:** Thank you, thank you. ((*points at David, who is raising his hand*))
19 **David:** If some aristocrat wanted to travel from Brno to Prague, it would take much more time. But we just board a train and are there in three hours.
20 **Teacher:** ((*writes "Length of journey" on the board*)) This means that the length of that particular journey influenced them?
21 **David:** Yep.
22 **Teacher**: OK, thank you. What about Eda, will he wake up from his slumber? Will he smile?
23 **Eda:** ((*smiles*))
24 **Teacher**: You got anything? Any ideas?
25 **Eda:** No.
26 **Teacher:** All right, no problem, we'll see.
27 ((…))

This extract shows the beginning of a teaching episode on traveling in the Middle Ages. The entire activity is propelled by a series of questions of low cognitive demand that Marek asked his students. As in the previous lesson, Marek chose which student would speak. He did not call on the students in the order in which they raised their hands. Interestingly, Marek even asked students who did not volunteer to speak to do so, such as Jenda (lines 3 and 8) and Eda (line 22). The student responses were rather on the longer side, yet they entirely lacked reasoning and argumentation. The students simply put forth whatever they free-associated with the topic: Jenda suggested that people traveled when they needed to buy goods, David proposed that traveling took longer, and so forth.

The episode shares some characteristics with the episode recorded in Lesson 4. The activity did not increase the values of the indicators, and the purposefulness principle was still not met, but the number of participating students rose across both ability groups. In sum, 11 of the 14 present students spoke in the episode, which is a successful outcome from the perspective of the principle of collectivity.

During the reflective interview, the researcher pointed out that the activity comprised questions of low cognitive demand to which students responded with snippets of information associated with traveling in the Middle Ages (e.g., Jenda spoke of traveling by chariot and Vasek about traveling to fairs):

Extract 6.10: Interview after Lesson 5

1 **Researcher:** Do you remember when we talked about the activity from the lesson before this?
2 **Teacher:** The one about knights.
3 **Researcher:** About knights. It was an activity where the students could start talking and it wasn't difficult for them to say something, but they answered less cognitively demanding questions and said something they knew and so the whole thing wasn't really much of a challenge for them.
4 **Teacher:** Hmm. (*agreeing*)
5 **Researcher:** So, this was really similar. How you asked them. I've got some of the questions here.
6 **Teacher:** Yeah, yeah.
7 **Researcher:** For example, how often those people traveled. How far they traveled. If they could just set off. How they made the money for their travels. And so on. ((*reading the questions the teacher had asked during his lesson*))
8 **Teacher:** Sure, yeah.
9 **Researcher:** And they just tried to somehow answer these questions.
10 **Teacher:** Yeah.

The teacher did not proceed to talk much about the activity. Unlike in the previous interview, Marek did not doubt the assessment of his questions as being of low cognitive demand nor did he justify their sequencing or length. He did not seem to want to comment and merely agreed with the researcher. It is likely that he expected the second activity that took place in the lesson to be in accordance with the indicators and principles of dialogic teaching.

In the second activity from Lesson 5, Marek divided the students into four groups of equally gifted students and tasked them with group work. There was one group of two students, one group of three, one of four, and then there was Karel, whom Marek left to work alone. The students were to create a set of questions that would enable them to find out as much information about Marco Polo that they found interesting as possible. This type of interaction did not involve the whole class, as had been promoted in the TPD program. Nonetheless, Marek wanted to include group work since he thought it would solve the discrepancy between the indicators and principles of dialogic teaching. He believed his students would be given a chance to speak without being affected by the shyness that accompanies whole-class interaction. In turn, he hoped they would be able to pass the requirements associated with tasks of high cognitive demand.

Since our two cameras were not enough to record the student group talk, we decided to employ one voice recorder for each student group. The following extract showcases the nature of student communication in the groups. We have chosen a recording of one of the groups that Marek labeled as "weak," specifically a group of girls. This short extract shows talk patterns that we observed among all of the other groups as well.

Extract 6.11: Lesson 5

1 **Pavla:** So, I would like to know when he kicked the bucket.
2 **Dita:** Where he came from. Yeah, alright, when he died and where he came from.
3 **Lucka:** When he died, huh?
4 **Dita:** Hmm 20 questions. (5) So when he died, where he came from ((*repeating to Lucka, who is writing it down*)).
5 **Lucka:** And I would ask (1) how old he was when he died.
6 **Dita:** Nope, that's gonna be the next question. ((*laughs*))
7 **Lucka:** Alright then.
8 **Pavla:** Damn.
9 **Dita:** So that was the second one, but there should be 20. So, (.) the second question: where was he born?
10 **Lucka:** When?
11 **Dita:** Where. And then when.
12 **Dita:** OK. (.) So, (.) when was he born? (2) And how old he was when he died.
13 **Lucka:** Yeah, but we already know that. (1) Like when we have there when he died and when he was born, those two are enough to know it.
14 **Pavla:** Yeah, but we won't have to do the math.
15 **Dita:** Where he was born, yes, that's also good. The fourth one – what was I saying?
16 **Pavla:** I don't know.
17 **Lucka:** When – how old he was when he died.
18 **Dita:** Well, maybe it's a redundant question, but at least we'll have more of them.

Several features of student group work can be deduced from Extract 6.11. The first among those is a clear preference for questions of a biographical nature (when and where Marco Polo was born and when he died). The students decided to inquire into these matters perhaps because they are typically included in biographies even though they were supposed to ask questions that they themselves found interesting. We can also presume that the students decided to favor questions that did not require creativity to create, which appears to be supported by the rest of the extract. Their

6.2 Series of Lessons Marek Taught During TPD Program

main aim was to make the completion of the task easier (line 14) but still arrive at the number of required questions (line 18). This approach was mirrored by students in the other groups as well. The students thus created questions that did not unearth new information but got them closer to the required number of questions.

Furthermore, the students did not build on what other students said. They proposed questions that were not elaborated on by their colleagues. Their questions were only accepted. It could even be stated that the students did not listen to one another. For example, when Dita asked what question she had proposed a moment ago, her classmate responded that she did not know (line 16). The final common feature—which is not captured in this extract—is the fact that the students spent most of their group work time discussing extra-curricular matters and returned to the assigned work only when the teacher approached.

How were Marek's expectations aligned with the real course of his students' group work? His students did talk with one another more than they did during whole-class interactions. This is a natural feature of group work since each group has a discourse of its own and this increases the talk time available to members of the group. However, the group work did not activate more students to speak. Only 11 of the 14 students spoke and so the numbers are identical to those recorded in the previous motivational activity. Some students preferred not to speak even in their small groups. From the perspective of the indicators, there was a decrease in the cognitive demand of the task because the students replicated questions commonly appearing in biographies instead of creating their own questions. Similarly, student thoughts with reasoning did not increase. In fact, this lesson contained the least number of student thoughts with reasoning out of all of the recorded lessons (see Fig. 6.1). Students did not appear to be willing to discuss with one another; instead, they accepted what their peers said in an effort to complete the task as quickly as possible. Thus, group work did not achieve the goal that Marek had expected it would. To summarize, the fifth recorded lesson clearly shows that increasing the communication space available to students does not necessarily result in an increase in dialogic teaching indicators nor does it guarantee a higher number of participating students.

Therefore, the aim for the next recorded lesson remained the same: to increase the values for the indicators and create conditions for higher student participation from various groups, i.e., to meet the principle of collectivity. As for the content of the lesson, Marek decided to use the questions created by students in the previous class and let the students answer them in a whole-class interaction. He explained as much in a reflective interview before the lesson. The researcher asked whether it would be prudent to require all students to report their answers, which would guarantee that students other than the purportedly gifted ones would speak.

Extract 6.12: Interview after Lesson 5

1 **Teacher**: The questions will be glaring from the board. We'll go through one after another and discuss what they learned about the topic. And we'll see whether they'll be willing to share the things they discovered, whether they'll be willing to tell these things to the others. And by doing that, I'll verify the assumption that they'll be willing to…
2 **Researcher**: Yeah, build on one another.

3 **Teacher**: Build on one another. That's my assumption. I don't think they will. They'll just be so shy that the gifted ones will control it as they see fit, but I'll see; perhaps I'll be surprised.
4 **Researcher**: And what if, hypothetically speaking, what if there was a rule that stated that each group needed to report something. So even if the gifted ones spoke, they would know that they couldn't speak anymore this round, which would enable the other groups to speak. Does that sound silly?
5 **Teacher**: It doesn't.

Having analyzed the transcripts of the recorded group communication and reflected on the nature of the recorded classroom talk, Marek decided to return to whole-class teaching. Nonetheless, he was not persuaded that it was an effective method that could overcome the existing social bonds in the classroom and students with different levels of academic achievement. Marek believed that these two obstacles would hinder discussion among his students, which from the next lesson on would be a monitored indicator. The third workshop, which focused on fostering student discussion, took place between Lesson 5 and the reflective interview. In an effort to strengthen the likelihood of student discussion, Marek decided to change the students' seating arrangement: "It's going to be a circle. They'll react if they're seated in circle." He held on to this plan as he entered the next recorded lesson.

Lesson 6: Unplanned absence of talkative students and its effect on classroom discourse

An unplanned occurrence played a vital role in the sixth recorded lesson: the talkative students were not present because of a trip abroad. Marek continued with the remaining students in his Marco Polo activity from where he had left off in the previous session. He asked the students the questions that they had created during their previous lesson, which he had photographed and thus could use. Marek asked some questions he himself had prepared. Since the activity was planned in advance, Marek could choose questions with answers that exercised skills of high cognitive demand. This enabled Marek to stop the ongoing decrease in cognitive demand in his instruction that was observed in his previous two lessons. However, only students about whom Marek had said they "have no clue" and "are too lazy to think" were present in class that day. The following extract shows the extent to which Marek was able to lead such students in a circular seating arrangement to participate and talk with reasoning.

Extract 6.13: Lesson 6

1 **Teacher**: So, if we considered what I said a moment ago, what would happen to Marco Polo if there were a financial crisis during his lifetime? If there were a crisis, what would happen? (1)
2 **Lucka**: He would go bust.
3 **Jana**: And lose everything.
4 **Teacher:** Why do you think so? ((*looking at Jana*))
5 **Jana**: Because he would have the money somewhere and so he would lose it.

6.2 Series of Lessons Marek Taught During TPD Program

6 **Teacher:** (1) Do you all agree with Jana?
7 **Ondra:** Yep. ((*the others remain silent*))
8 **Teacher**: Try to explain it a bit more ((*to Ondra*)) because I'm not sure I get what Jana…
9 **Jana**: He had his money. He had to stash it somewhere. And if there were a crisis, he could lose everything and all of the money as well.
10 **Teacher:** You all agree?
11 **Students:** ((*nodding*))

The teacher introduces a hypothetical situation in the form of a financial crisis taking place during the life of Marco Polo. Marek then asked his students to speculate as to how such a crisis would affect Marco Polo. He received immediate answers from Jana and Lucka, both students whose ability Marek had questioned because he presumed they were shy and the questions would be above their level. However, the answers given by Jana and Lucka clearly show they understood Marek's instruction well and were capable of applying information about a financial crisis to a different epoch (lines 2 and 3). Even students whom Marek labeled as lazy thinkers made use of the opportunity to speak without being limited by their more active peers. For Marek, this lesson served as evidence that even such students can be partners for challenging talk.

The nature of the interaction between Marek and the so-called lazy thinkers changed in Lesson 6. Marek no longer praised these students for their willingness to join the talk (as was the case in Lesson 4). Instead, he used uptake to highlight weaker points in their answers. As is apparent from the extract, Jana was not in the least discouraged by Marek's claim that he did not understand her. Instead, she took the floor and elaborated her point, even though Marek had asked a different student to do so (line 8). In the subsequent elaborate answer, which clearly shows that Jana was capable of creating a response longer than 30 words, Jana makes her point clearer. She mentions Polo's savings, their hypothetical location, the decrease in their value, and the resulting loss of Polo's net worth. Jana did not specify the institution in which Polo would keep his money, but the rest of her talk is understandable and so her peers find it agreeable. By speaking in front of her peers of her own volition and on more than one occasion, Jana fulfilled Marek's instructions even though he questioned whether such a scenario could take place. Interestingly enough, Jana's initiative represents only one example of many similar ones that we recorded.

As far as the values for indicators are concerned, Lesson 6 can be understood as a leap. The decrease in recorded values was halted and the values even increased (see Fig. 6.1). The number of open questions of high cognitive demand asked by Marek turned out to be similar to the values recorded in Lesson 3. Surprisingly, the number of student thoughts with reasoning was the highest from all of the recorded classes—even though the students whom Marek had expected to use argumentation the most were not present in the class. In addition, Marek's activity enabled him to meet his teaching goals and so it can be considered purposeful. The principle of collectivity was also met: 11 of the 14 present students spoke. The number of participating students in Marek's whole-class activity was exactly the same as in the previously recorded group work. For the first time, the dialogic teaching indicators and principles were not opposing forces. This outcome also came about because the typically talkative students were not present in the class.

In the subsequent reflective interview, Marek suggested that his planned activities took more time than usual. Nevertheless, he added that he had noted the increased participation by the students. He expressed a hint of surprise about the girls' ability to put individual pieces of information into a coherent whole. He was also surprised that the girls managed to connect information acquired from different classes within his class, as was the case of the hypothetical financial crisis and its presumed influence on the life of Marco Polo. He therefore started to see them differently than in the previous interviews.

Extract 6.14: Interview after Lesson 6

1 **Teacher:** It all took longer than I expected. I thought we would manage to do all the questions, that we'd go through them. On the other hand, more students participated than usual. Even those who normally don't say anything participated through eye contact at least. And I had this feeling that at least five girls started to connect the dots. But that was just a feeling. If it's also accurate or not … I was really influenced by the absence of Vojta, Olda, Nikos, and the others.

2 **Researcher:** I tried to count how many of your students spoke and if I decoded well who spoke when, which wasn't always easy, it seemed to me that there were 14 of them and of those 11 spoke.

This lesson convinced Marek that even students who usually do not assert their voice can participate in talk driven by open and cognitively demanding questions. How to maintain this achievement even with all of the students present in the classroom remained to be solved.

Lesson 6 aimed to strengthen student discussion. In accordance with this plan, the indicator of open discussion increased in this lesson for the first time during the development of the program (see Fig. 6.1) since the students built upon what their peers said. Marek noticed this and mentioned it several times with pleasure during the interview. In the following extract, Marek talks about a situation in which students explained how they reached their conclusion and why it was correct. They did not consider Marek to be an umpire, which he described as one of his goals.

Extract 6.15: Interview after Lesson 6

1 **Teacher:** They normally say "yes" or "no" just to make me happy. They don't say it because they're convinced of it. But in this situation, they had all the information and they competed with one another. Well, they weren't really competing, they just wanted to talk it through among themselves.

2 **Researcher**: And that's the moment where they just looked at one another. You're completely outside the circle when they talk to one another.

3 **Teacher:** Well, that's great. I didn't really notice it, but I'm happy about it.

4 **Researcher**: So here, he really nicely explained his position, and how he reached it, and how he had thought about it before, but … I mean, this was just great. It's not that he's telling them new information, but he is also telling them where he'd been and how he got there. And notice how long those responses are.

6.2 Series of Lessons Marek Taught During TPD Program

5 **Teacher:** So, what I wanted to happen really happened. As I was saying, when a student learns something they can substitute for the teacher and we can really see it here. Like that it is possible. They need to learn something first, that is the essential precondition. And, of course, there has to be the thing that worked in this class from the very beginning. That they listen to one another, they don't interrupt when somebody else is speaking, nobody is showing off, nobody is pretending to be better.

Marek acknowledged that sometimes his students answered his questions because they knew he would be pleased. In the recorded session, however, Marek suddenly saw the inner motivation of students who wanted to say something because they had just established it. Finally, Marek expressed his opinion that his teaching had proceeded exactly as planned and as he had presumed it would go. We believe that it was only Marek's experience that changed his opinion.

Lesson 7: Creating space for the participation of all students

Lesson 7 was the last lesson in which Marek focused on Marco Polo, but this time, students from both groups were present. An unexpected change occurred: Oldrich moved with his parents to a different town. Marek's final lesson plan was identical to the one presented in the reflective interview. Over 45 min, Marek planned to implement dialogic teaching via three activities. He started with a tested activity in which students answered questions prepared in advance. This activity proceeded in the same way as its first iteration; there were not many questions left and so it quickly concluded.

Marek wanted his students to reach an understanding as to why Polo's travelogue was called *One Million Lies* and why Polo himself was perceived as an unreliable narrator. This end was planned to be facilitated by a discussion in which students would express what they expected to find in a travelogue even if they had never traveled. This much is shown by the following extract:

Extract 6.16: Lesson 7

1 **Teacher**: What type of information would you expect to find in a travelogue? I mean, if you were a person who had never traveled more than 10 km.
2 **Dita:** ((*raising her hand*))
3 **Teacher:** ((*points at Dita*))
4 **Dita:** Whether drinking water is available on the way.
5 **Teacher:** ((*nods*))
6 **Lucka:** ((*raises her hand*))
7 **Teacher:** (*points at her*)
8 **Lucka:** Whether they'll give me food.
9 **Vasek:** ((*raises his hand*)) If there's a war.
10 **Teacher:** Well. ((*2 – scanning the room*)) Anything else?
11 **Jana:** I was thinking about whether there's going to be a war.
12 **Teacher:** Whether there's going to be war, whether you'd be safe. So. And now try to see this through the eyes of a person who has never left their home city. And they have never seen (.) any other city (1). Try to see it this way.

13 **Jana:** Will we have any tools available to us?
14 **Teacher:** What would tools be good for?
15 **Jana:** Like a rope.
16 **Teacher:** I see.
17 **Vojta:** Jana would build a house.
18 **Students:** ((*laughing*))
19 **Jenda:** ((*raises his hand and says hesitantly*)) Will there be a place for us to stay?
20 **Teacher:** ((*nodding hesitantly*)) You're still dealing with the fundamentals, I like that. (.) So.
21 **Dana:** If there are any wild animals.
22 **Student:** How far it is, I guess.
23 **Student:** How much food costs there.
24 **Teacher:** Hmm. Alright.

Marek was hoping that his students would list some paranormal fears that they would expect in a travelogue. He also supposed that he would be able to inform his students that it was the lack of the paranormal that made contemporaries of Marco Polo question the credibility of the work, which included ordinary, factual information. However, the students' suggestions were of a predictable nature (whether food and water would be available, how much both cost, whether the roads would be safe, etc.). These ideas mirrored their own experiences with traveling. There was no conclusion to this activity and no follow up. Thus, the activity stands in contrast to the others since it was not purposeful. The subsequent educational communication was in no way related to the activity.

The subsequent activity lasted for most of the lesson and presented a clear turn since it was purposeful. The activity also aptly captures how classroom discourse developed in Marek's lessons. He asked his students to put themselves into the situation of medieval people who had never left their home village. They were then to decide and explain which travelogue they would find more credible: one with descriptions of fabulous beasts and monsters or one with information on the state of the roads, cities, and natural world along the way. The aim of this activity was to make students understand why medieval people would find the travelogue with beasts and monsters more trustworthy.

Extract 6.17: Lesson 7

1 **Teacher:** So imagine you are told by someone (1) who just may be a traveler that you will definitely encounter a cyclops along the way and dragons too and you'll meet beasts the size of a house who can eat you up with one bite (1). And then there's another guy who describes the destination, tells you where the road goes, where you can eat, and so on. So, which one of these will you trust? Think about this on your own.
2 **Nikos:** ((*raises his hand*)) The guy (.) with the monsters.
3 **Teacher:** Why?
4 **Nikos:** Because it's cool.
5 **Students:** ((*laughing*))

6.2 Series of Lessons Marek Taught During TPD Program   127

6   **Teacher:** ((*points at Kamila who was raising her hand*))
7   **Kamila:** I would trust the one who had really been there because it is less probable that he is lying if he's only describing how it looks and what it's like.
8   **Teacher:** ((*nodding while looking at the others*)) Talk to me. Do you agree with Kamila (((*pointing at her*))?
9   **Dita:** ((*raises her hand*))
10 **Teacher:** ((*nodding in her direction*)) Dita?
11 **Dita:** I would trust the guy with boring descriptions because it would be strange if they had so many monsters and we had none. (.) And the truth is usually also kind of (.) boring.
12 **Teacher:** ((*points at Dita*)) There. That's a great answer. (1) Does anybody want to add anything?
13 **Vojta:** I didn't hear it.
14 **Teacher:** Try to pay more attention. I heard it and we are equally far away. Just look at the person ((*points at Dita*)) and watch them as they speak. Only that will help. Dita, can you repeat your answer?
15 **Dita:** ((*is silent*))
16 **Teacher:** Don't be afraid. You can say it in other words. It doesn't have to be word for word.
17 **Dita:** I would trust the guy who describes it without monsters because ((*1 – shaking her head and looking at the teacher*)) I don't know what I said.
18 **Kamila:** The truth. (.) That she is going to trust the person who tells the boring story because that is usually more truthful.
19 **Pavla:** Also it would be weird that we have zero cyclopes and they have lots of them.
20 **Nikos:** ((*raising his hand*))
21 **Teacher:** Yes, Nikos?
22 **Nikos:** Well, I wanted to say the same thing that they just said. ((*pointing at the girls*))

Marek has specified in his opening question that he is interested in hearing not only what the students would prefer but also why (line 1). As usual, Nikos spoke first and suggested he would rather trust the traveler describing monsters (line 2). Yet, since he did not explain his choice, Marek asked him to do so. Nikos replied with a joke that was clearly intended to amuse his classmates, at which he was successful. A change is apparent in Marek's behavior: Marek does not react in any way. Previously, Marek's behavior had been different. When Nikos made a joke in Lesson 4, Marek laughed at it and modified his teaching so that it would include the subject of the joke. In Lesson 7, however, Marek instead asked a female student to speak. Apparently, when Marek decided that the "gifted" students should not dominate the classroom talk, he gradually came up with ways to accomplish this goal.

This was also facilitated by the "slow" thinkers who—once they'd found out that the teacher was interested in hearing their answers—clearly showed that they would like to participate in classroom talk. Kamila disagreed with Nikos and supported her choice with reasoning: a traveler who has visited the destination is necessarily more trustworthy than one who has not (line 7). When Marek asked his students to evaluate the answer, Dita chose to do so. She supported Kamila's response by adding that the truth is typically uneventful (line 11). Marek appreciated Kamila's response and then—in an effort to create discussion—asked his students for their opinions. Instead of a response discussing Kamila's opinion, Vojta said that he did not hear Dita, who indeed spoke in a very quiet voice. We take Marek's reaction as another little step out of many that enabled him to build an environment in which all students could participate. Marek said that he could understand Dita even though he was as far from her as Vojta. He further instructed Vojta to also watch Dita speak since that aids comprehension too. He then asked Dita to repeat her answer once more, which emphasized the worth of her answer. Since Dita was not able to repeat her answer, Marek reassured her that he would like to hear the gist of her response and not a word-for-word reproduction. Dita eventually mustered her courage; nonetheless, she could not repeat her answer and remained uncertain (line 17). Kamila came to the rescue (line 18) as she tried to complete Dita's response in her place while restating Dita's initial idea: the truth is boring. Pavla followed up of her own volition and made Dita's and Kamila's answer more specific and personal: "we have zero cyclopes and they have lots of them" (line 19). This part of the extract aptly illustrates how an answer becomes the product of student co-construction (see Sect. 1.3.4). This also shows the way the supportive principle of dialogic teaching can be met.

The end of the extract (line 22) shows that Nikos reached the same conclusion that a moment previously had been vocalized by the girls. We can observe a reversal of roles for the first time during the program: the "slow" thinkers were the ones who came up with an opinion. This is a reversal of the process recorded in Lesson 3, in which Marek instructed the girls to listen and then agree or disagree with the boys' opinions (see Extract 6.3).

The questions asked by Marek could for the most part be considered to be open questions of high cognitive demand. As for their number, the peak for Marek was in Lesson 7. Marek also constantly emphasized to his students that they need to defend their positions. This helped the increase in student thoughts with reasoning that had occurred in Lesson 6 continue into Lesson 7 (see Fig. 6.1). A downturn is noticeable only in relation to student discussion, which Marek explained by the presence of both groups of students in the classroom, with one group not being accustomed to giving space for communication to the other. Both the principle of purposefulness and that of collectivity were met in this lesson despite the decrease in student discussion. Only 12 students were present that day in the classroom and 10 students spoke. Eda and Karel were the only students who at this point in the program had not spoken at all. In comparison with the previous two sessions, the students spoke less with one another and more often directed their responses to Marek. Marek's aim for the last two sessions was to maintain the numbers for student thoughts with reasoning (since it was a key indicator), strengthen open discussion, and maintain the overall level of student participation.

Lessons 8 and 9: At the end of the program: elements of dialogic teaching aligned

Marek had a detailed plan prepared for the last two recorded lessons. The students were first acquainted with a short text that they discussed. Their discussion started with content-specific questions and then proceeded further. In Lesson 8, the students

6.2 Series of Lessons Marek Taught During TPD Program

read a text on the graduation exam and expressed their reactions to it. In Lesson 9, they read an extract from a short story that described how a boy ended up in an orphanage because his mother was arrested during the 1948 Communist takeover of Czechoslovakia. The task in this lesson was to look for connections between the extract and the history of the Czech Republic. The overall aim for both lessons was to continue with the previously established dialogic trends in classroom discourse. The students were to use reasoning, members of both student groups were to participate, and all of them were supposed to build on their utterances. While the first two goals had already been met (and thus were just to be maintained), the strengthening of student discussion still eluded Marek.

The following extract captures the nature of the classroom discourse in the last recorded lesson as the students discussed the extract about a boy's childhood heavily influenced by World War II.

Extract 6.18: Lesson 9

1. **Teacher:** So, what do we know about that family? Vasek.
2. **Vasek:** I think that the family is Jewish.
3. **Teacher:** Why do you think so?
4. **Vasek:** Because, like, Communists moved into their flat where they were living and put them in the cellar and at the end it says that he saw unknown men walking in their flat, some men he didn't know. And the Communists typically didn't like the Jews.
5. **Ondra:** Yeah, the bad guys.
6. **Vasek:** And I think that his father is in a concentration camp, I guess.
7. **Teacher:** But it's said several times that all this took place after the war.
8. **Nikos:** (*raises his hand*) I just wanted…
9. **Teacher:** Just a moment, let's give Vasek space to finish his thought.
10. **Vasek:** Even though this was after the war, they still really must have hated them.
11. **Teacher:** Yes, they didn't really like them; that's correct. Well thought out. Jana?
12. **Jana:** Well, it was en-, it was enough if somebody just disagreed with the Communists, went to demonstrations, and so their house got inspected for any illegal materials, leaflets. They didn't have to be Jewish.
13. **Dana:** Jana's probably right.
14. **Lucka:** They could have hated more things.
15. **Teacher:** Elaborate.
16. **Lucka:** ((*shrugs her shoulders*)) I dunno.
17. **Teacher:** Shhh. ((*2 – looking at Lucka*)) So, in which category would you put the story and why? Well, Nikos?
18. **Nikos:** I'd like to get back to what Vasek said ((*points at Vasek*)). Because he said that the Communists hated the Jews, which I think is incorrect. The Nazis hated the Jews, no?
19. **Teacher:** ((*shrugs*)) Well, express your opinion.
20. **Nikos:** ((*looks at Vasek*)) Yes, Vasek? Tell us how you see it.
21. **Vasek:** ((*shrugs and smiles*)) You're right.

22 **Nikos:** So the whole thing just got even more tangled. So they don't really have to be Jews. In that case, I agree with Jana. ((*points at Jana*))

23 **Kuba:** I don't think they were Jews. They disagreed with the Communists after the war.

24 **Teacher:** I see. (1) Dana?

25 **Dana:** Well, he could also have been, like, a Czech person. It could have taken place in Czechoslovakia and they could (1) – and his mother could have been against the Communists. Something like that. And so they inspected their house.

26 **Teacher:** This is a very interesting line of thought. I have to honestly say that I like the way you're approaching this.

27 **Dana:** So listen, there was this type of police that Hitler had.

28 **Nikos:** The Gestapo.

29 **Dana:** They were under Hitler and he thought from time to time that it was a good idea to inspect a few houses, so he had more people to put into concentration camps, so they were full.

30 **Teacher:** Are we talking about a situation during the war or after the war?

31 **Ondra:** After the war.

32 **Pavla:** Yeah, after the war.

33 **Nikos:** ((*still raising his hand and speaking to Dana*)) So why did you talk about the Jews and concentration camps?

34 **Dana:** I didn't realize this.

35 **Teacher:** Yes, it seems as if you jumped from one timeline (1) after the war right back into another one during the war. I don't know how your thinking went and how it got back to the war.

36 **Dana:** OK, so let's talk about the first one, the first one, the first one (1) that they were against the Communists.

In the extract, students were trying to establish the narrator's family situation. The students did connect information from the short story with their knowledge of history. This means that Marek chose an extract that was both cognitively challenging and open ended for his students as their interaction did not end with only one correct solution. The students attempted to talk with reasoning. As for uptake, Marek used it to provide his students with relevant information. He also modified his uptake based on the nature of the given response instead of who was responding (e.g., lines 7, 11, 17, 30). As for open discussion, the students built on what Marek said but also reacted to what their peers said as well. Marek himself participated less in the classroom talk and instead managed it (see lines 9 and 17). As a consequence of this, open discussion increased in the last two recorded lessons and constituted almost half of the last lesson. It should also be noted that the class discussion was related to the subject matter and so the classroom dialogue was purposeful.

Since 13 students out of 16 present actively participated, the extract captures a segment of collective participation. Also, students from both groups spoke (Vasek and Nikos represented the "gifted" students and Dana, Jana, Pavla, Lucka, Kuba, and Ondra the "slow" thinkers). The participation of the female students changed as well. The principle of collectivity was thus met.

To summarize the features of classroom discourse in the last two sessions, the key indicator of dialogic teaching—student thoughts with reasoning—continued to increase. The quality of the discussion in the last two sessions also increased: the students were capable of reacting to one another without usurping the communication space of others. Consequently, the indicators of open questions of high cognitive demand and uptake decreased. As Marek said in one of the reflective interviews, when a student has learned something, that student can fill the role of the teacher. Student reactions and questions thus replace the questions and uptake provided by the teacher. Marek could in turn focus on leading the discussion and only intervene when necessary.

6.3 How to Understand Inner Tensions and Conflicts in a Dialogic Teaching System

This section presents some more general conclusions from Marek's case. We chose his case since it illustrates the complex nature of the transformation toward dialogic teaching and the troubles with the inner tensions among its elements.

At the beginning of the TPD program, Marek thought that dialogic teaching was aligned with his teaching style, and he presumed that a change would be minor and easy to achieve. Nevertheless, as the previous pages have shown, Marek's teaching had to undergo significant changes on several levels: his organization of student classroom work, his preferred way of teaching (from independent work to group work), his approach to teaching and students, and the expectations placed on the students. The final change was markedly more pronounced than what Marek had expected at the beginning of the program. Completing the TPD program thus demanded a significant amount of energy from Marek.

This was due to the complexity of dialogic teaching. In Marek's case, it was clear that while he was improving certain aspect of his teaching, he was often in danger of failing in another aspect. As stated in Sect. 2.3.3, the complex nature of dialogic teaching represents a significant obstacle that makes its implementation demanding and difficult for teachers (Hennessy and Davies 2020). Simply said, dialogic teaching cannot be reduced to one element or even a set of several elements (see Boyd and Markarian 2011, 2015; Molinari and Mameli 2013), and its individual elements cannot be assessed on their own. The coordination among individual elements is what matters. When implementing dialogic teaching, it is necessary to monitor whether a particular improvement has undesirable and unintended consequences (see Sect. 5.3.2) that could undermine the full-blown implementation of dialogic teaching.

A study by Emanuelsson and Sahlstrom (2008) described how a Swedish math teacher increased student participation—a key element in dialogic teaching. However, the enhanced student participation led to the trivialization of classroom tasks and limitation of the mathematical content of the classes. To make the students participate, the teacher provided them with clues that would enable them to solve the tasks in the least challenging way possible. The study is an illustration of the inner tension between various elements of dialogic teaching. We think this tension was also apparent in the case study of Marek.

When planning the TPD program, we were aware of the existence of several elements of dialogic teaching, specifically indicators, principles, and teaching methods, and we acknowledged the necessity of coordinating them. During the program's run, we observed whether individual teaching practices led to increases in dialogic teaching indicators and whether the indicators were aligned with the principles, and together with the teachers we sought suitable teaching methods. However, we did not foresee the extent to which the interplay and the reciprocal dynamics among all of the elements might be complicated and render the outcomes of the TPD fragile. We realized this only during the course of the TPD program, specifically during the reflective interviews with the teachers.

In the course of data analysis, we noted that individual elements can support one another and can also conflict with one another. Furthermore, progress in one indicator can inhibit progress in another. In Marek's case, we observed that when he started asking more open questions of high cognitive demand, his students started to talk more with reasoning and the lesson become purposeful. The indicator of open questions positively influenced a rise in the indicator of student thoughts with reasoning, and the increase in both indicators strengthened the purposefulness of Marek's teaching. On the other hand, the increase in the indicator of open questions of high cognitive demand led to a violation of the principle of collectivity. Since the principle and indicator clashed at this point, Marek's teaching moved further away from the ideal of dialogic teaching. This only changed once the conflict, which we observed in subsequent classes as well, was resolved.

We did not perceive the temporary clash between elements of dialogic teaching as a fault in Marek's practices nor in those of any of the remaining teachers from the program. Instead, we took this clash to be a logical consequence of the implemented change, which is broad and complex. We viewed it as a clear sign that the teachers were in transition (Billings and Fitzgerald 2002), or, in other words, that a change was truly taking place.

A whole range of conflicting constellations can occur among elements of dialogic teaching. These can occur between an indicator and a method or between an indicator and a principle. Also, they can occur among indicators, as the strengthening of one can lead to a weakening of another—e.g., in Marek's case, enhancing open discussion was accompanied by a decrease in open questions of high cognitive demand.

We think that conflicts within the system of dialogic teaching during its implementation are not all equally significant. A method that repeatedly leads to a violation of a principle or the weakening of an indicator can be easily replaced with another method. For example, when it came to student work, Marek preferred independent student work with worksheets, which conflicted with all of the indicators and was thus completely unfit for dialogic teaching. Nevertheless, this conflict was easily solved by Marek and his choice of a different teaching method. Therefore, we consider conflicts that involve methods as not very significant and easily solvable.

Conflicts among indicators present a greater defect. Nonetheless, a deficit in one indicator can be compensated by an increase in another, as long as the key indicator of student thoughts with reasoning is not weakened in the end. The case of Marek shows how a decrease in the indicators of open questions of high cognitive demand and uptake was compensated by an increase in open discussion and student thoughts with reasoning in the last two lessons. In sum, even this conflict was not harmful.

Harmful conflicts are those in which principles are heavily involved. This is due to the fact that principles represent essential norms of good teaching. Probably the most visible conflict involving principles occurred when Marek violated the principle of collectivity when he tried to increase the indicator of open questions of high cognitive demand. The same result occurred when the situation was reversed: Marek strengthened the principle of collectivity, which in turn decreased the measured indicators. These conflicts were problematic—they could not be solved by letting go of either of their constituting elements. There is no way to cut corners with either indicators or principles, and they do not compensate for one another (as was the case with conflict among various indicators).

Conflicts among different principles are equally serious. In Marek's case, purposefulness clashed with collectivity. When Marek tried to engage more students in dialogue, he weakened the principle of purposefulness. Marek communicated with the allegedly slow students in a way that had nothing in common with the teaching goals of our TPD program. Interestingly enough, Marek was not even aware of this as he was fully focused on increasing the principle of collectivity. We consider conflicts involving principles to have the greatest potential of going unnoticed. Indicators can be easily measured; principles are less open to simple measurement.

During the TPD program, we noticed a variety of tensions and conflicts involving principles. Most often, the principles of purposefulness and collectivity were somehow violated. We induce from this that these two principles are the hardest for teachers to maintain while striving to transform their teaching toward a more dialogic one. Therefore, the following section discusses in detail what happens with classroom dialogue when purposefulness and collectivity are not maintained.

6.3.1 *When Dialogue is Not Purposeful*

Purposelessness occurs when individual activities or tasks do not lead to a desired goal: they do not acquaint students with the subject matter or skills comprising the studied subject (Herbel-Eisenmann et al. 2013). During our cooperation with teachers, we repeatedly noticed that teaching can formally fulfill all of the indicators of dialogic teaching and yet remain purposeless. In such cases, the teachers provide students with adequately demanding questions that the students can discuss or reason about and yet such talk might have no merit. Meeting the principle of purposefulness is vital since it is this very principle that connects dialogic teaching with the subject matter.

When we analyzed purposeless segments,[1] we noted four repeating patterns, which we call purposeless riddles, quasi-evocations, quasi-reflections, and neighborly chatter.

6.3.2 Purposeless Riddles

Purposeless riddles are situations in which the teacher requires students to come up with an answer that they do not know and have no way of establishing. In short, the students are required to guess what the teacher is thinking. For example, the teacher either has the students guess a historical date that they do not know and cannot guess or give the name of characters from a book they have not yet read. In such situations, the principle of purposefulness is typically in conflict with the principle of collectivity because the teacher uses such activities to give all of the students the same chance to establish the correct answer. By doing so, the teachers hope to engage their students in an equal way. This goal is often met because the nature of the activity is random. One needs luck to answer such questions correctly and so none of the students has an unfair advantage. Nonetheless, this comes at the price of classroom talk becoming purposeless.

Marek's instruction for his students to guess the medieval class that would become the topic of their lesson is a prime example of a purposeless riddle. The students went on to name individual classes of people without having any other way of answering correctly than simply guessing (see Extract 6.7). Since the students could not have learned anything from mere guessing, they would not have been cheated of any cognitive benefit had Marek identified the group. Purposeless riddles were the most represented type of purposeless passages in Marek's case and in the teaching of the remaining teachers.

6.3.3 Quasi-Evocations

The aim of evocations is to activate student pre-concepts related to the topic of the given class. The role of evocation as a starting point is to help build new understanding, as the constructivist approach to education claims. This activity can be very purposeful if it is aligned with the subject matter. Nevertheless, there are passages in our data in which evocation had no connection to the subject matter or goals. Instead, the connection was of a purely associative nature. The students were often at a loss as to how to connect the associated matter with the subsequent activities since it was

---

[1] We only paid attention to purposeless passages that occurred during a whole-class interaction between the teacher and students. Our data also included purposeless passages that were produced either by a single speaker or a group of students. We will not examine those passages here.

mostly not even possible. Therefore, we think of this as of a faulty form of evocation and call it quasi-evocation.

Marek's instruction in which he asked students to list examples of information they would expect to find in a travelogue (even if they had never traveled) was an example of quasi-evocation given that the subsequent student responses were not in any way connected to the content of the lesson. Nonetheless, this was one of the few episodes of quasi-evocation in all of the data from Marek's recorded sessions. Such episodes did appear frequently in the data from other teachers. They were often connected to sharing of personal experience related to various extracurricular activities. An example can be taken from Daniela's case when she asked her students to state which animals they liked and why, since the topic of that particular class was fables (see Extract 4.3 in Chap. 4). The examples provided by students had zero influence on the rest of the lesson.

As was the case with purposeless riddles, quasi-evocations also embody the conflict between the principles of collectivity and purposefulness. The teacher chooses a method that enables the greatest participation by students, which also explains why the teacher does not modify student answers. The teachers attempted to do so in all of the mentioned examples.

It was apparent from reflective interviews and analysis of lesson plans that quasi-evocations typically happened when teachers had expected students to deal with the task differently than they actually did, as we could see in both Daniela's and Marek's lessons. They both expected that their students would sooner or later provide the correct answer and then they would be able to build upon that. Daniela expected her students to list animals that are typically featured in fables. Marek believed his students would end up naming supernatural fears around traveling. However, these expectations were not met in either case and the activities fell flat.

6.3.4 Quasi-Reflections

We use the term quasi-reflections to describe situations in which it seems that students reflect and summarize newly learned knowledge even though this is not really the case. While quasi-evocations typically open a lesson or an activity, quasi-reflections generally close them. These activities could be purposeful if they served as a space for students to recognize how they increased their knowledge. However, quasi-reflections do not meet these criteria. Teachers do not strive to use them for students to acknowledge how much new information they learned and how they have increased their previous knowledge. Instead, students respond with superficial truisms without engaging in deeper thought.

In Marek's case, quasi-reflections could be exemplified by the teacher's invitation to students to tell him what new information they had learned about Marco Polo in Lesson 6. The students responded by saying that Polo traveled a lot, providing a banal fact of which they had been aware even before the start of first lesson on Marco Polo. Quasi-reflections are another example of a conflict between purposefulness and collective student participation. Since every answer is correct during quasi-reflection, all of the students can share their opinion, which comes at the cost of the activity being purposeless.

6.3.5 Neighborly Chatter

As the name indicates, neighborly chatter is characterized by lively interactions among students since all of them have something (seemingly worthy) to say and all can express their opinion on the discussion subject. The students react to one another and so neighborly chatter can appear to be similar to a discussion, at least in terms of classroom organization. Nonetheless, such an activity is purposeless as it lacks aim and direction. This is facilitated by the fact that these student responses are not modified by the teacher.

We observed chatter in Marek's class when he asked his students how their lives would change if they had started traveling at a young age. He allowed them to respond in any way they saw fit as he wanted to increase the number of participating students. He was not interested in the purposefulness of the activity as a whole. Students soon diverged from the topic, and some started talking about the niece of one of their peers who lives abroad and speaks Italian.

Neighborly chatter is characterized by the teacher's attempts to initiate a dialogue and by the students' non-corresponding answers. The dialogue thus degenerates. The teacher very often does not correct student responses. Furthermore, the teachers do not define what a valid student response should be or are unable to maintain the standard for valid responses. Even though Marek stopped his students once they had diverged from the topic, there are many several-minute-long passages recorded in the classes of other teachers that did not lead to any goals and were not modified by the teachers.

6.3.6 Why Does Purposefulness Occur in Teaching?

We identified four types of situations in which the principle of purposefulness is not met in teaching and thus the teaching is not dialogic, even if the required indicators are met. The central conflict that causes failure in purposefulness is the clash between the principle of purposefulness and the principle of collectivity. Such situations stem from teachers' desire for higher student participation (even at the cost of disregarding teaching aims), which explains why the teachers did not stop chatter even when it veered off course. Apparently, the teachers found it difficult to engage students in collective participation, and in order to achieve the goal they abandoned their teaching aims, both consciously and unconsciously. This phenomenon is in accordance with our previous study in which teachers reported that dialogic teaching is valuable but there is no time for it in real-life teaching as it hampers the teaching of content

(Sedova et al. 2014). In their attempts at implementing dialogic education, teachers apparently face the problem of matching content (in accordance with the principle of purposefulness) and form (e.g., student participation). These elements clash with one another and teachers are not capable of solving such an issue. Therefore, they shy away from dialogic teaching.

Why do purposeless activities occur in teaching? The first explanation includes a teacher who prepared a content-related discussion activity but has students who behave differently than the teacher predicted. The teacher does not adjust their lesson plan and, consequently, the interaction is not useful from the perspective of aims. This is often the case with both neighborly chatter and quasi-evocation. The risk of unexpected development is apparently closely connected with dialogic teaching. Twiner et al. (2014) noted that teachers switch between two trajectories in dialogic education: the intended one (which is based on activities and ready-made materials prepared by the teachers) and the immediate one (which arises spontaneously in the lesson as a consequence of unpredictable student communicative activities). These authors perceived immediate trajectories as very important and useful as they can support and deepen student understanding. Our analysis, however, shows that immediate trajectories are risky. They present a digression from lesson plans and thus put greater demands on teacher expertise. Furthermore, at the start of such activities, teachers cannot predict where they will go and how they will be connected to the planned lesson aims. Our findings show that it is very difficult for teachers to use immediate trajectories productively.

The second explanation concerns the implementation of purposeless activities in teaching: teachers include purposeless activities to increase student participation in discussion even though they know that such activities do not help fulfill teaching aims. This is the case with purposeless riddles, which only lead students to guessing at the topic of a given class.

The literature provides only a few suggestions as to how to solve the problem. Alexander (2006) stated that during the implementation of dialogic teaching it is necessary first to focus on principles related to form (i.e., collectivity) and only later address principles related to content (i.e., purposefulness). On the other hand, Hammond (2016) argued that formal and content principles need to be pursued simultaneously and content principles should become the driving force in the process. Both authors agreed that it is more difficult to fulfill the content principles than the formal principles.

6.3.7 When Dialogue is Not Collective

Dialogue is non-collective when, for example, only a few students or one group of students participate in classroom talk, as we repeatedly saw in Marek's recorded lessons. Empirical studies show that student participation in classroom discourse is uneven (Myhill 2002; Black 2004; Kovalainen and Kumpulainen 2007; Jurik et al.

2014; Clarke 2015), which means that there is always a risk that the classroom dialogue will not be collective.

A paper by Black (2004) drew attention to the existence of patterns of uneven participation in whole-class discussions and proposed a typology for identifying productive and non-productive interaction, classifying students into several types: students who participate in a productive way on an ongoing basis, students who tend to only participate in a non-productive way (involuntarily, abruptly, and only when called upon by the teacher), students characterized by a balanced proportion of productive and non-productive participation, and students with a generally low participation rate. The variability of participation patterns was highlighted by Kovalainen and Kumpulainen (2007), who distinguished: (a) vocal participants, who are very active and respond to the teacher's questions, but also pose questions themselves—they take part in feedback and react to both the teacher and other students, (b) responsive participants, characterized by a medium degree of participation—they are focused on interaction with the teacher and mostly respond to the teacher's questions, (c) bilateral participants, characterized by a medium degree of participation—they are focused on interaction with the teacher, but also with their classmates, and they will respond to questions and pose questions themselves, and (d) silent participants who rarely take part in communication.

In the dialogic approach to teaching, students are encouraged to participate as much and as productively as possible, but the question is whether this opportunity is used to the same extent by all students. The studies cited above demonstrate that participation in classroom discourse is usually unevenly distributed and student behavior can be placed on a scale ranging from vocal to silent participants (Kovalainen and Kumpulainen 2007). This raises the question of whether and how the implementation of dialogic teaching affects student participation patterns. If the nature of classroom discourse changes, does participation in fact change? Are the existing participation patterns transformed, or are vocal students provided with even more space for their talk?

There are certain indications that collectivity in dialogic teaching can be difficult to achieve. Helgevold (2016) indicated that teachers perceive different characteristics among students in the class—in particular, different cognitive capabilities and motivation—as a barrier to establishing whole-class dialogue. Based on a long-term field study comprising classroom observations and interviews with teachers, Lefstein and Snell (2014) argued that teachers view student capabilities as fixed and believe that few of their students are able to participate in classroom dialogue. They think that only those students who are bright and articulate can participate in, and benefit from, cognitively challenging dialogic teaching and learning (Snell and Lefstein 2018). This was described in Sect. 2.3.2 as the teacher's mindset obstructing the full implementation of dialogic teaching.

Looking back at how teachers tried to meet the principle of collectivity, there were a number of situations in which the chances for certain students to participate were decreased. Such situations occurred because the teachers either deliberately created uneven opportunities to talk for different students or passively accepted students' differing willingness to talk. This differentiation leads us to delineate two types of situations in which the principle of collectivity was violated.

6.3.7.1 Teacher Nominations

The first source of non-collectivity stems from the fact that teachers nominate some students to speak more often than others. This phenomenon was apparent in Marek's case. Students that Marek considered gifted (such as Oldrich and Nikos) were called upon more frequently than students whom he thought of as slow thinkers. The latter group was more often instructed to pay attention and listen to what the others were saying (at the beginning of the program, Marek often instructed the group of girls in this way). It could be said that Marek and the other teachers most probably wanted to meet their teaching aims by following this method of uneven nomination.

Marek's preference for the "gifted" students was subtly disguised. At the beginning of the program, he followed a rule that students were called upon in the order in which they raised their hands. This seemingly neutral decision resulted in the same students being asked to speak over and over because the high achievers volunteered first. Thus, Marek ensured that his teaching would go according to his plan and meet his goals.

6.3.7.2 Dominance of Vocal Students

Even students themselves can break the principle of collectivity. This happens when a teacher does not nominate students to speak and the students claim speaking space on their own without any modification from the teacher. In such situations, it often happens that one or two students dominate the classroom discourse. Again, this pattern could be observed in Marek's recorded lessons in which the communicatively more active students spoke more often, even in situations in which Marek did not ask them to speak.

Teachers are aware of the dangers arising from some students dominating the discourse and attempt to prevent it. Nonetheless, active students are still capable of controlling a large portion of classroom talk (as, for example, Nikos often did in the recorded lessons). On the other hand, such students can follow instructions well. They therefore help the lesson progress in the direction chosen by the teacher who is therefore less inclined to modify the communicative dominance of such students.

6.3.7.3 Why Does Non-collectivity Occur in Teaching?

There are many reasons that students do not participate. It is virtually impossible for students to participate if teachers do not nominate them to do so. It follows from our data analysis that teachers nominate students in relation to their willingness to participate. It is also valid that those students interested in participation are often high achievers (Myhill 2002; Black 2004; Kovalainen and Kumpulainen 2007). Therefore, teachers talk more with high achievers simply because they react to spontaneous responses from their students. It is likely that there are students in the classroom who would like to participate but are not nominated by the teacher because they do not send clear enough signals. It is also valid that students who are often nominated to speak tend to become vocal and claim the right to speak even without teacher nominations. This again solidifies the groups of those who speak and those who do not.

A question arises as to why certain students participate in communication while others do not. We have mentioned the connection to academic achievement. Students who are perceived as weak choose not to speak because they fear they would reveal themselves as incompetent or as not knowing the right answer. Such students want in this way to prevent their peers and teachers from perceiving them even more negatively. A study by Clarke (2015) put the connection between achievement and participation in an interesting context. Clarke showed that students verbally participate primarily when they think they know the right answer. Not knowing the right answer was indicated as the main obstacle to participation. Through an analysis of student narratives, however, Clarke also found that high talkers are able to transcend this conception of knowledge as a precondition for participation and are willing to risk entering the communication even when they do not know the right answer. These findings are supported by our data. The desire of non-participating students to avoid risk is common to both types of collectivity violation discussed above. Only students who know the right answers or do not fear negative appraisal speak. Student willingness to speak is an essential element in dialogic teaching. Much the same can be said about the willingness to provide teachers with answers that may not be correct because students can only be certain about the correctness of their answer in traditionally conceived teaching in which teachers lecture first and test second. Since knowledge is constructed during the lesson in dialogic teaching, students by definition talk about things that they do not yet fully know or are not yet certain of.

6.3.8 Overcoming of Inner Tension in the Dialogic Teaching

During the TPD program, Marek gradually discovered how to deal with inner tension in his teaching. In his case, the main task was to overcome the non-collectivity of the classroom dialogue. Chapter 5 shows that it was similarly challenging for Daniela to discover how to keep the classroom dialogue purposeful. Both these two teachers and other teachers in our sample thus faced serious challenges with harmonizing various elements of dialogic teaching.

Chapter 5 outlined how the unintended consequences of implemented change can lead teachers to return to gestalts, resulting in stagnation rather than in a transformation toward dialogic teaching. We identified reflection and experimentation with teaching methods as the tools for overcoming stagnation or regression. Both these tools were also effective in dealing with tension and conflict inside the system. This was apparent in the case of Daniela. Through the lens developed in this chapter, some of her struggles can be interpreted as a conflict between achieving the indicators of dialogic teaching and maintaining the principle of purposefulness.

Nearly all of the examples of purposeless patterns that we identified in this chapter can be purposeful if the teachers modify their teaching methods. This would happen once the teachers better thought through the ways to connect activities to their own lesson aims (which is particularly the case with quasi-evocations and quasi-reflections) and continually adjusted these activities so that they would proceed in the desirable direction (which is particularly relevant for neighborly chatter). Teachers should therefore not focus only on whether their students will participate but also on the merit of student responses. If, for example, the students paid attention to the subject matter instead of chatting and were asked by their teacher to explain their opinions, such an activity would certainly be purposeful. We realize it can be difficult to reach this goal. The same applies to quasi-evocations and quasi-reflections, which can become valuable methods of evocation and reflection once their purpose in teaching is thought through.

During the TPD program, we found that it was not easy for teachers to notice whether the classroom dialogue was purposeful. They were able to do it only in reflective interviews when they were led by researchers to compare their plans for the particular lesson with the actual teaching outcomes in the given lesson. Thus, to recognize this important aspect of dialogic teaching requires careful reflection on the side of teacher. When this condition is met, then the teacher is able to think about using alternative teaching methods to overcome the conflict in the future.

In this chapter, we followed Marek dealing with tension in relation to including collectivity, which was difficult for him to achieve. However, as the case study shows, Marek's teaching got closer to meeting the collectivity principle over the duration of the recorded lessons. To do so, he had to change his mindset about student abilities. This study shows that Marek's mindset was firmly fixed, and the change required a lot of experimentation with teaching methods and the help of a lucky coincidence (the absence of the talkative students in Lesson 6). Only then was the experience of seeing how the underestimated students were capable of productive interaction utilized for reflection, resulting in new patterns in teacher-student interactions. Once Marek revised his beliefs about his students, he intentionally started to create space in class for them to verbally participate. This completely changed his teaching, making it equal in distributing learning opportunities.

6.4 Summary

This chapter utilized the case of Marek to demonstrate that dialogic teaching is a complex system of elements (indicators, principles, and methods) that influence one another either in a synergistic or discordant way. The tensions or even conflicts can arise between them which makes the full-blown implementation of dialogic teaching challenging for teachers.

The tension between elements occurred multiple times in Marek's lessons during the TPD program. The collectivity principle was violated in instances in which the values of the indicators of dialogic teaching were high. There were also situations in which the collectivity principle was met and the purposefulness principle was broken.

We claimed in this chapter that conflicts among the elements vary in their significance. Conflicts including principles can be considered the most significant because the principles cannot be replaced or exchanged in the way that, for example, methods can. Therefore, we discussed in detail the situations quite frequently present in our data in which the dialogue stopped being purposeful or collective. We showed the main sources of these situation—unexpected developments in the lesson blocked purposefulness, and teacher mindset about student abilities interfered with collectivity.

Finally, we identified the main tools for overcoming tensions and conflicts that teachers used during the TPD program: a careful reflection of what was happening in the class and how this corresponds with teaching goals for the given lesson and subsequent planning of alternative teaching methods enabling harmonizing all the elements.

References

Alexander, R. J. (2006). *Towards dialogic teaching: Rethinking classroom talk* (3rd ed.). Cambridge: Dialogos.

Billings, L., & Fitzgerald, J. (2002). Dialogic discussion and the Paideia Seminar. *American Educational Research Journal, 39*(4), 907–941. https://doi.org/10.3102/00028312039004905

Black, L. (2004). Differential participation in whole-class discussions and the construction of marginalised identities. *Journal of Educational Enquiry, 5*(1), 34–54.

Boyd, M. P., & Markarian, W. C. (2011). Dialogic teaching: Talk in service of a dialogic stance. *Language and Education, 25*(6), 515–534. https://doi.org/10.1080/09500782.2011.597861

Boyd, M. P., & Markarian, W. C. (2015). Dialogic teaching and dialogic stance: Moving beyond interactional form. *Research in the Teaching English, 49*(3), 272–296.

Clarke, S. N. (2015). The right to speak. In L. B. Resnick, C. S. C. Asterhan, S. N. Clarke (Eds.), *Socializing intelligence through academic talk and dialogue* (1st edn.). American Educational Research Association: Washington, D.C.

Emanuelsson, J., & Sahlström, F. (2008). The Price of Participation: Teacher control versus student participation in classroom interaction. *Scandinavian Journal of Educational Research, 52*(2), 205–223. https://doi.org/10.1080/00313830801915853

Hammond, J. (2016). Dialogic space: Intersections between dialogic teaching and systemic functional linguistics. *Research Papers Education, 31*(1), 5–22. https://doi.org/10.1080/02671522.2016.1106693

Helgevold, N. (2016). Teaching as creating space for participation—establishing a learning community in diverse classrooms. *Teachers and Teaching, 22*(3), 315–328. https://doi.org/10.1080/13540602.2015.1058590

Hennessy, S., & Davies, M. (2020). Teacher professional development to support classroom dialogue: Challenges and promises. In N. Mercer, R. Wegerif, & L. Major (Eds.), *The Routledge international handbook of research on dialogic education*. Abingdon: Routledge.

References

Herbel-Eisenmann, B. A., Steele, M. D., & Cirillo, M. (2013). (Developing) teacher discourse moves: A framework for professional development. *Mathematics Teacher Education, 1*(2), 181–196. https://doi.org/10.5951/mathteaceduc.1.2.0181

Jurik, V., Gröschner, A., & Seidel, T. (2014). Predicting students' cognitive learning activity and intrinsic learning motivation: How powerful are teacher statements, student profiles, and gender? *Learning and Individual Differences, 32,* 132–139.

Kovalainen, M., & Kumpulainen, K. (2007). The social construction of participation in an elementary classroom community. *International Journal of Education Research, 46*(3–4), 141–158. https://doi.org/10.1016/j.ijer.2007.09.011

Lefstein, A., & Snell, J. (2014). *Better than best practice: Developing teaching and learning through dialogue.* Abingdon, New York: Routledge.

Molinari, L., & Mameli, C. (2013). Process quality of classroom discourse: Pupil participation and learning opportunities. *International Journal of Education Research, 62,* 249–258. https://doi.org/10.1016/j.ijer.2013.05.003

Myhill, D. (2002). Bad boys and good girls? Patterns of interaction and response in whole class teaching. *British Education Research Journal, 28*(3), 339–352.

Sedova, K., Salamounova, Z., & Svaricek, R. (2014). Troubles with dialogic teaching. *Learning, Culture and Social Interaction, 3*(4), 274–285. https://doi.org/10.1016/j.lcsi.2014.04.001.

Snell, J., & Lefstein, A. (2018). "Low ability", participation, and identity in dialogic pedagogy. *American Education Research Journal, 55*(1), 40–78.

Twiner, A., Littleton, K., Coffin, C., et al. (2014). Meaning making as an interactional accomplishment: A temporal analysis of intentionality and improvisation in classroom dialogue. *International Journal of Education Research, 63,* 94–106. https://doi.org/10.1016/j.ijer.2013.02.009.

Chapter 7
Teachers' Self-understanding and Emotions as the Catalysts of Change

Abstract This chapter focuses on the role of teachers' self-understanding and emotions in the process of change toward dialogic teaching. During the TPD program, we noticed that participating teachers differed in how they saw themselves, as well as in what emotions they expressed toward TPD, researchers, students, and their own teaching. We became interested in whether these differences could affect the outcomes of TPD, as individual teachers differed in the extent of the implemented changes. The analysis of the data presented in this chapter confirmed our expectations.

In this chapter, we first introduce concepts of self-understanding and emotions and then categorize participating teachers into four types according to their self-understanding and the emotions they experienced during the TPD program. Finally, we look at how different types of teachers differed in the extent of the changes they implemented. Our main finding was the positive role of negative emotions experienced during the TPD program.

7.1 Concepts and Data Analysis in This Chapter

We view teachers' self-understanding as a way for teachers to define themselves for themselves and for others. Kelchtermans (2005) identified five components of self-understanding. These are (a) self-image, the manner through which teachers define themselves, (b) job motivation, the driving force in their profession, (c) future perspective, the expectation teachers have of their future selves, (d) self-esteem, an assessment of their teaching, and (e) task perception, an ethical dimension containing assumptions as to what teachers have to do to become good teachers in the best interests of their students. These components in conjunction affect how teachers deal with professional challenges and how they approach their further education and development (Uitto et al. 2016). This is because teachers' self-understanding can explain their commitment to change along with behavior that accompanies it.

Researchers agree that teachers' self-understanding is strongly connected to their emotions (Lasky 2005; Van Veen et al. 2005; Zembylas 2003, 2005). Mulligan and Sherer (2012) define basic characteristics of emotions by claiming that they (a) have an episodic nature (i.e., a certain duration with a beginning and an end), (b) have intentionality (in the sense that they are directed toward achieving an objective), (c) include appraisal (which evaluates the objective as good or bad), and (d) are connected with bodily changes. Emotions are typically defined as feelings produced after certain stimulations (Pekrun et al. 2002). When thinking about the TPD program, the program itself and its components are the stimuli invoking emotions. Emotions can be seen as adaptation mechanisms that organisms use to regulate their social and organic survival. Emotions control human behavior because in themselves they are basic forms of decision making used by humans to respond appropriately in different situations (Immordino-Yang and Damasio 2007). Therefore, when people are acting, they are thinking about the situation and following their thoughts about what to do, but they are also feeling and following their emotions with the intention of feeling good.

There is agreement that teacher learning evokes a diverse range of emotions and that professional development programs often initiate strong emotional reactions in teachers (Lasky 2005; Reio 2005). Yoo and Carter (2017) identified four different types of emotions experienced by participants in teacher development program: (a) energy, excitement, passion, (b) inner conflict, frustration, discouragement, (c) vulnerability, engagement, hope, and (d) generosity, gratitude, inspiration. This line of research shows that every change, reform, or development in teaching is accompanied by various emotions, a considerable number of which are negative. We can assume that any process of change activates emotions. Darby (2008) and Van Veen et al. (2005) emphasized the important role of emotions, as emotions can instigate change, but they can also hinder it.

The analysis in this chapter aims to (a) identify emotions experienced by teachers who participated in our program, (b) explore how these emotions are related to teachers' self-understanding, and (c) identify what role these emotions played in the process of change. We analyzed the interviews with all eight teachers participating in the TPD program. The interviews were conducted before the program started, during the program, and after it finished (see Chap. 3).

For this chapter, we assigned coding focused on teachers' self-understanding based on Kelchtermans' five indicators (2005,2009): *self-image, job motivation, future perspective, self-esteem*, and *task perception*. In the next stage of analysis, we focused on emotions according to Pekrun et al. (2002) of: *enjoyment, anticipatory joy, hope, joy about success, satisfaction, pride, relief, gratitude, empathy, admiration, sympathy and love, boredom, hopelessness, anxiety, sadness, disappointment, shame and guilt, anger, jealousy and envy, contempt,* and *antipathy and hate*. For all the interviews, we coded passages that expressed these individual emotions. Subsequently, we linked the declared emotions to the teachers' self-understanding. Finally, we combined these analytic outcomes with quantitative data from classroom video recordings (see Chap. 4).

7.2 Self-understanding of Teachers Participating in the TPD Program

The following section describes a typology of self-understanding that we introduced through an analysis of teachers' utterances during workshops and individual reflective interviews. We divided teachers into four groups according to how they perceived themselves: (a) perfect—Marek, (b) eager-to-learn—Daniela, Vaclav, (c) positive—Radek, Hana, Marcela, and (d) insecure—Jonas, Martina.

7.2.1 Perfect Teachers

One teacher who participated in our project, Marek, perceived himself as a perfect teacher. As he said: "You know, I got the reputation that, probably, I am the best English teacher at this school. So, as I'm saying, like the kids know that I translate and they know I'm like super capable." According to Marek, his reputation is well known since his greatness is no secret to his students, their parents, or Marek's colleagues. Throughout the duration of the program, Marek's self-image was based on pride and positive self-evaluation.

Marek did not perceive his participation in the project as an opportunity to learn. He believed that he taught in accordance with the principles of dialogic teaching even before he joined the project. Marek mentioned that he saw the method of Socratic dialogue as an essential part of his teaching practice. In short, Marek saw his participation as an opportunity for the researchers to see what good teaching practice looks like. It was clear that he consistently created himself as the image of the perfect teacher, which corresponded with his high self-esteem.

During the project, Marek behaved in accordance with his construed self-understanding. In the video-stimulated interviews, Marek was generally content with his own performance and how his lessons went. He remained content with his own teaching even when the researcher Zuzana, who worked in a pair with Marek, critiqued a particular aspect of his teaching practice. Typically, during reflective interviews, Marek saw his approach as the best approach he could choose.

Regarding emotions, Marek experienced most often the emotions of pride and anger during the TPD program. He felt proud of himself, as can be seen from his perception of himself quoted above, and he was angry at others. In many cases, the recipients of Marek's anger were his students, who in his eyes did not react quickly enough, seemed unmotivated, and whose answers lacked the sophistication that Marek would have expected. For example, Marek described a situation in which his students needed more time to find the right answer than he found reasonable by saying: "I think I was generous enough by giving them this vast amount of time during which they could have formed their answer. Then I got fed up with it all since it they could not get it even after ten minutes."

Another recipient of Marek's anger was the researcher Zuzana. During reflective interviews, Marek repeatedly expressed his discontent with how the researcher assessed the situation in the classroom, tried to avoid critical reflections of his own practices, and challenged Zuzana's comments and suggestions. Sometimes, Marek shortened the time for reflective interviews (less than 60 min) or ignored the researcher's e-mails with comments on the observed lessons despite insisting on receiving them. He explained his behavior as due to having limited time and being constantly in high demand. We interpret this behavior as signs of not feeling completely comfortable during the TPD program.

It could be concluded that the *perfect* teacher's self-understanding and negative emotions limited the potential and impact of the project and the potential for learning through the reflective interviews. It seemed that for Marek, maintaining his self-image was more important than improving his teaching. Yet the findings of the video recordings (see Chap. 6) showed that Marek's classroom discourse changed positively. Even though Marek did not admit that he learned anything during the TPD program, repeated video recordings of his lessons clearly showed that learning happened.

7.2.2 Eager-to-Learn Teachers

Teachers with self-understanding as being eager-to-learn teachers were represented by Daniela and Vaclav, who saw themselves as ready to learn, improve, and do their job as well as possible. For example, both Daniela and Vaclav suggested that they always prepare their own lesson plans and teaching materials for each lesson without relying on course books and prescribed lesson plans. At the same time, they did not think that their teaching was always perfect. In an initial interview, Vaclav said: "I have to say that I do not always leave each lesson feeling great. But, as I see it, there are several ways that I can tell whether things worked." Vaclav acknowledged that a teacher can fail to an extent and can then actively investigate how the classes went, for example, by asking the students for feedback. When these teachers felt that their classes did not go as planned, they sought the cause in themselves. As the following statement by Daniela shows: "It can sometimes happen that they're [students] not paying attention, that they're having a bad day, but I take it a sign for myself. I mean they're not paying attention because maybe something is troubling them or they don't get it."

Throughout the TPD program, Daniela and Vaclav behaved in accordance with this description. They saw the aims of the program as compatible with their own task perception and hence tried to maximize the amount of input from researchers. They actively tested tools introduced in workshops. These teachers were eager-to-learn even when they were given challenging tasks. In situations in which they thought they improved, they committed to further improvements, as they saw individual improvements as temporary stages. They also accepted researchers' critiques and perceived them as a feedback tool.

Both Daniela and Vaclav felt a wide range of emotions during the project. Those were mostly positive, such as hope and joy. In the interviews, both of them often said "I hope I will do it well" (before their lessons) and "I hope I did it well" (after their lessons). Daniela expressed joy because using new teaching methods helped her achieve better results. As for their relationships with the researchers, the eager-to-learn teachers expressed sympathy and gratitude. Daniela, for example, expressed her gratitude to the researcher working in tandem with her by saying: "I learned so much thanks to Klara." Such positive emotions coincided with the teachers' self-reflection because the researchers kept them on task. This in turn strengthened the teachers' self-esteem and improved their self-image: the teachers wanted to learn and improve, and the researchers supported them in this.

Yet, even these teachers experienced negative emotions during the project. When Vaclav's lesson did not go according to plan despite all his preparations, Vaclav was disappointed. Disappointment can evoke yet another negative emotion: anxiety. These teachers did not feel anxiety when trying the new methods for the first time but after partial failures. Daniela described how she felt anxious and nervous about using the new methods in future lessons. Yet her perseverance and ability to learn led not to rejection of the new methods but to their continual testing until she learned to use them well.

7.2.3 Positive Teachers

Positive teachers in this research project were Radek, Hana, and Marcela. These teachers had healthy self-esteem and believed they did not encounter problems doing their job. They also told the researchers that they received positive feedback from their students and colleagues, which pleased them. Their self-image also reflected their affection for teaching in general and their subjects in particular.

The most common emotions these teachers experienced were enjoyment and satisfaction. They also emphasized a particular sense of a community within the school. In contrast with perfect teachers, positive teachers did not see themselves as exceptional and better than the others. Instead, they felt themselves to be part of a community that shares similar values and acts in similar ways.

Positive teachers were visibly interested in the well-being of their students and wanted them to be happy and enjoy classes. Sympathy and empathy dominated their relationships with their students. For instance, Hana said it is important to "have a good time" in class. Positive teachers showed their care by trying to engage their students and being interested in their thoughts and opinions. On the other hand, these teachers may relax the difficulty of their subjects and emphasize shared fun.

Similar to their relations with students, positive teachers were understanding and empathetic toward the researchers. They wanted their shared time to be as pleasant as possible and wanted the researchers to be satisfied. This motivated them to do what the researchers asked of them. These teachers generally evaluated the whole project positively and appreciated the presence of impartial and knowledgeable observers in the classroom. These teachers aimed to fulfill researchers' expectations, and they also cared for the mental well-being of the researchers and hoped they would not regret conducting the project with their chosen teachers.

The positive teachers were friendly and sociable to the point of preparing snacks for their interviews and asking about personal matters. While the teachers looked forward to talking to the researchers, they took the video recordings as a task that just needed to be done. During her interviews, teacher Hana often asked researcher Klara, "Will this be enough?" and inquired whether her lesson included a satisfactory amount of the observed indicators. Positive teachers generally attempted to make progress that would be above a certain minimal threshold so that the researchers would be content and, in turn, the teachers as well. In this, they differed from the eager-to-learn teachers who understood progress as a temporary stage on a continuum of success that needed further work and attempted to achieve more and more.

When the researchers suggested that a teacher's performance was not entirely satisfactory, the positive teachers tended to avoid discussion or downplay its significance. The positive teachers did not appreciate it when their good times were questioned. Nonetheless, they could skillfully change the direction of a conversation, soften the critical reflection (or completely avoid it), and reestablish mutual understanding between themselves and the researchers.

7.2.4 Insecure Teachers

There were two insecure teachers in our sample: Jonas and Martina. These teachers were not confident that they could perceive themselves as good teachers. They wanted to see themselves this way, which explains why they chose to participate in this development program. As for their teaching practices, they were unsure whether their methods were the right ones and whether their practices would be approved by the researchers, which worried them. Their insecurity was apparent in both their self-image and task orientation, which is indicated in Martina's perception of herself as a teacher: "I don't know. I think that the way I teach is related to my character, I don't like orders... I'm non-directive and that maybe it's a problem, I don't know... but maybe it's wrong, I don't know."

Insecure teachers regularly experienced negative emotions during the project. They often showed their disappointment regarding their performance and anxiety whether they would be at all capable of changing it in the future. The researchers hardly critiqued these teachers, since these teachers tended to be highly critical of themselves. These teachers often questioned their own teaching methods, and they accepted researchers' suggestions without reservations, appreciated their input, and were often thankful to the researchers since they believed that the researchers tried to help them become better teachers.

The insecure teachers showed disappointment with themselves and even guilt for not having acted as the researcher suggested, as indicated by Martina's remarks: "So why didn't I actually do that? I think I didn't really think it through." She also showed gratitude to the researcher, which meant acknowledging the researcher's knowledge. The insecure teachers shared thoughtfulness and eagerness to understand with the eager-to-learn teachers. Yet the insecure teachers were more skeptical about their expectations of their future ability and in their critical reflections. Even when these teachers identified partial successes in their video recordings, they showed no signs of higher self-esteem or success in the reflective interviews that followed.

Another feature typical of the insecure teachers was questioning the possibility of their ever improving, as Martina suggested: "That seems to be beyond me." Expressing hopelessness, to them, did not mean giving up attempting to improve. The insecure teachers were active in trying to understand how they could use the methods proposed by the researchers in their teaching practice. After accepting what the researchers suggested to them, the insecure teachers asked follow-up questions for specific details about using proposed methods in their teaching practice. Hence, hopelessness as a negative emotion did not prevent these teachers from attempting to improve. We are of the view that the insecure teachers used self-critique and self-reflection as a defensive strategy.

The insecure teachers were generally surprised when researchers pointed out their progress in video-recorded sessions. For example, Jonas commented on a successful interaction with a female student as follows: "Wow, she's really cool. I didn't even notice that, you know, in the lesson." If something went well, insecure teachers believed it was thanks to the students and not because of their own abilities. Consequently, they expressed low self-esteem through considerable self-critique. At the same time, this was not a strategy for becoming passive: the insecure teachers were keen to learn. Yet, they did not expect any significant improvement, and they did not acknowledge when they did improve.

7.3 Connection Between Self-understanding, Emotions, and Change in Teaching Practices

The previous section showed that teachers experienced emotions related to their type of self-understanding during the education development program we conducted, as Table 7.1 shows. In this section, we closely examine whether there is a connection between the experienced emotions and the effects of the TPD program (by effects, we mean changes in the teaching practices of the participating teachers).

To assess the difference in teaching practices, we compared episodes recorded before the program started and after it ended (see Chap. 3). We perceived that the change was represented by the presence of selected indicators of dialogic teaching, with student thoughts with reasoning considered the most important. Our analyses showed that classroom discourse changed significantly during the observed lessons. There were on average 2.41 student thoughts with reasoning in one lesson before the program started; there were 8.93 thoughts after the program ended. On average, there were 6.52 more student thoughts with reasoning per each lesson. However,

Table 7.1 Typology of teachers according to their self-understanding and experienced emotions

Type	Selected teachers	Self-understanding	Emotions
Perfect	Marek	I'm a good teacher because I'm the best at everything	Pride, Anger
Eager–to-learn	Daniela, Vaclav	I'm a good teacher because I want to learn and improve	Hope, Joy about success, Sympathy, Anxiety, Disappointment
Positive	Radek, Hana, Marcela	I'm a good teacher because I have good relationships with students and teach without having any problems	Enjoyment, Satisfaction, Empathy
Insecure	Jonas, Martina	I'm not sure if I'm a good teacher	Hopelessness, Anxiety, Disappointment, Shame and Guilt, Gratitude, Admiration

Table 7.2 shows that the results for individual teachers differed: Jonas, for example, improved significantly, while the improvements by Radek, Hana, and Marcela were below average.

Combining the results in Table 2 with our previous analysis shows that the teachers who changed little (Radek and Marcela) or not at all (Hana) belonged to the positive teacher group. They were content with themselves and felt no need to improve. Even though they showed willingness to meet up with the researchers, their results in Table 7.2 show that their teaching practices did not transform or transformed very little during the program.

Table 7.2 Distribution of student thoughts with reasoning in lessons

	Pre					Post					
	Mean	N	SD	Min.	Max.	Mean	N	SD	Min.	Max.	Difference
Jonas	2.00	5	2.82	0	7	27.00	2	1.41	26	28	25.00
Radek	1.75	8	1.75	0	5	4.00	3	3.61	0	7	1.86
Hana	3.33	6	5.20	0	11	3.33	6	3.61	0	9	0.00
Vaclav	3.57	7	3.31	0	10	13.83	6	14.99	3	40	10.26
Marcela	3.00	5	3.16	0	8	6.14	7	6.81	0	21	3.81
Daniela	1.36	11	1.56	0	5	8.63	8	10.04	0	23	8.68
Marek	0.00	2	0	0	0	8.66	6	6.62	0	17	8.66
Martina	3.43	7	3.95	0	10	10.20	5	10.37	0	26	6.94
All	2.41	51	3.04	0	11	8.93	43	9.72	0	40	6.52

7.4 Why Do Emotions and Self-understanding Make a Difference?

In this chapter, we identified different types of teachers' self-understanding that corresponded with recurring combinations of emotions. We showed that interactions between the participants and the researchers were often affected by the teachers' emotions and their need to maintain a positive self-understanding. We established that experienced emotions are related to whether a change in teaching practices occurs. A number of authors pointed out that teacher behavior is to a considerable degree driven by emotions (Korthagen 2017; Immordino-Yang and Damasio 2007). Our analysis is in concordance with this.

Further, our findings showed that the emotions the teachers experienced were related to their self-understanding. In this aspect, our findings corresponded with some previous research concerning teachers' emotions in a process of reform. Zembylas (2005) and Van Veen et al. (2005) claimed that teachers experience positive emotions if a required change is in accordance with their subjective ideas about good teaching (Kelchtermans 2005). If the teachers are asked to make a change that is not in accordance with their task perception, it provokes a negative emotional response (Van Veen et al. 2005).

Our data indicated a more complex reality. In fact, none of the teachers who participated in the TPD program was against dialogic teaching. On the contrary, all the teachers wanted to participate in our project and agreed with its theoretical background. Yet, nearly all teachers (with the exception of positive teachers) experienced both positive and negative emotions. We believe that it was not task perception (i.e., the teachers' conception of good teaching) but their self-esteem and self-image (see Kelchtermans 2005) that was in charge of teachers' emotions. Hence, the questions of if and why our teachers perceived themselves as good proved to be central. The teacher's behavior could therefore be attributed to their preservation of positive self-esteem and self-image (in the cases of perfect teachers, eager-to-learn teachers, and positive teachers). Alternatively, it could be attributed to wanting to make themselves feel that way (as was the case of insecure teachers).

Marek, our example of a perfect teacher, believed that he had all the necessary skills. He rejected critical suggestions from the researcher, reacting with anger, antipathy, and ostentatious rejection of his support. Yet the results in Table 7.2 show changes in his behavior. These changes were most probably caused by his wish to prevent further critical comments and maintain his self-understanding as a perfect teacher.

Eager-to-learn teachers described themselves as people who like to learn and improve. Critical comments from the researchers did not cause negative emotions in these teachers. Such emotions arose only when they could not achieve certain aspects of dialogic teaching in their classes the way they would have wished. These minor failures were understood as signals of their slow or inefficient learning, which in turn threatened their self-understanding. These teachers tried hard to overcome early setbacks and they succeeded. Hence, their positive self-understanding was maintained.

Positive teachers were the only ones who did not experience negative emotions. They were understanding of the researchers but accepted their critical suggestions only when these could be accommodated with minor changes in their teaching practices. When positive teachers received more substantial critique, they retreated, though they were not angry or hostile. Sustaining good relations with both their students and the researchers was important to them, and this was reflected in their behavior. They did not make substantial changes in order not to jeopardize the relaxed atmosphere in their classes. On the other hand, they did make some minor changes so as to not threaten their good relationships with the researchers. Positive teachers commented on these partial changes and emphasized their significance and usefulness.

Insecure teachers did not strive to maintain positive self-esteem and self-image. Yet it should not be overlooked that they wanted to improve during the project. Insecure teachers used the negative emotions they experienced (hopelessness, anxiety, disappointment, shame, and guilt) as a certain protective shield. Researchers minimized their own critique once they were presented with the insecure teachers' self-critique and tried to emphasize that they perceived these teachers as capable of making change. This encouraged these teachers who consequently changed their behavior. This further improved their positive image in the eyes of the researchers and improved their self-esteem and self-image.

A key finding of our analysis was that negative emotions fuel change. The group of teachers who did not improve were the ones who did not experience negative emotions. This finding contradicted the current understanding according to which teaching and teacher development are facilitated by positive emotions (see for example Danner et al. 2001; Fredrickson 1998, 2001; Fredrickson and Joiner 2002; Wyer et al. 1999).

Our key finding according to which negative emotions stimulate teaching is supported by the research by Darby (2008) examining a school undergoing a reform initiative due to the poor academic achievement of its students. During the reform, teachers' practices were found to be ineffective. This caused negative emotions of fear and intimidation as teachers' professional self-understanding (especially their self-esteem and self-image) were challenged. The facilitators involved in the reform helped the teachers to overcome their nervousness and fear of being judged. Eventually, both the academic achievement of students and the instructional practices of teachers improved. These positive changes made the involved teachers feel proud and excited. Darby (2008) argued that strong negative emotions at the beginning of the reform stimulated the teachers to change. In order to improve their self-understanding (which was challenged by negative emotions), the teachers were highly willing to change their teaching practices. According to Darby (2008), negative emotions were necessary for the teachers to improve because they served as stimuli for learning. We believe that the same message emerged from the analysis of teachers' emotions experienced during our TPD program. Negative emotions have strong potential to work as catalysts during TPD as they guide teachers toward some kind of a change as a means of restoring a positive self-understanding.

7.5 Summary

In this chapter, we strove to explain possible sources of the differences in the extent of the change of classroom discourse between teachers participating in our TPD program. We investigated their self-understanding and emotions. We identified four different types of teachers' self-understanding: perfect, eager-to-learn, positive, and insecure. These types of self-understanding corresponded with specific combinations of emotions that teachers experienced during the TPD program.

The perfect teacher experienced pride and anger. Eager-to-learn teachers dealt with hope, joy, sympathy, anxiety, and disappointment. Positive teachers expressed enjoyment, satisfaction, and empathy. Insecure teachers reported feelings of hopelessness, anxiety, disappointment, shame and guilt, gratitude, and admiration. This enumeration indicates that the spectrum of emotions emerging in the process of teacher development was broad and included both positive and negative emotions.

A key finding of our analysis in this chapter was that when negative emotions were absent, the extent of the change of classroom discourse was limited. Thus, we understand the negative emotions as a catalyst for change. They serve as stimuli for learning, as they threaten teachers' self-understanding, and this motivates teachers to change their teaching to restore or establish positive self-esteem and self-image.

Only one group of teachers in our research did not experience negative emotions. We called them positive teachers. These teachers stayed happy and relaxed throughout the whole TPD program, and they kept the teaching practices they were used to. By contrast, the other teachers in the sample (perfect, eager-to-learn, and insecure) were pushed by their negative emotions to make a change in their practices.

References

Danner, D. D., Snowdon, D. A., & Friesen, W. V. (2001). Positive emotions in early life and longevity: Findings from the nun study. *Journal of Personality and Social Psychology, 80*(5), 804–813. https://doi.org/10.1037//0022-3514.80.5.804

Darby, A. (2008). Teachers' emotions in the reconstruction of professional self-understanding. *Teach Teach Educ, 24*(5), 1160–1172. https://doi.org/10.1016/j.tate.2007.02.001

Fredrickson, B. L. (1998). What good are positive emotions? *Rev Gen Psychol, 2*(3), 300–319. https://doi.org/10.1037/1089-2680.2.3.300

Fredrickson, B. L. (2001). The role of positive emotions in positive psychology: The broaden-and-build theory of positive emotions. *American Psychologist, 56*(3), 218–226. https://doi.org/10.1037//0003-066X.56.3.218

Fredrickson, B. L., & Joiner, T. (2002). Positive emotions trigger upward spirals toward emotional well-being. *Psychological Science, 13*(2), 172–175. https://doi.org/10.1111/1467-9280.00431

Immordino-Yang, M. H., & Damasio, A. (2007). We feel, therefore we learn: The relevance of affective and social neuroscience to education. *Mind Brain Educ, 1*(1), 3–10. https://doi.org/10.1111/j.1751-228X.2007.00004.x

Kelchtermans, G. (2005). Teachers' emotions in educational reforms: Self-understanding, vulnerable commitment and micropolitical literacy. *Teaching and Teacher Education, 21*(8), 995–1006. https://doi.org/10.1016/j.tate.2005.06.009

Kelchtermans, G., Ballet, K., and Piot, L. (2009). Surviving diversity in times of performativity: Understanding teachers' emotional experience of change. P. A Schutz and M. Zembylas (Eds.) *Advances in Teacher Emotion Research: The Impact on Teachers' Lives* (pp. 215–232). New York: Springer.

Korthagen, F. (2017). Inconvenient truths about teacher learning: Towards professional development 3.0. *Teachers and Teaching: Theory and Practice, 23*(4):387–405. https://doi.org/10.1080/13540602.2016.1211523

Lasky, S. (2005). A sociocultural approach to understanding teacher identity, agency and professional vulnerability in a context of secondary school reform. *Teaching and Teacher Education, 21*(8), 899–916. https://doi.org/10.1016/j.tate.2005.06.003

Mulligan, K., & Scherer, K. R. (2012). Toward a working definition of emotion. *Emotion Review, 4*(4), 345–357. https://doi.org/10.1177/1754073912445818

Pekrun, R., Goetz, T., Titz, W., et al. (2002). Academic emotions in students' selfregulated learning and achievement: A program of qualitative and quantitative research. *Educational Psychology, 37*(2), 91–105. https://doi.org/10.1207/S15326985EP3702_4

Reio, T. G., Jr. (2005). Emotions as a lens to explore teacher identity and change: A commentary. *Teaching and Teacher Education, 21*(8), 985–993. https://doi.org/10.1016/j.tate.2005.06.008

Uitto, M., Kaunisto, S.-L., Kelchtermans, G., et al. (2016). Peer group as a meeting place: Reconstructions of teachers" self-understanding and the presence of vulnerability. *International Journal of Education Research, 75,* 7–16. https://doi.org/10.1016/j.ijer.2015.10.004

Van Veen, K., Sleegers, P., & van de Ven, P.-H. (2005). One teacher"s identity, emotions, and commitment to change: A case study into the cognitive-affective processes of a secondary school teacher in the context of reforms. *Teaching and Teacher Education, 21*(8), 917–934. https://doi.org/10.1016/j.tate.2005.06.004

Wyer, R. S., Jr., Clore, G. L., & Isbell, L. M. (1999). Affect and information processing. *Advances in Experimental Social Psychology, 31,* 1–77. https://doi.org/10.1016/S0065-2601(08)60271-3

Yoo, J., & Carter, D. (2017). Teacher emotions and learning as praxis: Professional development that matters. *Australian Journal of Teacher Education, 42*(3), 38–52. https://doi.org/10.14221/ajte.2017v42n3.3

Zembylas, M. (2003). Emotions and teacher identity: A poststructural perspective. *Teaching and Teacher Education, 9*(3), 213–238. https://doi.org/10.1080/13540600309378

Zembylas, M. (2005). Discursive practices, genealogies, and emotional rules: A poststructuralist view on emotion and identity in teaching. *Teach Teach Educ, 21*(8), 935–948. https://doi.org/10.1016/j.tate.2005.06.005

Chapter 8
Generic Processes Behind Dialogic Teaching Implementation: Discussion and Conclusion

Abstract This chapter concludes the story of our TPD and research project. First, we will summarize the main results reported in the individual chapters to briefly review what we have found. Second, we open a discussion about what led to any changes. We consider how the participating teachers surpassed various obstacles associated with dialogic teaching that are usually seen as critical. We also describe the general processes that we see as responsible for the success of participating teachers in transforming their teaching practices—appropriation of teaching tools and reflection. Finally, we share some concluding remarks, including our thoughts on possible directions for future research.

8.1 What Have We Found?

In this book, we described a teacher development program aimed at changing classroom talk. In developing this program, we were inspired by theories postulating that speech can stimulate student thinking and learning (see Chap. 1). Although these theories and their related pedagogies have become very popular in recent decades, teachers who teach accordingly can only rarely be found in mainstream schools. As reported by Wilkinson et al. (2017), teachers find the implementation of dialogic practices to be highly challenging. This has motivated many researchers and research teams to try to establish how this situation could be changed. One way to achieve such a change lies in the professional development of teachers (see Sect. 2.2). However, actual TPD projects in this field have reported variable outcomes—some proved successful in achieving change; some did not. This motivated us to attempt our own teacher development program and analyze its effects. We wanted to succeed in getting dialogic teaching into classrooms and to acquire substantive knowledge about the mechanisms of change. As stated by Hofmann (2020), there is a need to identify generative mechanisms that can bring about change. This is what we attempted when analyzing the data.

We carried out a TPD program based on theoretical input (workshops), experiences in authentic settings (lessons taught during the TPD program), and reflection (reflective interviews). The aim of the TPD program was to help teachers to implement indicators of dialogic teaching (open questions of high cognitive demand, uptake, open discussion, and student thoughts with reasoning) and to maintain the principles of dialogic teaching (collectivity and purposefulness). To measure the change, we compared lessons before the program started and at its end. When evaluating the effects of the program (see Chap. 4), we found that the occurrence of dialogic teaching indicators increased in the participating classes. Teachers started asking more open questions of high cognitive demand and giving more uptake to students, students started formulating more thoughts with reasoning, and the amount of open discussion time was prolonged. We also found that the measured indicators correlated. The more teachers used open questions of high cognitive demand, uptake, and open discussion, the more student thoughts with reasoning occurred. This means that teachers can change the talk behavior of their students. We see this as an important result of our research. Teachers sometimes argue that implementing dialogic teaching is questionable, as students are not ready to take part in authentic and challenging dialogues or discussions (see Pimentel and McNeill 2013; Snell and Lefstein 2018). Our results show that students are very sensitive to teacher talk behavior. When the teacher goes dialogic, students respond accordingly.

Our analysis showed that the TPD program strengthened two principles of dialogic teaching: collectivity and purposefulness. As a consequence of the program, more students spoke in the lessons and, at the same time, more time during the lessons was focused on curriculum and devoted to the educational goals set by teachers. Moreover, we found that a symbiotic relationship was created between the implemented indicators and the principles of dialogic teaching. Asking open questions of high cognitive demand strengthened the purposefulness of teaching and the occurrence of open discussion had a positive impact on collectivity. These results show that the concept of dialogic teaching is a coherent system of elements that can work in synergy with each other.

The statistical analyses we performed confirmed the effectiveness and success of the TPD program. However, we were not only interested in whether teachers improved in their implementation of features of dialogic teaching; we also inquired as to how such a process of change took place. Therefore, we monitored the development trajectories of individual teachers during the TPD program with the aim of studying the microgenetics of teacher learning (see Walkoe and Luna 2020). In this book, we presented two case studies (Chaps. 5 and 6) that we consider representative because the phenomena depicted in each study were observable across the whole sample of participating teachers. We discovered that change did not take the form of a gradual step-by-step improvement. Instead, it occurred in phases of progress that alternated with phases of stagnation and, in some cases, even of regression. It commonly happened that a teacher's effort to improve one aspect of their teaching led to the deterioration of another aspect. We termed this the phenomenon of unintended consequences. Moreover, when a teacher felt insecure, there was an apparent tendency to go back to the habitual behavioral patterns established prior to entering

TPD program. Both unintended consequences and returns to gestalts explain why the progression of change was occasionally interrupted.

Also, we demonstrated that the complex nature of dialogic teaching (see Sects. 2.1 and 2.3.3) generates tensions and conflicts between partial elements. We see these tensions and conflicts as side effects of the implementation of new talk patterns in the classroom. Their incidence during the development process is natural, but they have to be monitored and considered in order to be overcome. We examined two serious conflicts that we diagnosed during the TPD program in detail. The first conflict occurred when the teacher focused on engaging students in lively conversation and neglected curricular matters, thereby making the dialogue purposeless. The second conflict happened when the teacher invited only some students perceived as capable into dialogic conversation, thereby making the dialogue uncollective. The case studies showed that when conflicts, unintended consequences, and gestalts were recognized, the teachers were able to work actively to overcome them, primarily through experimenting with their teaching methods.

During the TPD program, we became aware that teachers' self-understanding and emotions are at play and affect the scope of change. We noticed individual differences among the teachers and tried to ascertain why some of them underwent a more comprehensive change than others (see Chap. 7). We showed that the process of change puts teachers' self-understanding at stake and that this generated strong and often negative emotions. Surprisingly, our data emphasized the importance of negative emotions. Our data show that the desired change does not occur (or is limited in its extent) if negative emotions are not activated and teachers do not attempt to overcome them.

8.2 What Made Change Happen?

While designing the program, we relied on a number of recommendations formulated in the literature that describe the features of programs that are effective in stimulating teachers' professional development (Borko et al. 2008; Desimone 2009; Ponte et al. 2004; Van de Pol et al. 2017; Wayne et al. 2008; Wilkinson et al. 2017). The TPD program we implemented included three components: theoretical, experiential, and reflective. At the workshops, teachers were introduced to the concept of dialogic teaching and its indicators and principles (thus they encountered the theoretical component), experimented with the introduced indicators and principles in their own teaching (thus encountering the experiential component), and reflected on their teaching experience in tandem with a researcher (thus encountering the reflective component). The program was designed as an experiential learning program with a strong foundation in theory and support in reflection.

Thanks to the procedures used in the program implementation, data collection, and analysis, we developed a successful teacher development program and proved its effectiveness, and we opened new perspectives on how to understand the situation of teachers who are trying to significantly transform their teaching practices. This allows us to enter into discussions on how to support teachers through effective professional education. However, our focal point is not to present the traits of a successful TPD program. We believe that the success of a TPD program was (and always is) founded in the actions of the participating teachers. Therefore, in the following discussion we will concentrate on how teachers acted during our TPD program and how they—with the support of researchers—managed to change.

8.2.1 Troubles with Dialogic Teaching Overcome

In Sect. 2.3, we summarized the troubles that teachers have to face when they decide to start with dialogic teaching. Based on literature in the field, we identified three clusters of obstacles that could prevent the transformation to dialogic teaching: organizational constraints, teacher mindset, and complexity of change. We now discuss how teachers participating in our TPD program overcame these obstacles. According to our analysis, these three clusters are interconnected, and finding a way to cope with one cluster can help in coping with the other clusters.

8.2.1.1 Coping with Organizational Constraints

The scheduled time and duration of a lesson, the pre-defined content given by the curriculum, and a high number of students in the classroom are often seen as constraints against dialogic teaching in ordinary classrooms (see, e.g., Lefstein 2010; Michaels and O'Connor 2015; Resnick et al. 2018; Sedova et al. 2014). In our two case studies (see Chaps. 5 and 6), we showed that during our TPD program, the teachers faced all these constraints.

Time constraints are perceived to be serious because in dialogic teaching teachers elaborate ideas introduced by students (Lefstein 2010), and the duration of this is difficult to predict. Interestingly, the teachers participating in our TPD program coped with the time pressure quite smoothly. This was due to careful lesson planning and due to instruction from the researchers that it is not necessary to keep the whole lesson dialogic. Rather, the researchers recommended that teachers rhythmize classroom discourse through alternating between dialogic and non-dialogic phases (see Scott 2008; Nurkka et al. 2014). This enabled the teachers to be economical with time as the non-dialogic phases were easier to control for the pace and duration. Despite this, sometimes the teachers had difficulty estimating the time demands of a dialogic activity they had planned for the given lesson, which resulted in the necessity of leaving out part of the planned lesson. When this happened, in the next lesson the teacher modified their teaching methods or reduced the lesson plan so as to not be under time pressure again. However, teachers became quickly habituated to the fact that to give authentic voice to students means to devote more time to the interaction with them. They learned not to overfill the lesson plan and not to insist on keeping everything in the lesson. They developed the capacity to spontaneously modify the course of the lesson in order to get on with time schedule. This development was in accordance with notion of Twiner et al. (2014) that flexible interplay is needed between a teacher's planned discourse trajectory and the trajectories that spontaneously emerge from the interactions between teacher and students.

For the participating teachers, troubles with the curriculum and with the high number of students were more painful. Concerning curriculum, the teachers repeatedly digressed from the content they felt obligated to teach for the sake of enhancing student participation in classroom talk. This was apparent in both case studies, more prominently in Daniela's lessons (e.g., Lessons 6 and 7). The teacher designed the lesson to let the students talk, but the educational goals were repressed (Lesson 6), or vice versa the educational goals were accomplished but the talk patterns were authoritative ones (Lesson 7). The quantity of students in the classroom was also challenging, as was demonstrated primarily in Marek's case study. This teacher had chosen which students would be nominated to talk and he saw it as impossible to address the class as a whole. As a consequence of this, part of the class was always left aside waiting for a turn.

The teachers gradually learned how to deal with the curriculum and the students when teaching dialogically. This went in parallel with how they changed their own mindsets and gained control over the complexity of the change. We discuss here the organizational constraints in connection with these two issues.

8.2.1.2 Shifting Teacher Mindset

As reported by Butler et al. (2004), changing teacher practices inevitably involves achieving a shift in teachers' conceptual knowledge about teaching. Hennessy and Davies (2020) claimed that a specific teacher mindset is needed for implementing dialogic teaching. First of all, these authors stress trust in dialogic teaching to be a necessary prerequisite for transformation. There is evidence that a strong theoretical background legitimizes the change in the eyes of teachers and thus increases the effectiveness of development programs (Adey 2006; Butler et al. 2004). Therefore, we based the TPD program on a strong theoretical and research background with which we tried to convince participating teachers to the benefits of dialogic teaching.

During the workshops, the teachers responded positively to the arguments for dialogic teaching. They were in favor of the idea of dialogic teaching even before the program started; this is why they voluntarily decided to take part. Moreover, some of them believed that they were already teaching dialogically, even before the program started. In sum, there was no serious problem with trust in dialogic teaching across the sample of participating teachers.

However, many more subtle facets of their thinking and beliefs had to be changed for the transformation to occur. The first mindset we discuss here is related to curricular constraints. If teachers were to overcome the tension between the limits defined by the curriculum and the extension of space for ideas introduced by students (see Lefstein 2010), they had to change their conception of what it means to let students talk.

Sedova et al. (2014) analyzed interviews with teachers and found that teachers perceived dialogue with students as desirable, as it makes students active and engaged and contributes to building positive relationships between teachers and students. At the same time, they did not believe that it was possible to construct disciplinary knowledge through dialogue. In this view, efficient teaching means delivering knowledge to students through authoritative methods of teaching—exposition of information and facts conveyed by the teacher. Only then, it is reasonable to give space to the students to let them express and share their opinions. The purpose of this sharing is to increase student engagement, interest, and well-being. Similarly, Resnick et al. (2018) claimed that teachers believe that students must learn facts (typically presented to them by the teacher) before they can take part in meaningful dialogue. In this interpretation, learning is seen as accumulating bits of information through drill and practice. Dialogue is not seen as tool for increasing the effectivity of instruction.

This viewpoint was also typical for the teachers in our sample. At the beginning, all of them wanted to enter in dialogue with their students, but they struggled to make this dialogue contribute to knowledge building. This struggle was manifested in purposeless dialogic sequences (see Sect. 6.3.1). Their conception of dialogue and discussion was primarily one of relaxation and fun in the classroom. During the TPD program, they shifted this mindset toward the belief that it is possible to build new knowledge through dialogic activity. This can be seen, e.g., in the difference between Daniela's Lesson 6 (students talked about what is in a picture, unrelated to the interpretation of a given literary text) and Lesson 9 (students talked about what it means to be heroic, strongly contributing to the interpretation of the given literary text). For Daniela, being able to plan and perform Lesson 9 required shifting from the mindset of dialogue as fun and relaxing to the mindset of dialogue as a tool for knowledge building. This achieved the vision of Mercer et al. (2019) concerning harmonizing curriculum and the dialogic approach, as dialogue develops learning and thinking skills in students and thus supports the curricular aims.

The second mindset to shift during the TPD program concerned students and their characteristics and abilities. There is agreement in the field that teacher understanding of student capabilities is essential for implementing dialogic teaching (Hofmann 2020). A number of studies reported that teachers commonly believe that not all students are capable of engaging in challenging dialogue (e.g., Pimentel and McNeill 2013; Resnick et al. 2018; Snell and Lefstein 2018). Snell and Lefstein (2018) see teacher beliefs about student ability as fixed and context-independent, and as a barrier to implementing dialogic teaching as at the core of this pedagogy is the requirement of active pupil participation in academically challenging classroom discourse. For a transformation to happen, a mindset about student ability as a product of that individual's interaction with the environment is needed (Snell and Lefstein 2018).

Troubles with mindsets about students were noticeable in Marek's case study. This teacher believed that it is not possible to address all of the students in the class with challenging questions and therefore excluded many students from authentic dialogue, nominating them to talk only when the conversation was easy and non-challenging. In this case study, implementation of full-blown dialogic teaching was clearly only possible after Marek overcame this mindset and involved all the students in demanding dialogic interaction. Daniela also had to rethink some assumptions about students and their ability and willingness to participate. She treated all students in the classroom similarly, but she struggled with how demanding the tasks she assigned to them should be, as she expected that demanding tasks and questions would undermine student zest for participation. For her, to abandon her mindset about student preference for effortless activities was essential. Similar movements were observable across the whole sample of teachers. All of them had to recognize that students do not have completely fixed abilities, preferences, and talk patterns; rather their behavior is shaped by the classroom context that they share with the teacher and their classmates (Gresalfi 2009). The teachers gradually recognized during the TPD program that their students are able to change their talk patterns when they get the chance. This was very clear in Marek's case study. When the students perceived as non-capable and "slow" had the chance to assert their voices, they did so. This convinced the teacher to shift his mindset about them.

A question arises of what caused the change in teacher mindset. Our data show that it was primarily the experience with how changes in the teaching modified the context. In other words, we do not think that a shift in teacher mindset preceded the change in teaching practices. Rather contrariwise, teachers experimented with altering their teaching practices and thus had the opportunity to observe how changeable student's reactions were and that it is possible to use dialogic teaching in the service of curricular goals. These unexpected experiences made them question their previous beliefs. Once the teachers shifted their mindsets, they started being open to new experiences confirming their newly emerging perspectives. This started a spiral on which both shifted mindsets and altered teaching practices came hand in hand.

8.2.1.3 Controlling the Complexity of Change

According to Hennessy and Davies (2020), one reason that TPD programs on dialogic teaching may have limited impact is the overwhelming complexity of the required change. In Sect. 2.1, we introduced various partial elements that are expected to work in synergy. Teachers should at the same time use an appropriate repertoire of teaching talk, implement adequate indicators of dialogic teaching, and keep all of the principles of dialogic teaching. This all has to co-create a dialogic stance in which students participate authentically and produce thoughtful utterances that build upon and relate to what has already been said by the teacher and their peers (Boyd and Markarian 2011).

However, it is not easy for teachers to control so many elements at the same time and therefore the transition to dialogic teaching is extremely challenging (Resnick et al. 2018). This was manifested in both of our case studies (see Chaps. 6 and 7) through phenomena of unintended consequence (see Sect. 5.3.2) and conflict between partial elements (see Sect. 6.3). Nevertheless, the participating teachers achieved harmonization in the end; the system started working in synergy with the individual indicators and principles supporting each other (see Sect. 4.4.2).

According to Van de Pol et al. (2017), when conducting a TPD program on dialogic teaching, it is important to choose the central conceptual framework around which the program is organized. Teachers must be given sufficient resources to understand the nature of the intervention, but they must not be overwhelmed by overlapping and related concepts. As reported by Gomez Zaccarelli et al. (2018), it is difficult for teachers to change classroom discourse as a whole. Bearing this in mind, we had to decide which level of system of dialogic teaching to make central. We chose indicators as a starting point because they are easy to measure, so it is possible to perform instant checks that reveal whether change is taking place. We did not intend to narrow change only to the level of indicators; instead, we assumed that by influencing this element of dialogic teaching we would influence the remaining elements as well.

Therefore, during the workshop stage of our project, we encouraged the teachers to use indicators in their lessons. In addition, we systematically discussed with them whether the use of indicators in their teaching led to the establishment of a dialogic talk repertoire (dialogue, deliberation, argumentation, or discussion). A case in point is presented in the study of teacher Daniela (Chap. 5): in one of the lessons, Daniela asked a substantially higher number of open questions of high cognitive demand, but the students remained relatively passive and no real discussion followed. In cases like these, we work with teachers on modifying their use of a particular indicator so that it better contributes to inducing dialogic talk repertoire.

We also wanted teachers to apply a set of dialogic principles as general rules governing the dialogue between teachers and students (Alexander 2020). Even though this set of principles is well known and often referred to in the literature, it is rarely used in empirical studies with the exception of the studies carried out by Lehesvuori et al. (2013) and van de Pol et al. (2017). We decided to incorporate these principles into the TPD program. We introduced the principles to the teachers in the workshops, and we observed the teachers to see if they succeeded in implementing them. We concentrated on two principles: collectivity and purposefulness.

We consider the collectivity principle to be crucial as it has a significant impact on the distribution of learning opportunities in the classroom. It is well known that participation in classroom discourse is usually unevenly distributed, and student behavior ranges from vocal to silent participants (Kovalainen and Kumpulainen 2007). Recent studies (Webb et al. 2014; Sedova et al. 2019; Larraín et al. 2019) show that learners who speak and argue more will learn more. If we accept this premise, then not implementing the collectivity principle signifies a serious violation of equality of educational chances in the classroom. Some empirical research shows that teachers are convinced that not all students are able to engage in dialogue of the same quality (Pimentel and McNeill 2013; Snell and Lefstein 2018). This may result in their tendency to exempt some students from classroom talk and prefer interaction with students whom they consider competent. In the early stages of the TPD program, teacher Marek demonstrated this belief and behavior during the video recording of his lessons (see Chap. 6). We consider equality of educational chances to be such a fundamental value that we decided to continuously monitor whether the teachers implemented the principle of collectivity and reminded them to do so.

8.2 What Made Change Happen?

We consider the principle of purposefulness to be equally important as it describes situations in which dialogue is used to provide students with content and practices constituting the subject matter (Herbel-Eisenmann et al. 2013). Hammond (2016) perceives the relationship between form (indicators) and content (the principle of purposefulness) in dialogic teaching as potentially problematic. He thus implies that focusing on talk structures and forms should not become an end in itself. Instead, it should lead to the promotion of student learning of certain curricular content. In the course of our project, we repeatedly observed how focusing on indicators led teachers away from focusing on their teaching goals. As in the case of the principle of collectivity, we therefore continuously monitored whether the teachers followed the principle of purposefulness during the course of our project.

The expected harmony between partial elements of dialogic teaching was hard to achieve for participating teachers during the TPD program. Occasionally, the efforts of the teachers resulted in some indicators being in conflict with some principles. We describe these situations in the case studies of teachers Daniela and Marek (see Chaps. 5 and 6). For example, Daniela found it difficult to align the indicator of open discussion with the principle of purposefulness. She implemented activities in her lessons in which students were very active, asked questions, and responded to each other. Nonetheless, the educational goal of interpreting literary texts was not met. Another type of conflict between an indicator and a principle occurred in the teaching practice of Marek. While he was implementing the indicator of open questions of high cognitive demand, Marek violated the principle of collectivity as he interacted only with a limited group of students whom he perceived as capable. On the other hand, when he was interacting with all the students, the cognitive level of his questions declined markedly, which resulted in a decrease in the value of this indicator.

We noticed an interesting phenomenon during the TPD program. Immediately after a workshop, teachers often did well in indicators—with Daniela, this is apparent in Lessons 3 and 6. Lesson 3 came just after the workshop focused on open questions of high cognitive demand and uptake; Lesson 6 came just after the workshop focused on open discussion. However, this straightforward success usually came at some cost—typically in neglecting principles or in struggling with organizational constraints. This was always discussed in the following reflective interview, and in the next lesson indicators were very often decreased as the teacher did not focus exclusively on them. In the subsequent lessons, the indicators started to increase again. There is a clear message from this observation. It is easy for teachers to change one partial element of their teaching. Complex change is more demanding and requires experimenting with teaching methods to find an equilibrium in which all elements are working in harmony.

The fact that teachers struggled with complex changes during the TPD program elucidates why the development during the program was nonlinear, alternating phases of progression and regression. This phenomenon should in no way be regarded as a sign of failure. We see it as a natural effect of the process of complex and extensive change. Since teachers need to experiment with teaching methods until they reach equilibrium, it is necessary to give them enough time for this during a TPD program.

This explains the well-known statement according to which an effective development program for teachers must have a sufficiently long duration (see, e.g., Adey 2006; Butler et al. 2004; Desimone 2009).

8.2.2 Implementation of Dialogic Teaching as Process of Appropriation

In previous chapters, we introduced teacher development during our TPD program as a process of overcoming the obstacles inherent in transforming to dialogic teaching. In this chapter, we examine the nature of teacher learning during that transformation. We ask how their understanding of new concepts and tools developed and how they advance toward the ability to use them in their practice.

We see the implementation of dialogic teaching as a process of appropriation (Grossman et al. 1999). This simply means that teachers do not passively accept the contents offered to them during a TPD program. On the contrary, they are agentic in creating their personal approach to these contents. Grossman et al. (1999) used the term *appropriation* to describe a process in which a person is learning how to use new teaching tools. These can be new ways of achieving certain educational goals (e.g., concepts and thoughts on the nature of teaching and learning) as well as practical techniques and strategies for acting in the school classroom (Grossman et al. 1999). Appropriation thus helps its users master a tool and always includes some modification of the tool to the needs and preferences of the user. Teachers who enter further professional education do not adopt educational tools unmodified. Instead, they adapt such tools by subjecting them to their personal interpretation. In this way, teachers creatively add such tools to their preexisting repertoire of skills and knowledge.

Although we acknowledge the importance of theory, when designing the TPD program, we did not adhere to the theory-to-practice approach in which educators present theory to teachers and assume that teachers rationally understand it, accept it, and adjust their teaching practices accordingly (Korthagen 2017). According to Korthagen et al. (2001), this model is not functional, as mere acquaintance with theory rarely affects the real behavior of teachers. Desimone (2009) stated that if a TPD program aims to be effective, it must include active learning components for teachers. Teachers cannot be mere recipients of information and knowledge; they must construct both themselves. Accordingly, our program was designed to allow teachers to try new ideas and construct knowledge about teaching and learning in an authentic context (Butler et al. 2004).

The program was designed to build on workshops that aimed to familiarize teachers with theories, concepts, and tools, and to experiment with new knowledge in authentic learning situations. The nature of individual indicators was introduced during the workshops. In the weeks following the workshops, teachers tried to use these indicators in their own lessons and were recorded on video. Our records show

8.2 What Made Change Happen?

that over the course of several consecutive lessons, teachers tried different specific procedures and techniques to implement the indicators. For example, in the case study of teacher Daniela (Chap. 5), we saw how she first induced open discussion through an activity in which students asked their classmates questions based on a picture (Lesson 6). In the next recorded lesson, Daniela induced open discussion through an intentionally partial narration that the students were to complete by asking her follow-up questions (Lesson 7). In the next recorded lesson, she achieved the same end by having the students discuss which characters from *The Lord of the Rings* trilogy can be considered heroes and which not (Lesson 8). Even though Daniela tried to reach same goal (i.e., to create a situation in which students talk to each other), she always invented a different path leading to this goal. Consequently, the lessons proceeded differently, and the effects of the chosen approaches were different as well.

Daniela's repeated experimentation can be seen as an effort to appropriate the concept of open discussion. According to Grossman et al. (1999), appropriation is a process in which a learner learns to use new pedagogical tools (i.e., means to achieve certain pedagogical goals). While some of these tools embody concepts and ideas that reflect the nature of teaching and learning, others embody practical practices and strategies for managing classroom interaction. Appropriation thus leads to a mastery of a tool by its user and always involves some degree of modification of the tool according to the user's needs and preferences. Consequently, teachers participating in development programs do not adopt new teaching tools in their complete form. Instead, they interpret the tools subjectively and integrate them creatively into their existing repertoire of professional knowledge and skills. During the final stage of appropriation, teachers understand the logic behind the tools and can therefore make adjustments to intensify the effects of their use.

According to Grossman et al. (1999), the results of professional development education can be represented with the following scale: (1) lack of appropriation: tools are rejected, perceived as overcomplicated, and not consistent with previous experience and knowledge; (2) appropriating a label: the individual subscribes to the use of tools and learns the terminology but fails to use the tools correctly; (3) appropriating surface features: some formal elements are appropriated, but without deeper epistemological understanding; (4) appropriating conceptual underpinnings: the individual understands the theory that governs the use of tools; and (5) achieving mastery: the individual gains the ability to use tools prudently and efficiently.

Dialogic teaching can be seen as a set of pedagogical concepts and tools; both case studies in this book (Chaps. 5 and 6) describe the story of their appropriation. The chapters describe how the teachers went through different phases of the appropriation process. At the beginning of the program, Marek appropriated the label. Even during the first interview, Marek claimed that he used elements of dialogic teaching routinely in his practice; the video recordings clearly show that this was not the case. Many of the complications described in the two chapters occurred when one of the teachers appropriated only some of the superficial features of dialogic teaching elements, which were fragmentary and unrelated, and their effectiveness was questionable. Adequate understanding of the tools and their use happens only when the individual elements are aligned and the indicators mutually reinforce the principles, together creating a dialogic talk repertoire. If a teacher starts to feel at ease while using the new tools and does not feel the need to exert extra effort, then that teacher has reached the stage of mastery (Grossman et al. 1999). This situation can be observed in the last recorded lesson taught by Daniela.

We demonstrated that when teachers try to approach the ideal of dialogic teaching, they do not proceed in a linear, step-by-step fashion. We repeatedly observed that a phase of progress was followed by a phase of regression. The regressions were caused by obstacles (see Sect. 8.2.1) as well as by phenomena naturally accompanying transformation—unintended consequences, returns to gestalt, and conflict between elements (see Sects. 5.3.2, 5.3.3 and 6.3). The effort of teachers to rise above the regressive phases and restore the previous growth was part of the appropriation process. Simply said, there is no easy straightforward path to mastery in using new teaching tools. The only way to achieve mastery of tool appropriation (Grossman et al. 1999) is through solving a series of gradually emerging problems. Thus, an effective TPD program must be long enough (Adey 2006; Butler et al. 2004; Desimone 2009) and must be flexible in terms of time, as it is not possible to predict how much time will be needed for change to take place since it is not possible to foretell the extent of problems that will emerge during the process of change.

Moreover, in an effective TPD program, teachers should be supported in agentic experimentation with new pedagogical tools in order to be able to understand how they work. We instructed the teachers how to ask good open questions of high cognitive demand, how to provide students with uptake, and how to open space for open discussion. However, we did not primarily follow the path of training specific talk moves, as was the case in some other projects (see O'Connor and Michaels 2019). Rather, we wanted the teachers to understand the conceptual logic behind open questions of high cognitive demand, uptake, open discussion, and student thoughts with reasoning so that they would be able to use them. On the one hand, this meant that teachers had to recognize these elements of dialogic teaching when they occurred. Interestingly, it often happened in the course of the project that the teachers thought they had used a particular indicator, when in fact they had not. Therefore, we continuously refined the empirical definitions of individual indicators throughout the duration of the program, using examples from video recordings. On the other hand, teachers had to learn to create and induce these desirable indicators themselves. We did not want them to practice using selected phrases: we wanted to teach them how to formulate phrases that would be aligned with the nature of selected indicators, such as open questions of high cognitive demand and uptake, or to create conditions for the occurrence of other indicators, such as open discussion and student thoughts with reasoning.

As reported by Butler et al. (2004), teacher education should enable teachers to find their own ways of implementing presented theoretical concepts in their own practices. Various specific practices aligned with the theory on which our teacher development program is built have always existed. In our project, the teachers gradually discovered these practices, while the relevant theory was used as a guide to their assessment and analysis. At the same time, observing how the teachers embraced the concepts (i.e., how they implemented indicators and principles to create talk repertoires) enriched our initial theoretical framework. For example, the realization that some principles can be strengthened with some indicators has become an original contribution to Alexander's (2020) theory. La Velle (2019) stated that teacher education is at its best when practice is informed by theory and theory is informed by practice. We were aligned with this statement in our TPD project.

8.2.3 There is No Profound Change Without Reflection

Transition toward dialogic teaching is extremely challenging as it requires change on the micro-level of interaction between teachers and students, which is typically outside of teachers' conscious control and so is ruled by ingrained habits and routines (Lefstein 2008). Therefore, even when teachers agree with the main ideas of dialogic teaching, they find it difficult to adapt their behavior and classroom practices accordingly. Moreover, the experiences a teacher had as a student can play a greater role than teacher education or intentional decisions; teachers often imitate what they observed from their teachers and mentors who were powerful role models (Lortie 1975; Gröschner et al. 2020). Therefore, as Gröschner et al. (2020) argued, reflecting on our own school experience is an important aspect of going dialogic. More generally, to get our own interaction behaviors under conscious control requires an explicit effort in changing established norms (Hofmann 2020). Therefore, during the TPD program, we not only encouraged teachers to experiment with new teaching tools, but also encouraged them to reflect on their own prior experiences.

There has long been consensus in academia regarding the necessity of a reflective element in teacher education (see, e.g., Beauchamp 2015; Hatton and Smith 1995; Korthagen et al. 2001; Lane et al. 2014). Berson et al. (2015) stated that education that aims to change the teaching practice of teachers needs to be supplemented with reflection. They argued that it is necessary to observe how new patterns of behavior emerge in the process of change and to try to understand the logic and nature of these patterns. Therefore, we incorporated a reflective component into the plan of TPD program.

According to Korthagen et al. (2001, p. 71), reflection is a special form of thinking that consists of structuring or restructuring a certain experience and one's perception of it. Reflection leads to analytical examination of past situations. When immersed in a situation, teachers act intuitively or automatically. Reflection makes it possible to return to the situation later and consciously examine its individual aspects. This enables change in the future. Both the teachers described in Chaps. 5 and 6 repeatedly found themselves in this situation: while teaching, they felt that the lesson was proceeding as planned. Yet later, during reflection, they found various aspects of the lesson that they taught to be problematic. For example, in Lesson 7, Daniela instructed her students to ask her questions related to the subject matter (fantasy). In the lesson itself, Daniela was happy because the students proceeded to ask questions and she was able to provide them with a lot of information. Only after the lesson did she realize that although she wanted to activate the students, they were paradoxically less active because most of the communication space was filled by Daniela's answers. Unintended consequences of various effects that were caused by the teachers' actions could be observed in many of the recorded lessons. With some exceptions, the teachers did not notice these consequences during the lessons, but only later during the reflection. Reflective interviews thus served as a space for identifying the unintended consequences of the introduced changes.

The term "reflection" refers to an intensive examination of a past experience. As such, reflection can only rarely take place during the course of teaching as teachers must react quickly and act immediately, and hence, their attention is focused elsewhere. Korthagen et al. (2001) use the term "gestalt" to describe such acting without thinking (see Sect. 5.3.3). A teacher's gestalt comprises an interplay of cognitive and emotional factors that make the teacher act in a specific and consistent way. A teacher's routine behavior, which teachers typically consider to be correct (cognitive factor) and feel good about using (emotional factor), comprises a set of gestalts.

Hence, any teacher training that aims to change teacher behavior is in fact a requirement of teachers to change their gestalts. In our TPD program, teachers strove to implement dialogic teaching. This required varied restructuring of their existing teaching practices, depending on how far their gestalts were from the desired ideal. Meeting some of the requirements was straightforward for the participating teachers as it involved strengthening existing tendencies in their teaching practices. Other requirements demanded a relatively large deviation from the methods that the teachers used up to that point.

If teachers are to acquire new practices or skills, they must transcend their gestalts and establish new forms of behavior. This is done through the appropriation of new tools and concepts and by reflecting on the effects of these changes. Yet the original gestalts do not disappear completely. Instead, they remain a part of the teachers' repertoire. They coexist with the newly acquired practices, and at some points can even prevail over them. We observed this in both case studies presented in this book. It turns out that teachers return to their original gestalts in situations in which they cannot implement the newly acquired procedures and yet they face new demands on their teaching practices. Hence, returning to well-practiced procedures induces in them a feeling of calm and a sense of control. However, this return to gestalts interrupts the process of change.

What we have written in this chapter has the potential to explain why the theory-to-practice model—a term describing situations in which teachers are acquainted with a new theory and change their practices accordingly—does not work in the field of professional teachers development (Korthagen et al. 2001). The transmission of new concepts and tools into teaching practice is very difficult without reflection, which links together the knowledge of teachers and their behavior in authentic situations (Smagorinsky et al. 2015). Hence, reflection is an essential prerequisite for appropriation of new concepts and tools. While reflecting, teachers look back and assess the effects of using new concepts and tools in the classroom. They identify the unintended consequences of introduced changes and seek ways to suppress or manage them. Bearing in mind their recent experiences, teachers can consider how

8.2 What Made Change Happen?

the new concepts and tools can be modified for future use. On the other hand, when teachers are immersed in the process of teaching, they tend to act automatically and under the influence of their gestalts. Reflection thus offers the opportunity to perceive one's own gestalts at a distance and analyze whether they are functional.

When designing the TPD program (see Chap. 3), we used Korthagen's model of reflection (Korthagen and Kessels 1999; Korthagen et al. 2001), which is based on teachers noticing elements of their behavior that would otherwise remain unconscious. This feature of the model is particularly useful in the context of dialogic teaching since talk patterns are typically characterized by being largely outside the conscious control of the actors. Reflecting on their own talk and interaction behavior enables teachers to develop practical wisdom (Lunenberg and Korthagen 2009), or, in other words, to build the ability to find and apply appropriate practices based on a judicious assessment of relevant aspects of the given situation. According to Lunenberg and Korthagen (2009), practical wisdom is the element that allows bridging between theory and experience, or between abstract theoretical principles and corresponding classroom methods.

In our opinion, these considerations accurately reflect the essence of the problem. It is not vital to acquaint the teachers with a "correct" theory and ask them to follow it. Instead, it is vital to enable them to develop practical wisdom that will in turn enable them to make use of the theory in their own teaching practice. As Lefstein and Snell (2014) stated, a method, tool, or principle that works in one context may not work in the same way in another. Therefore, universal manuals on how to teach are destined to be unsuccessful. In a way, the common presentations of good teaching practices that are often included in handbooks for teachers are similarly misleading. Effective teacher education should not be based on teachers either accepting or adopting new ideas and practices but on adapting them and monitoring their functionality during use, which is impossible without reflection.

A question arises as to how to support teachers in reflection and appropriation processes. The fundamental tools that we used to support teacher reflection were reflective interviews, led by a trained researcher who observed the lessons, and video recording, which made the process of reflection significantly easier (see Borko et al. 2008; Sherin and Han 2004). We first acquainted the teachers with new concepts and tools in workshops and then had them experiment with both in their own lessons. The lessons were recorded, and the recordings served as a basis for the subsequent reflective interviews. Analyses of the data from these interviews showed that there was a correspondence between the content of the interviews and the changes made in the following recorded lessons. In other words, the topics discussed in the interviews became a stimulus for change in the next lesson. This was clearly evident in both case studies presented in Chaps. 5 and 6. An example can be found in Marek's interview with the researcher after his third recorded lesson in which he mentioned that there was a large group of non-participating students in his class and an activity that he planned for next session that aimed to activate these students.

Many such situations were discussed in each of the paired interviews between the teachers and their researchers. A pattern repeated in all the interviews: some implemented changes were considered satisfactory, while others were considered unsatisfactory or problematic. An analysis of changes that occurred between consecutive lessons showed that the teachers always focused on those changes that were assessed as not sufficiently well managed. The teachers' self-critical reflection thus served as an engine that fueled their ongoing change. In light of the findings presented in Chap. 7, it may even be said that teachers' dissatisfaction with their own teaching and the negative emotions that emerged during the reflective interviews strongly facilitated the subsequent changes. Teachers who showed no dissatisfaction and negative emotions changed their teaching only to a small degree.

The fact that criticism and self-criticism drive change in the process of teacher development can be explained by the concept of dissonance (Delaney 2015; Gelfuso 2016), which describes the perceived discrepancy between what is expected and what actually happens. Dissonance is usually accompanied by discomfort (Bakkenes et al. 2010). Our data from reflective interviews show that the teachers repeatedly experienced dissonance along with related negative emotions. According to Gelfuso (2016), the experience of dissonance is closely linked to reflection, because it is only during reflection that dissonance is acknowledged. At the same time, as Gelfuso (2016) argued, dissonance is the basis for reflection as it makes reflection possible. This view is in accordance with the opinion of Ward et al. (2011), who stated that a profound change in a teacher's practice is not possible without the teacher experiencing and then managing to solve a conflict. In light of these propositions and our data, the experience of failure and dissatisfaction with one's own work can be seen as a component influencing the effectiveness of a teacher development program.

However, we also noted that teacher dissatisfaction with their own teaching and the related uncertainty and frustration can result in a return to gestalt. On the one hand, the researchers had to help teachers identify unintended consequences and suboptimal gestalts (and thereby induce dissonance). On the other hand, the researchers had to prevent returns to gestalts and, instead, stimulate the teachers to further experiment and appropriate new concepts and tools. A very complicated interplay of circumstances needs to exist if a sustainable change is to take place. It is necessary to induce dissonance because without it the change would not be deep enough; at the same time, it is necessary to prevent dissonance from causing intolerable frustration and retreats to gestalts. Teacher educators should not be afraid of invoking critique. Yet they should also provide teachers with sufficient support. Teacher educators can help teachers to design possible modifications of concepts and tools. In addition, they need to continuously appreciate the progress that teachers make and assure them that the direction chosen is good one and that it makes sense to persevere and consolidate changes. In other words, inducing dissonance must be accompanied with appreciation and recognition of the good work that teachers do. Any TPD program oriented toward changing teaching practices is challenging in all respects for the participating teachers. Therefore, it is necessary to offer the teachers a positive outlook on their professional identities.

8.3 Concluding Remarks

During the course of our teacher development program, we worked with the participating teachers to implement dialogic teaching in their classrooms and to learn something new about dialogic teaching and the professional development of teachers. This book offers a testimony of what we uncovered during the process.

8.3.1 What Did We Learn About Dialogic Teaching?

First of all, full-blown dialogic teaching is possible to achieve in ordinary Czech classrooms. Concerns have been expressed in the literature that dialogic teaching is depicted in such an idealized way that it is not possible to implement it into real teaching practice (Lefstein 2010). We therefore entered the project prepared to accept that some aspects of dialogic teaching would prove to be impossible or highly problematic to implement (see Sect. 2.3). However, we found that a complete implementation of dialogic teaching is possible, at least in the subjects of civics and Czech literature in Czech lower-secondary schools. The lessons our teachers taught at the end of their participation in the program met the demanding requirements described by the theory of dialogic teaching.

We intended from the beginning of the project to implement a comprehensive change in the teaching practices of the participating teachers. We therefore focused on three different elements—indicators, principles, and talk repertoires—in order to achieve their alignment. Before we gained experience in the classrooms, we were unable to estimate how difficult it would be to achieve their alignment and how much work it would take. However, we believed that a change that was not comprehensive would not be adequate. We presumed that it would be relatively easy for teachers to implement a selected indicator if they did not try to also implement the other indicators and principles of dialogic teaching. However, such a change would only be superficial.

We found that because of the complexity of the concept of dialogic teaching, as elaborated by Alexander (2017), its individual components clash with each other on different levels. A teacher's effort to implement one component can lead to the neglect or violation of another. At the same time, we discovered a significant and optimistic finding: if concepts and tools of dialogic teaching are appropriated well, then the individual components act in synergy with one another. For example, our teachers learned to increase the effectiveness of their teaching through the questions they asked their students. They also increased the collectivity principle of their teaching by establishing open discussion.

One of the most important things that we learned about classroom talk is that if a teacher's talk patterns change, then the talk patterns of students change quite immediately as well. As soon as the teachers began to implement the indicators and principles of dialogic teaching, student utterances became longer and contained more arguments. We consider this to be a valuable finding, because some teachers argue that average students are unable to have rational discussions with their teachers or classmates. Our data show that dialogic teaching is truly effective in stimulating pupils to produce elaborate and thoughtful utterances. This means that dialogic teaching proved to be a way to include students in productive participation (see Black 2004). If we accept the argument according to which utterances reflect the level of student thinking (see Vygotsky 1978; Sfard 2008), then this is a very important finding. Teachers' use of their classroom talk can also influence how their students think and learn.

8.3.2 What Did We Learn About the Professional Development of Teachers?

We designed our TPD program as a combination of theory, experimentation in classrooms, and reflection. It turned out that all these components had meaning in the program and were mutually supportive. We used theory as a basis to explain the purpose of change and to introduce the concepts and tools of dialogic teaching. However, the ideas embedded in theory were introduced to teachers provisionally rather than prescriptively (Hennessy et al. 2011). This, in the next step, enabled the teachers to feel free to experiment with the concepts and tools and gradually appropriate them. Without appropriation, the outcome of the TPD program could easily slip into a mere appropriation of the label or surface features of dialogic teaching (Grossman et al. 1999), so this dimension of the program was extremely important. Appropriation could not take place without reflection, so the reflection in the program was enhanced through video-supported interviews and with the participation of independent researchers.

Our research shows that if teachers are to profoundly transform their teaching practices, then step-by-step linear improvement cannot be expected. We have come to the conclusion that alternating between stages of acceleration and stagnation or regression is not an anomaly but is inevitable if the change is to be profound. In such cases, various components will easily get into mutual disharmony or conflict with one another, often resulting in the teacher returning to gestalt and interrupting their positive development. We consider the phenomenon of unintended consequences to be an important discovery, since it describes a situation in which a teacher's effort to improve one aspect of teaching leads to a deterioration in another aspect. These findings show why effective professional development programs have to be of sufficient length. The cases of all the participating teachers show that their development proceeded as a series of gradual adjustments to partial problems, many of which arose during the development as unintended consequences of the newly introduced practices or forms of action. This leads us to an important statement: change represents uncertainty and results are not always beneficial. Hence, implementing dialogic teaching principles and indicators requires a great deal of courage from teachers as they have to step outside the boundaries of what they know. It requires patience as it takes a long time before the newly adopted teaching tools start to function well. All of this requires a considerable (and not predictable) amount of time and, of course, energy as well.

This is also related to the fact that teachers experience strong negative emotions during the change. Our analysis showed that this need not be perceived as a threat; on the contrary, it is a necessary condition for the change to be profound. Negative emotions accompany dissonance without which there is no effective reflection and without which no effective appropriations of concepts and tools can take place. At the same time, teachers must be appreciated and assured that they are going in the right direction. Otherwise, dissonance can easily result in teachers returning to their gestalts to soothe negative emotions.

Our development program was meticulously prepared in advance, but it still gave considerable freedom to both teachers and researchers. Even though the teachers were given precise instructions in the form of a list of which indicators they need to implement, it was left to them as to how they would go about it. Further, while the researchers guided the teachers in their reflection of the recorded lessons, the conclusions drawn from the reflections were made by the teachers, who also decided how they would change their plans for subsequent lessons. As researchers, we were repeatedly surprised by the actions of the teachers, their choice of procedures, and their resulting effects. We now believe that it was beneficial that the program balanced both structure and freedom. This setting created conditions that facilitated the learning process and left a large part of the initiative in the hands of the teachers, who could take responsibility for their own learning. Further, the researchers could learn from the teachers. As a result, we were able to see how teachers approach change and what effects it brings. Therefore, at the very end of this book, we thank the teachers who participated in our program for making this possible.

8.3.3 An Unexpected Epilog

In 2018, we conducted another research project focused on the relationship between student participation in classroom talk and student achievement (see, e.g., Sedova et al. 2019; Sedova and Navratilova 2020). A lucky coincidence brought teacher Daniela (see Chap. 5) to the sample of teachers participating in this project. This gave us a chance to observe this teacher three years after she had completed the TPD program described in this book.

The long-term impact of dialogic teaching TPD initiatives is often questioned (see Hennessy and Davies 2020). When we look at how challenging it is for teachers to achieve change, concerns about its sustainability may arise. What happens after the support from researchers and educators is gone? Unfortunately, there is nearly no data about this. Hennessy et al. (2018) reported observing two teachers who continued using a dialogic approach ten weeks after they completed a TPD program (see also Hennessy and Davies 2020). More elaborated findings were published by Osborne et al. (2019), who conducted a TPD program to enhance elementary teachers' ability to engage their students with argumentation in science. The data were gathered longitudinally (over four years in total), with the last collection one year after the end of the TPD program. The authors found a rapid increase in dialogic teaching practices in the first year of teacher participation in TPD, and then the pace of change decelerated. When measured one year after completing the program, the values of indicators were lower than during the program, although still higher than before the program started. Osborne et al. (2019) concluded that changes in teaching practices might be difficult to sustain. Newly mastered teaching skills may fade without additional TPD opportunities and support.

When we met Daniela again in 2018, we decided to use video recordings of her lessons collected in the new project for comparison with the older data. We recorded four lessons of Czech literature taught to ninth graders. We then counted the indicators of dialogic teaching in this lesson, just as we had in the original project. This allowed us to compare the occurrence of indicators in the pre-lesson (before the TPD program), post-lessons (at the end of the TPD program), and in the follow-up lessons (three years after the TPD program ended). Figure 8.1 displays the results.

The trend is not the same for all indicators. The open discussion and students' thoughts with reasoning indicators show the same pattern: a rapid increase from the pre-lesson to the post-lessons and a moderate decrease between the post-lesson and follow-up lessons. Open questions of high cognitive demand increased heavily due to the program, but three years later, they were used with very similar frequency as before the program had started. Uptake increased only mildly between pre- and post-lessons, but the increase continued over time, reaching its maximum in the follow-up

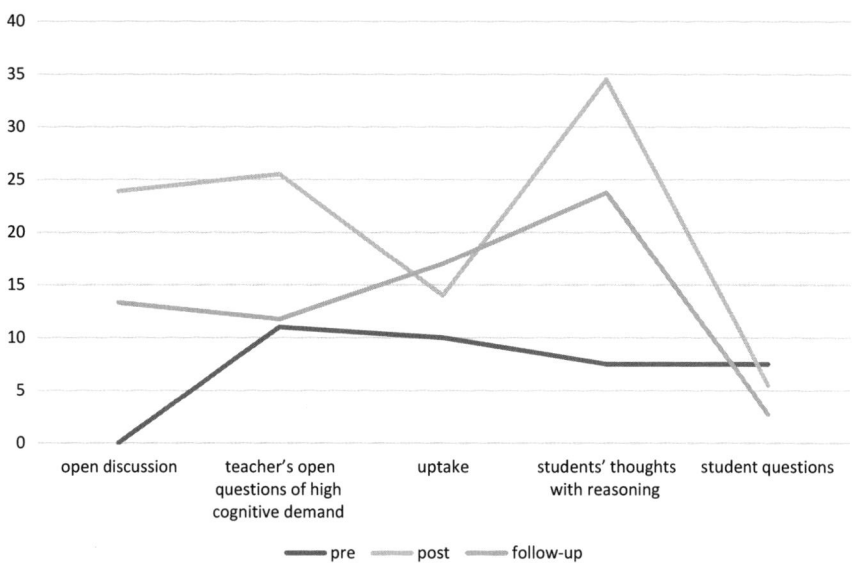

Fig. 8.1 Comparison of pre-, post-, and follow-up lessons

lessons. In sum, some things the teacher learned in the TPD program strengthened over time (uptake); some things remained, but not in the top form (open discussion and student thoughts with reasoning); and some things seemed to be lost (open questions of high cognitive demand).

We believe the data might be viewed as optimistic. Three years after the TPD program, three indicators are higher than they were before it started. A moderate decrease between the post-lessons and follow-up lessons in open discussion and student thoughts with reasoning may be attributed to the changed conditions of data gathering. The context of the lessons recorded during TPD was somewhat unnatural—teachers were strongly encouraged to teach in compliance with the TPD conception of good teaching. In contrast, the lessons some time after the TPD program reflected more the teacher's own conception of what is good. From this perspective, we can see that Daniela appreciated some of the indicators enough to keep them, but she did not achieve the extreme values that she was able to reach when being monitored and mentored by the researchers.

The open questions of high cognitive demand returned to the same frequency as before the TPD program; on the other hand, uptake continued to increase after the completion of TPD. These findings indicate that after some time, the teacher performed dialogic teaching, but not exactly as she had been taught to: she autonomously reinterpreted and recreated the concept. Some things were accentuated by her and some things were de-emphasized. We stated that during TPD, teachers appropriate new teaching tools (Grossman et al. 1999). Our follow-up data can be understood as an indication that the teacher continued with appropriation even after the end of the TPD program.

In addition to video recordings, we interviewed Daniela to find how she viewed the TPD program and its effects after some time. We found her full of trust in dialogic teaching, enthusiastic about its effects for student learning, and very self-confident about her ability to teach dialogically. The reunion was comforting and led us to feel that the energy devoted to the TPD program was meaningful.

8.3.4 Where to Next?

In this book, we presented the main findings from the research investigating the implementation of dialogic teaching in classrooms through a TPD program for teachers. We focused on processes of teacher learning and, we believe, broadened the knowledge about how they learn when they undergo a deep transformation of their teaching. However, there are still many blank areas worth closer investigation.

Our research was limited to a small sample of teachers with similar characteristics. It would be beneficial to conduct similar research with a broader sample of teachers with more varied characteristics (e.g., teaching different subjects). Also, an international comparison based on conducting a study of this kind in different countries would be very beneficial.

Further, we feel that specific topics in our data deserve closer inquiry. Thanks to a close analysis of the data from interviews and observations, we noticed how personally challenging the process of teacher development may be. We addressed this issue in Chap. 7 but there is much more to discover in this field. How do teachers feel during TPD programs, and what goes on with their professional identities? What are their relationships to their educators, and what tensions and struggles can emerge between them? Until now, these questions have been overshadowed by more technical concerns, e.g., how to choose TPD content, how to deliver information to teachers, what technological platform to use, etc. Our findings highlighted the overlooked personal and emotional side of TPD, and we believe future research should focus on this. If TPD is expected to make a difference, it has to go deep and thus necessarily become personal and emotional, both for teachers and their educators. Therefore, our knowledge about this should be richer and more detailed.

In Sect. 8.3.3, we indicated our concern with the long-term impact of the change. For the dialogic teaching movement, it is absolutely essential to examine these concerns. If the quality of teaching changes only temporarily, and the changes are not sustainable, then investing effort and money in TPD focused on dialogic teaching is in vain. Therefore, we think the sustainability of implemented dialogic teaching is perhaps the most important agenda for future research.

8.4 Summary

In this chapter, we summarized the main findings presented in this book and tried to explain some generative mechanisms underlying the transformation. We surveyed what the teachers had to do to overcome obstacles associated with implementing dialogic teaching—they coped with organizational constraints, shifted their mindsets, and took control over the complexity of the change. Only when all these aspects met the deep change of teaching practices was possible. Further, we labeled the key processes responsible for the learning and development of the teachers: appropriation and reflection. Appropriation means agentic and creative adapting of new (dialogic) teaching tools to serve a particular teacher's needs and preferences. This happened in our TPD program through teacher experimentation with new tools in their lessons and subsequent careful reflection on their experiences.

At the end of this chapter, we described a reunion with one participating teacher after a few years, through which it became possible to think about the sustainability of the change. Finally, we considered some possible directions for future research.

References

Adey, P. (2006). A model for professional development of teachers thinking. *Think Skills Creat, 1*(1), 49–56. https://doi.org/10.1016/j.tsc.2005.07.002

Alexander, R. J. (2017). *Towards dialogic teaching: Rethinking classroom talk* (5th ed.). Cambridge: Dialogos.

Alexander, R. J. (2020). *A dialogic teaching companion*. London: Routledge.

Bakkenes, I., Vermunt, J. D., & Wubbels, T. (2010). Teacher learning in the context of educational innovation: Learning activities and learning outcomes of experienced teachers. *Learn Instr, 20*(6), 533–548. https://doi.org/10.1016/j.learninstruc.2009.09.001

Beauchamp, C. (2015). Reflection in teacher education: Issues emerging from a review of current literature. *Reflective Practice, 16*(1), 123–141. https://doi.org/10.1080/14623943.2014.982525

Berson, E., Borko, H., Million, S., et al. (2015). Practice what you teach: A video-based practicum model of professional development for elementary science teachers. *Orbis Scholae, 9*(2), 35–53. https://doi.org/10.14712/23363177.2015.79

Black, L. (2004). Differential participation in whole-class discussions and the construction of marginalised identities. *Journal of Educational Enquiry, 5*(1), 34–54.

Borko, H., Jacobs, J., Eiteljorg, E., et al. (2008). Video as a tool for fostering productive discussions in mathematics professional development. *Teaching and Teacher Education, 24*(2), 417–436. https://doi.org/10.1016/j.tate.2006.11.012

Boyd, M. P., & Markarian, W. C. (2011). Dialogic teaching: Talk in service of a dialogic stance. *Language Education, 25*(6), 515–534. https://doi.org/10.1080/09500782.2011.597861

Butler, D. L., Novak, H., Jarvis-, S., et al. (2004). Collaboration and self-regulation in teachers' professional development. *Teaching and Teacher Education, 20*(5), 435–455. https://doi.org/10.1016/j.tate.2004.04.003

Delaney, K. K. (2015). Dissonance for understanding: Exploring a new theoretical lens for understanding teacher identity formation in borderlands of practice. *Contemporary Issues in Early Childhood, 16*(4), 374–389. https://doi.org/10.1177/1463949115616326

Desimone, L. M. (2009). Improving impact studies of teachers' professional development: Towards better conceptualisation and measures. *Educational Research, 38*(3), 181–199. https://doi.org/10.3102/0013189X08331140

Gelfuso, A. (2016). A framework for facilitating video-mediated reflection: Supporting preservice teachers as they create "warranted assertabilities" about literacy teaching and learning. *Teaching and Teacher Education, 58*, 68–79. https://doi.org/10.1016/j.tate.2016.04.003

Gomez Zaccarelli, F., Schindler, A.-K., Borko, H., et al. (2018). Learning from professional development: A case study of the challenges of enacting productive science discourse in the classroom. *Professional Development in Education, 44*(5), 721–737. https://doi.org/10.1080/19415257.2017.1423368

Gresalfi, M. S. (2009). Taking up opportunities to learn: Constructing dispositions in mathematics classrooms. *Journal of the Learning Sciences, 18*(3), 327–369. https://doi.org/10.1080/10508400903013470.

Gröschner, A., Jähne, M.F., Klass, S. (2020). Attitudes towards dialogic teaching and the choice to teach: The role of preservice teachers' perception on their own school experience. In: Mercer N, Wegerif R, Major L (eds) The Routledge international handbook of research on dialogic education. Routledge, Abingdon

Grossman, P. L., Smagorinski, P., & Valencia, S. (1999). Appropriating tools for teaching English: A theoretical framework for research on learning to teach. *American Journal of Education, 108*(1), 1–29. https://doi.org/10.1086/444230

Hammond, J. (2016). Dialogic space: Intersections between dialogic teaching and systemic functional linguistics. *Res Pap Educ, 31*(1), 5–22. https://doi.org/10.1080/02671522.2016.1106693

Hatton, N., & Smith, D. (1995). Reflection in teacher education: Towards definition and implementation. *Teaching and Teacher Education, 11*(1), 33–49. https://doi.org/10.1016/0742-051X(94)00012-U

Hennessy, S., Dragovic, T., & Warwick, P. (2018). A research-informed, school-based professional development workshop programme to promote dialogic teaching with interactive technologies. *Professional Development in Education, 44*(2), 145–168. https://doi.org/10.1080/19415257.2016.1258653.

Hennessy, S., Warwick, P., & Mercer, N. (2011). A dialogic inquiry approach to working with teachers in developing classroom dialogue. *Teach Coll Rec, 113*(9), 1906–1959.

Hennessy, S., Davies, M. (2020). Teacher professional development to support classroom dialogue: Challenges and promises. In: Mercer, N., Wegerif, R., Major, L. (eds). The Routledge international handbook of research on dialogic education. Routledge, Abingdon

Herbel-Eisenmann, B. A., Steele, M. D., & Cirillo, M. (2013). (Developing) Teacher Discourse Moves: A Framework for Professional Development. *Math Teach Educ, 1*(2), 181–196. https://doi.org/10.5951/mathteaceduc.1.2.0181

Hofmann, R. (2020). Dialogue, teachers and professional development. In: Mercer, N., Wegerif, R., Major, L. (eds). The Routledge international handbook of research on dialogic education. Routledge, Abingdon

Korthagen, F. A. J., & Kessels, J. P. A. M. (1999). Linking theory and practice: Changing the pedagogy of teacher education. *Educ Res, 28*(4), 4–17. https://doi.org/10.3102/0013189X028004004

Korthagen, F. A. J., Kessels, J. P. A. M., Koster, B., et al. (2001). *Linking practice and theory: The pedagogy of realistic teacher education.* Mahwah: Erlbaum.

Korthagen, F. (2017). Inconvenient truths about teacher learning: Towards professional development 3.0. *Teachers and Teaching: Theory and Practice, 23*(4):387–405. https://doi.org/10.1080/13540602.2016.1211523

Kovalainen, M., & Kumpulainen, K. (2007). The social construction of participation in an elementary classroom community. *International Journal Educational Research, 46*(3–4), 141–158. https://doi.org/10.1016/j.ijer.2007.09.011

La Velle, L. (2019). The theory–practice nexus in teacher education: New evidence for effective approaches. *Journal of Educational Teaching, 45*(4), 369–372. https://doi.org/10.1080/02607476.2019.1639267

Lane, R., McMaster, H. J., Adnum, J., et al. (2014). Quality reflective practice in teacher education: A journey towards shared understanding. *Reflective Practice, 15*(4), 481–494. https://doi.org/10.1080/14623943.2014.900022

Larraín, A., Freire, P., López, P., et al. (2019). Counter-arguing during curriculum-supported peer interaction facilitates middle-school students" science content knowledge. *Cognition Instruct, 37*(4), 453–482. https://doi.org/10.1080/07370008.2019.1627360

Lefstein, A. (2008). Changing classroom practice through the english national literacy strategy: A micro-interactional perspective. *American Educational Research Journal, 45*(3), 701–737. https://doi.org/10.3102/0002831208316256.

Lefstein, A. (2010). More helpful as problem than solution: Some implications of situating dialogue in classrooms. In: Littleton K, Howe C (eds) Educational dialogues: Understanding and promoting productive interaction, 1st edn. Routledge, Abingdon, New York

Lefstein, A., & Snell, J. (2014). *Better than best practice: Developing teaching and learning through dialogue.* Abingdon, New York: Routledge.

Lehesvuori, S., Viiri, J., Rasku-Puttonen, H., et al. (2013). Visualizing communication structures in science classrooms: Tracing cumulativity in teacher-led whole class discussions. *J Res Sci Teach, 50*(8), 912–939. https://doi.org/10.1002/tea.21100

Lortie, D. C. (1975). *Schoolteacher: A Sociological Study.* Chicago: The University of Chicago Press.

References

Lunenberg, M., & Korthagen, F. A. J. (2009). Experience, theory and practical wisdom in teaching and teacher education. *Teach Teach, 15*(2), 225–240. https://doi.org/10.1080/13540600902875316

Mercer, N., Hennessy, S., & Warwick, P. (2019). Dialogue, thinking together and digital technology in the classroom: Some educational implications of a continuing line of inquiry. *Int J Educ R, 97,* 187–199.

Michaels S, O'Connor C (2015) Conceptualizing talk moves as tools: Professional development approaches for academically productive discussions. In: Resnick LB, Asterhan CSC, Clarke SN (eds) Socializing intelligence through academic talk and dialogue, 1st edn. American Educational Research Association, Washington, D.C.

Nurkka, N., Viiri, J., Littleton, K., et al. (2014). A methodological approach to exploring the rhythm of classroom discourse in a cumulative frame in science teaching. *Learn Cult Soc Inter, 3*(1), 54–63. https://doi.org/10.1016/j.lcsi.2014.01.002

Osborne, J. F., Borko, H., Fishman, E., Gomez Zaccarelli, F., Berson, E., Busch, K. C., et al. (2019). Impacts of a practice-based professional development program on elementary teachers' facilitation of and student engagement with scientific argumentation. *American Educational Research Journal, 56*(4), 1067–1112. https://doi.org/10.3102/0002831218812059.

O'Connor, C., & Michaels, S. (2019). Supporting teachers in taking up productive talk moves: The long road to professional learning at scale. *Int J Educ Res, 97,* 166–175. https://doi.org/10.1016/j.ijer.2017.11.003

Pimentel, D. S., & McNeill, K. L. (2013). Conducting talk in secondary science classrooms: Investigating instructional moves and teachers' beliefs. *Science & Education, 97*(3), 367–394. https://doi.org/10.1002/sce.21061

Ponte, P., Ax, J., Beijaard, D., et al. (2004). Teachers' development of professional knowledge through action research and the facilitation of this by teacher educators. *Teach Teach Educ, 20*(6), 571–588. https://doi.org/10.1016/j.tate.2004.06.003

Resnick, L.B., Asterhan, C.S.C., Clarke, S.N. et al. (2018). Next generation research in dialogic learning. In: Hall, G.E., Quinn, L.F., Gollnick, D.M. (eds.), *The Wiley handbook of teaching and learning*, 1st edn. Wiley, Hoboken.

Scott, P. (2008). Talking a way to understanding in science. In: Mercer, N., Hodgkinson, S. (eds.), *Exploring talk in schools: Inspired by the work of Douglas Barnes*, SAGE, London.

Sedova, K., Salamounova, Z., & Svaricek, R. (2014). Troubles with dialogic teaching. *Learn Cult Soc Inter, 3*(4), 274–285. https://doi.org/10.1016/j.lcsi.2014.04.001

Sedova, K., Sedlacek, M., Svaricek, R., et al. (2019). Do those who talk more learn more? The relationship between student classroom talk and student achievement. *Learn Instr, 63,* 101217. https://doi.org/10.1016/j.learninstruc.2019.101217

Sedova, K., & Navratilova, J. (2020). Silent students and the patterns of their participation in classroom talk. *Journal of the Learning Sciences.* https://doi.org/10.1080/10508406.2020.1794878

Sherin, M. G., & Han, S. Y. (2004). Teacher learning in the context of a video club. *Teach Teach Educ, 20*(2), 163–183. https://doi.org/10.1016/j.tate.2003.08.001

Smagorinsky P, Shelton SA, Moore C (2015) The role of reflection in developing eupraxis in learning to teach English. Pedagogies: An International Journal 10(4): 25–308. https://doi.org/10.1080/1554480X.2015.1067146

Snell, J., & Lefstein, A. (2018). "Low ability", participation, and identity in dialogic pedagogy. *American Educational Research Journal, 55*(1), 40–78.

Twiner, A., Littleton, K., Coffin, C., et al. (2014). Meaning making as an interactional accomplishment: A temporal analysis of intentionality and improvisation in classroom dialogue. *Int J Educ Res, 63,* 94–106. https://doi.org/10.1016/j.ijer.2013.02.009

Van de Pol, J., Brindley, S., & Higham, R. J. E. (2017). Two secondary teachers" understanding and classroom practice of dialogic teaching: A case study. *Educ Stud, 43*(5), 497–515. https://doi.org/10.1080/03055698.2017.1293508

Vygotsky, L. S. (1978). *Mind in society: The development of higher psychological processes.* Cambridge: Harvard University Press.

Walkoe, J. D. K., & Luna, M. J. (2020). What we are missing in studies of teacher learning: A call for microgenetic, interactional analyses to examine teacher learning processes. *Journal of the Learning Sciences, 29*(2), 285–307. https://doi.org/10.1080/10508406.2019.1681998.

Ward, C. J., Nolen, S. B., & Horn, I. S. (2011). Productive friction: How conflict in student teaching creates opportunities for learning at the boundary. *Int J Educ Res, 50*(1), 14–20. https://doi.org/10.1016/j.ijer.2011.04.004

Wayne, A. J., Yoon, K. S., Zhu, P., et al. (2008). Experimenting with teacher professional development: Motives and methods. *Educ Res, 37*(8), 469–479. https://doi.org/10.3102/0013189X08327154

Webb, N. M., Franke, M. L., Ing, M., et al. (2014). Engaging with others" mathematical ideas: Interrelationships among student participation, teachers" instructional practices, and learning. *Int Journal of Educational Res, 63,* 79–93. https://doi.org/10.1016/j.ijer.2013.02.001

Wilkinson, I. A. G., Reznitskaya, A., Bourdage, K., et al. (2017). Toward a more dialogic pedagogy: Changing teachers" beliefs and practices through professional development in language arts classrooms. *Lang Educ, 31*(1), 65–82. https://doi.org/10.1080/09500782.2016.1230129

Appendix

See Tables 1, 2, 3, 4, 5 and 6.

Table 1 Test of changes in frequency of open-ended questions of high cognitive demand in pre- and post-TPD episodes

	Wilcoxon signed rank t test		Paired samples test					Cohen's d
	Z	p	t	df	p	Lower bound[a]	Upper bound[a]	
Pre_Post	2.24	0.02	−2.74	7	0.03	0.79	10.70	0.86

[a]The difference is calculated with the usual confidence level of 95%

Table 2 Tests of changes in uptake frequency in pre- and post-TPD episodes

	Wilcoxon signed rank t test		Paired samples test					Cohen's d
	Z	p	t	df	p	Lower bound[a]	Upper bound[a]	
Pre_Post	1.26	0.21	−1.41	7	0.20	–	–	–

[a]The difference is calculated with the usual confidence level of 95%

Table 3 Tests of changes in open discussion length in pre- and post-TPD episodes

	Wilcoxon signed rank t test		Paired samples test					Cohen's d
	Z	p	t	df	p	Lower bound[a]	Upper bound[a]	
Pre_Post	2.52	0.02	−3.40	7	0.01	84.40	472.66	>0.90

[a]The difference is calculated with the usual confidence level of 95%

Table 4 Tests of changes in frequency of student talk with reasoning in pre- and post-TPD episodes

	Wilcoxon signed rank t test		Paired samples test					Cohen's d
	Z	p	t	df	p	Lower bound[a]	Upper bound[a]	
Pre_Post	2.37	0.01	−2.55	7	0.03	0.54	14.03	0.59

[a]The difference is calculated with the usual confidence level of 95%

Table 5 Tests of changes in the number of verbally participating students in pre- and post-TPD episodes

	Wilcoxon signed rank t test		Paired samples test					Cohen's d
	Z	p	t	df	p	Lower bound[a]	Upper bound[a]	
Pre_Post	0.98	0.32	−1.43	7	0.14	–	–	–

[a]The difference is calculated with the usual confidence level of 95%

Table 6 Tests of changes in the length of effective teaching in pre- and post-intervention episodes

	Wilcoxon signed rank t test		Paired samples test					Cohen's d
	Z	p	t	df	p	Lower bound[a]	Upper bound[a]	
Pre_Post	2.52	0.01	−3.35	7	0.01	54.17	310.85	0.88

[a]The difference is calculated with the usual confidence level of 95%